Participatory IT Design

Keld Bødker
Finn Kensing
Jesper Simonsen

Participatory
IT Design

Designing for
Business and
Workplace Realities

The MIT Press
Cambridge, Massachusetts
London, England

This book was set in Palatino by Jan Speiermann.
Printed and bound in the United States of America.

Library of Congress Cataloging-in-Publication Data
Bødker, Keld.
    Participatory IT design : designing for business and workplace realities / Keld Bødker, Finn Kensing, Jesper Simonsen.
    p. cm.
    Includes bibliographical references and index.
    ISBN 0-262-02568-X (alk. paper)
    1. System design. 2. Information technology. I. Kensing, Finn. II. Simonsen, Jesper. III. Title.

QA76.9.S88B65 2004
004.2'1–dc22

2004042588

10   9   8   7   6   5   4   3   2   1

Overview

Contents

Contents

Contents

Illustrations

Preface

This book is about IT design. IT design is carried out as a project in a company to design sustainable IT usage. The project produces a decision-making foundation for the company regarding potentials and opportunities for implementing IT usage that answer the problems and challenges that the company is facing.

The book is the result of a ten-year research collaboration between the authors and Danish and American companies to develop and test a method for IT design. We made it a goal to explore whether it was possible to set sensible, general, and, not least, workable guidelines for IT design projects.

This book is our answer.

Acknowledgments

We would like to thank the corporations that cooperated with us in our study. Over the first few years, we conducted ten IT design projects in cooperation with Danish and American businesses, in which we experimented with different elements of our method. The corporations included:

- an American airline
- Stanford University
- an American research center
- The Danish Film Institute
- The Danish Broadcasting Corporation (DR)
- a Danish pharmaceuticals company
- Roskilde University

On the basis of these ten projects, we noted that the method worked when we ourselves took part in the design project. In recent years, we have been cooperating with three Danish companies as part of a research project sponsored by the Danish National Centre for IT Research. In these projects, we limited our role to introducing the method, which was then applied under our guidance. This offered us opportu-

nities to evaluate and revise the method. For their cooperation in these recent experiments, we are grateful to:

- The Community of Copenhagen Hospitals, Information
  Technology Department
- The Danish Broadcasting Corporation, DR Radio
- WM-data Consulting A/S, Tax Audit Solutions

A draft of this book was used in informatics programs at
business colleges and in information systems and computer
science programs at Danish universities. Reactions to the
first draft of the book were positive, and suggestions for
improvements have been a great help in our ongoing
efforts. Finally, a draft of the book was read closely by experienced developers, consultants, educators, and researchers.

We welcome any comments or questions regarding the content of this book from students, teachers, or practitioners.
Please direct all questions and comments to:

Keld Bødker: keldb@ruc.dk

Finn Kensing: kensing@itu.dk

Jesper Simonsen: simonsen@ruc.dk

Copenhagen, July 2004

Introduction

Changing organizations is always a major challenge. Realizing new business goals, accommodating a company's needs for change to its work organization, or solving problems of business processes is difficult. However, when the means to such change also require introducing new information technology (IT), the process becomes even more complex and risky. We use the term "IT design" to describe the beginning of this process. An IT design project runs from the emergence of an initial idea for change in a company to the development of a cohesive vision for overall change.

How to go about carrying out an IT design project is entirely dependent on the specific situation. It may depend on a company's management style, its staff's attitude toward change, and its corporate culture. Likewise, it may depend on a company's business and IT strategies and its past experiences with adapting new technology to its existing IT systems.

Is it possible to set sensible, general, and, not least, workable guidelines for such IT design projects? This was the question we set out to answer when we started the research program that has resulted in this book. This book is relevant for readers who

- acknowledge that IT projects can be highly problematic and may fail disastrously, unless they systematically take into account organizational conditions as well as staff qualifications and competencies;
- realize that carrying out an IT design project is difficult—both for students trying to gain competencies in the field as part of their education and for experienced IT designers who have worked with systems development for many years;
- recognize that systems development in general is undergoing change—as companies outsource their internal IT functions, customized IT solutions are replaced by complex and modifiable generic systems, and conventional, detailed requirement specifications

come up short and Web-based IT systems offer companies new opportunities;

- work in companies that must carry out a design project that leads to a well-planned competitive bid (for instance, companies working according to an outsourcing strategy following European Union tender regulations);
- want to become acquainted with the latest systems development research in this area—where IT design consistently takes a business-oriented approach, where management and staff actively participate during the entire project, where firsthand knowledge of users' work practices constitutes an important condition of the visions for change, and where the focus consistently is on anchoring the results with all impacted stakeholders.

This book presents a method for IT design. The method includes terminology identifying the most significant elements of a design project and offers a number of overall guidelines, techniques, and representation tools for the execution of a design project. The method was developed in a research program called MUST (a Danish acronym for theories and methods of initial analysis and design activities) and is known as the MUST method. As mentioned in the preface, the MUST method was developed and tested in thirteen industrial design projects. Here is what experienced IT designers have said about the method:

- It covers all relevant aspects of a design project.
- It ensures better anchoring of the visions.
- It promotes active management participation in the process.
- It offers specific directions for engaging staff in a design project.
- It serves as a means to present and explain the process to a company's customers.
- It helps a project manager plan and manage a design project in a structured manner.
- It helps new employees begin working with IT design.
- It breaks with the major dependency of past projects on overly detailed specifications as the basis of a competitive bid.
- It provides simple yet highly effective techniques for IT design.

- It introduces representation tools with no formalisms that are effective for involving professionals who do not have much experience with IT development.
- It can be used at all levels of education: in introductory tool-based courses, as a methodological primer on project-based work, and in advanced courses in IT strategy.

Target Audience and Structure

This book's target audience is IT designers—that is, people with IT competencies who plan and carry out a design project in cooperation with a company. Accordingly, the primary audience for this book is

- people who already work in systems development, or people with a systems development or programming background who will be carrying out a design project;
- students and educators looking to develop qualifications in IT design.

After reading an early draft of this book and receiving lessons on the MUST method, IT designers tested the method in their own projects. Similarly, students in computer science and information systems programs have conducted small-scale design projects in private and public corporations. The book in its present form is the result of incorporating the experiences gained from this work and comments from IT designers and educators.

Management and staff who will be participating in an IT design project will also profit from reading parts of the book. Managers on a steering committee, for instance, will benefit from reading part I and the overviews in chapters 3–7, which provide examples of the content of reports submitted to a steering committee for a decision. Staff members who will be part of a project group will likewise benefit from reading part I, as well as part II, which reviews the objective and content of the MUST method's phases.

The book is designed both as a textbook for IT design and as a reference work giving specific and experience-based directions that have proven useful in industrial design projects (see the epilogue for ideas on how to make use of the book).

Part I introduces the concepts that are used in the rest of the book. It presents arguments for the necessity of IT design projects, while describing what they involve and what their results are. Finally, it discusses the four principles of the MUST method, which serve as guidelines for a project group planning and conducting a design project.

Part II describes the four phases of the MUST method, which present the method's suggestions for organizing a design project:
- Initiation phase
- In-line analysis phase
- In-depth analysis phase
- Innovation phase

Each phase is described with reference to the following concerns:
- Objective
- Motivation
- Situations and ambitions
- Examples
- Possible phase activities
- Possible results of the phase

Each description starts by specifying the objective and motivation of the phase, namely, the arguments for conducting the phase. The phases can be planned and implemented at varying levels of scope and ambition, depending on the specific design project situation. Accordingly, different situations for each phase are sketched out, from a "MUST lite" situation to one that includes every activity a phase might possibly contain. Examples are provided of different situations that call for attaching greater or lesser importance to each phase. All potential activities of a phase are then described in depth, and aids for each activity are suggested in the form of relevant techniques and representation tools. In addition, the potential results of each phase are described in terms of their relevance, with respect to the design project, implementation project, business strategy, work practices, IT systems, and IT platform.

Part III describes the MUST method's suggested techniques and representation tools. Techniques are meant for individual activities (or aspects of activities) for data gathering, analysis and presentation, or project management. These can be used separately, regardless of how the design project is organized. The techniques provide specific suggestions for performing a certain activity. The representation tools are suggestions for drawings, diagrams, and models that support the technique and capture and communicate its results. Part III also presents an overview of the method's techniques and related representation tools. Figure 8.1 allows for comparing and selecting techniques with respect to the phases and principles where they principally apply, while indicating the type of knowledge to which they contribute. Each technique and representation tool is then described in detail in separate sections. The descriptions of individual techniques and representation tools are intended to serve as points of reference, featuring introductory and action-oriented text adapted to the individual tools and techniques.

For practitioners: Part I introduces the underlying concept of the MUST method and, as such, should be considered background reading for parts II and III, which are more practice-oriented. We recommend that project groups, in preparation for using the method, review and discuss the concepts and principles (introduced in part I) and relate them to their own practice. Parts II and III are designed as a practical "toolbox." Thus, the aim of each phase description in part II is for project participants to spend a few hours reading up on the phase prior to an initial project meeting about it. The activities and results reviewed for each phase may be regarded as a checklist of potentially relevant activities and results. Part III should be regarded as reference material. Only the introductory overview needs to be read in full, while individual tools and techniques can be studied as one considers implementing them. The epilogue describes some of our general experiences in working with IT practitioners on disseminating the MUST method in ways that allow them to include (parts of) the method in their repertoire.

For students and educators: We, especially in part I, describe the MUST method in a way that makes comparison with other methods easy—for instance, by explicitly describing the method's application and relating it to other methods. Part II is organized in a way that makes it possible to follow and employ the phases in a practical study project that will provide initial experiences with IT design. Part III provides an overview and practical review of individual tools and techniques. Each tool and technique may also be used separately, regardless of the choice of method—for instance, at an early stage of a study course. For more in-depth studies of tools and techniques, literature references are provided. The epilogue gives an example of how we have used this book as a textbook for a university course.

I
Concepts and Principles

Chapter 1

IT Design

Chapter 2

Principles of the Method

1
IT Design

This book is about IT design and IT design projects, as well as the methodological support for them in the form of the MUST method. This chapter describes IT design and outlines the MUST method. We illustrate the necessity of conducting IT design projects and review different ways of organizing and managing design projects. Five examples of design projects, demonstrating many different situations where the method has proven its usefulness, conclude the chapter.

1.1 What Is IT Design?

Our understanding of what IT design involves, and its definition in relation to an overall IT project, is inspired by better-established design traditions, such as architecture. Architects perform extensive study and design activities, forming the basis for a call for bids to choose a contractor for the construction. Architects analyze a client's wishes and needs, specifying a building's form and function over several iterations—first generally and conceptually, then in greater detail—in order to plan the construction process.

We think of IT design in similar terms: Initial efforts of analysis and design that form the basis for deciding which of the outlined visions for future IT usage best meet business goals and user needs for IT support in their work. An IT design project thus constitutes an important element in an organizational clarification process leading to descriptions of one or more sustainable uses of IT. In this book, we argue for an explicit upfront design component of an IT project. This can be realized in many ways. In section 1.6, we present five examples of such activities to illustrate the diversity of IT design in an industrial context. In many projects, we have experienced the necessity of dividing an IT project into a design project and an implementation project, separated by a call for tenders (see figure 1.1). We have chosen to present our approach using this model as our reference. Based on the design project and, possibly, supplementary detail specification of parts of a chosen vision, suppliers can judge whether their present systems meet their needs or whether they should make bids involving new development.

As mentioned, we have chosen the project model depicted in figure 1.1 as our reference for identifying the IT design project. The MUST method, including its techniques and tools, may be used in other contexts as well. For example, a product development company we have worked with uses the method when it prepares proposals for implementation

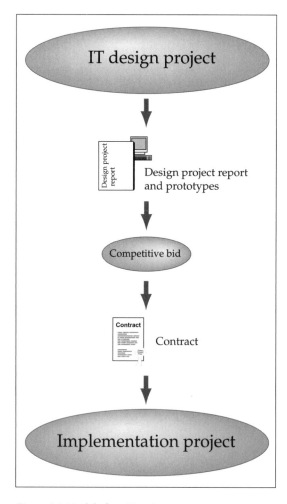

Figure 1.1 Model of an IT project

of its generic IT products for potential customers, as well as in the implementation projects.

In the construction industry, a centuries-old, established tradition determines how the construction process is conducted and how architects cooperate with the client and the many trade groups that, at one time or another, may be drawn into the project. In this process, a wealth of experiences is gained and consensus is reached in many of the areas involved in the construction process, as well in terms of the content and detail of various specifications developed in the process. No such tradition exists in the IT world. A marked difference is the construction industry's better-established and standardized interfaces between phases, which enable calls for tenders to be issued at several different points and in a varied scope. There is currently no such tradition in IT projects. So far, IT projects do not involve tenders similar to architectural competitions, in which a series of prequalified firms—for a fee—are invited to submit bids for possible solutions based on the client's designated needs. This book may be considered a contribution to the development over time of a well-established project processes in the IT industry. We consider the IT designer to be responsible for the design project, underscoring the importance of the element of design in such projects and, in turn, the analogy to the function of the architect in construction.

IT design project: A project conducted at a company that reveals goals, defines problems, and indicates solutions, with the aim of designing sustainable uses of IT based on a specific problem within the company.

The IT design project produces a decision-making basis for the company regarding the potentials and opportunities for implementing IT usage that solve the problems. The results of the design project provide a point of departure for a subsequent call for tenders and an implementation the design project's visions.

Definition 1.1 IT design project

> **IT designer:** A person with competencies in IT design projects and IT in general who, in cooperation with a company, plans and conducts a design project.

Definition 1.2 IT designer

The MUST method provides a perspective on IT design projects that takes a broad view of IT usage. This involves viewing IT systems within the work organization context of which they will be part and considering what new qualifications will be required for users to contribute to desired changes. Another important characteristic is the extensive participation of people from the company—that is, management and the future users of new IT systems, along with any internal IT designers who will be participating in the implementation. A third characteristic is the method's insistence on not taking for granted a company's premise for a design project or any ready solution proposals. There is good reason to be skeptical of ready solution proposals and to base proposed changes on a firm knowledge of a company's existing organizational and work practices. Accordingly, the MUST method rests on *four* principles that aim to represent these characteristics in a design project.

An IT design project, or design project for short, will produce a foundation for deciding whether to undertake an implementation project. A broad anchoring should be ensured for this foundation. Accordingly, a design project involves

- analyzing the company's business and IT strategies, as well as its present goals, needs, and potentials;
- designing one or more visions for overall change;
- weighing the design visions in relation to the company's business and IT strategies in relation to different personnel groups, interdepartmental relations, and with regard to customers and suppliers;

> **IT usage:** IT systems considered within a usage context, including work organization and the qualifications required for users to perform their work using the new technology and within the new work organization.

Definition 1.3 IT usage

- setting down a strategy and plan for technical and organizational implementation, and developing cost estimates for implementing the visions;
- guaranteeing continued feedback from the relevant actors.

These steps can be summed by defining design projects as identifying problems, clarifying goals, and outlining solutions.

Figure 1.2 outlines the function of a design project within an IT project, according to the MUST method.

A design project is undertaken because management wishes to pursue certain business goals, because one or more groups within the company have experienced a problem, or because somebody has a relatively clear idea of how a problem or new tasks can be handled with the help of new uses of IT. In any of these cases, the situation at the start of the design project, depicted as "the current situation" in figure 1.2, can be characterized as marked by various degrees of uncertainty. It is the design project's job to sort through these uncertainties.

The result is a report, possibly supplemented by prototypes, outlining one or more coherent visions for change in terms of technology, work organization, and required employee qualifications—shown as "visions of future situations" in figure 1.2. Moreover, the report includes an evaluation of the effects of implementing the visions, a cost estimate, along with a strategy and plan for implementing the visions. The report is the basis for a decision about an implementation project. This decision is typically followed by a call for tenders and contract negotiations with the chosen supplier or suppliers that will be implementing the IT systems. In some design projects, the specifications of new IT systems will be so far advanced that the design report may more or less directly serve as the basis for a call for tenders. In other cases, the design projects outline a number of possible alternatives the company's management could choose. Tender documents are then prepared based on the design that is selected.

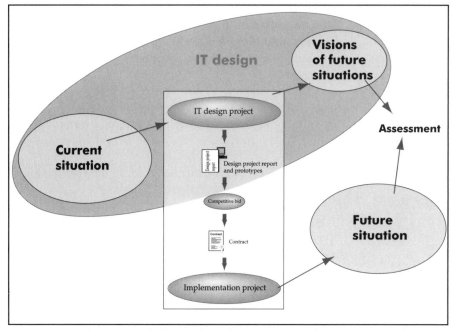

Figure 1.2 How the MUST method views the IT design project in relation to the overall project

The implementation project can then be conducted by the chosen supplier. The supplier is usually an external company, but may in some cases be a partner or a subsidiary of a big corporation. In special cases, the chosen "supplier" may be the company's own internal IT department. The implementation project leads to a future situation for the company as envisioned in the design project. During or after the implementation project, it will be possible to assess the results by comparing the design project's documented visions with the company's newly realized situation.

> **Supplier:** The supplier is a key actor with regard to the implementation part of the overall IT project (see figure 1.1). The supplier is usually an external company, but may in some cases be a partner or subsidiary of a corporation. In special cases, the chosen "supplier" may be the company's own internal IT department. Based on the deliverables of the design project (and possibly on supplementary detail specification of parts of a chosen solution), suppliers can judge whether their present IT systems meet the needs or whether they should make an bid involving new development.

Definition 1.4 Supplier

1.2 Overview of the MUST Method

The various elements of the MUST method should be considered resources for supporting IT designers in planning and conducting a design project (see figure 1.3). First, the method provides specific concepts for the most significant elements of a design project. Second, it provides four principles upon which a design project must generally build. Third, it provides certain overall guidelines in the form of four phases according to which a design project can be organized and planned. Fourth, the method provides a range of specific techniques and representation tools for use in the activities of the various phases.

No two design projects are alike. Any design project depends on the actual situation of a specific company at a given time. The design project should be planned and conducted accordingly. Responsibility for doing so rests with the IT designers. According to the MUST method, the central part of the figure (the IT design project) is an empty shell for the IT designers to fill.

At the top of figure 1.3 are concepts and principles introduced by the MUST method, including specifications of the phase concept, the design project and its results, as well as IT usage and the IT project. Also described are the method's

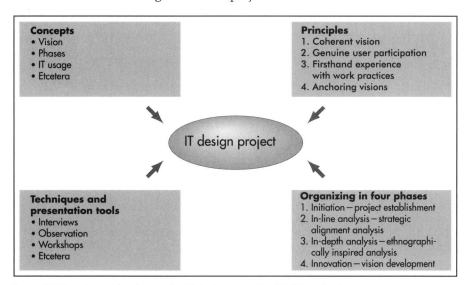

Figure 1.3 Four types of resources for IT design using the MUST method

basic assumptions, its application area, the central actors, and so forth.

These principles should be considered general guidelines for the method, regardless of the situation to which it is applied. As mentioned, the principles express the perspective that the project group should take on the design project.

The lower right-hand corner of figure 1.3 shows the phases of the method. As a starting point, we recommend planning a design project in four phases. Each phase has its own objective, content, and focus, supporting an incremental decision-making process via the intermediate and final products generated in each phase.

A phase is a collection of activities performed between two points in time, taking the design from one decision-making situation to the next. Accordingly, this involves a progression of content in the scope and detail of decisions. Such a phase concept is familiar from baseline planning, as described in section 9.1, and milestone planning. When working with this definition of a phase, it makes no sense to talk about iterating or returning to a phase once it has been completed and a decision to continue has been made. How-

---

Principles: The principles express the method's outlook, or perspective, according to which the project group should think and act when planning and conducting a design project. The principles should be considered general guidelines for the method, regardless of the situation to which it is applied. The principles express the method's reasoning for the design project (content and organization) and the design project's object field (the company and its actors).

Definition 1.5 Principles

Phase: A phase is a collection of activities performed between two points in time, taking the design project from one decision-making situation to the next. A phase will typically contain both analytical and design-oriented activities.

Definition 1.6 Phase

> **Activity:** A defined work process with a specific aim. An activity may be supported by techniques and representation tools.

Definition 1.7 Activity

ever, certain activities in a given phase may very well have to be done over and improved, if the decision-making foundation to which they contribute is found lacking. Similarly, certain activities may have to be taken up again at a later phase, if new insight has been gained that makes this necessary.

The lower left-hand corner of figure 1.3 shows the techniques and representation tools included in the method, while figure 1.4 offers an overview of MUST method techniques and representation tools.

The techniques suggest ways of approaching the various activities of the phases, while the representation tools support the processing and presentation of knowledge contributed by the activities. These techniques and representation tools should be considered additions to the "toolbox" already used by IT designers.

The MUST method is not a design recipe to be followed blindly. The method should always be adapted to the specific project. It is up to the design project's IT designers to decide how to follow the principles, how to plan and organize individual phases in greater detail, and, finally, how to choose which techniques and representation tools to apply. The method may be employed as a resource and inspiration for such efforts. It provides certain overall guidelines for conducting a design project, while offering guidelines for how to plan individual activities according to the specific situation. The descriptions of the individual phases provide examples of different situations and identify the most relevant aspects of the method to apply to these situations. In other words, the method is not a "cookbook." Its aim is not to describe, step by step, how to carry out a design project. Design projects are simply too dependent on the given situation and too complex to ever make this possible.

Techniques	Representation tools
Baseline planning	Baseline plan
Review	Summary
Hearing	Summary
Interview In situ interview	Summary
Document analysis	Notes
Functional analysis	Functional model
SWOT analysis	SWOT model Risk matrix
Observation	Summary
Thinking-aloud experiments	Notes
Workshop	Freehand drawing Collage Dead Sea Scroll Affinity diagram Role list Communication model Timeline Design sketch Data model
Future workshop	Open notes on big sheets of paper
Mapping	Diagnostic maps Virtual maps
Prompted reflection	Freehand drawing Notes Summary
Company visit	Summary
Experimenting with prototypes	Mock-ups Prototypes
Developing scenarios	Scenario

Figure 1.4 MUST method techniques and representation tools

Figure 1.5 outlines the four phases of the MUST method, their focus and results in the form of related intermediate and end products, plus the decisions they support. This figure illustrates how a design project may be conducted to produce knowledge and insight that make up a viable foundation for a decision to run a subsequent implementation project.

> **Technique:** A technique is a specific direction for performing a certain activity. It may involve activities for data gathering, processing and presentation, or project management. Techniques may be used independently of how the design project is planned.

Definition 1.8 Technique

> **Representation tools:** Representation tools are suggestions for graphics, figures, and models to support the processing and presentation of knowledge contributed by a technique.

Definition 1.9 Representation tools

> **Product:** The result of one or more activities. In baseline planning, a product corresponds to the result of a phase's activities on the baseline.
>
> **Intermediate product** refers to any product preceding an end product.
>
> **End product** refers to products on a design project's final baseline.

Definition 1.10 Product, intermediate product, and end product

Phases	Focus	Results—decisions
Initiation phase —project establishment	Scope of the design project: timetable, content, finances, and participants	Project charter + plan —premise and scope of the design project
In-line analysis phase —strategic alignment analysis	Aligning the design project's goals and the company's business and IT strategies	Strategic alignment report —choice of work domains to be examined
In-depth analysis phase —ethnographically inspired analysis	Work practices in selected work domains	Analysis report + work practice descriptions —prioritizing goals to be met and ideas for IT support to be specified
Innovation phase —vision development	Visions of IT systems and their relation to work organization and qualifications Implementation project	Design project report + mock-ups and prototypes —visions to be realized, and how to realize them

Figure 1.5 The four phases of the MUST method, their focus, and results

1.3 Why IT Design?

From our more than a decade of teaching and research collaborations with public and private corporations, it has been our experience that IT projects often run a troublesome course. They exceed budget and timetable, or are implemented without producing results that match the original intentions. A significant reason for these problems is the lack of a viable decision-making foundation for such projects. This may be due to the following factors:

- An unrealistic ambition level exists regarding the necessary organizational anchoring process or technical possibilities and limitation.
- The choice of technology is primarily guided by standalone technical solutions in identifying individual areas to be automated or supported.
- IT projects are undertaken as technical responses to problems that are basically organizational, without qualified interlocking of technical possibilities with organizational and human goals and needs.
- No systematic efforts are made to develop and anchor visions for overall change. There is a significant risk of

the desired goals not being achieved when such visions are not anchored with management, with those who will be implementing the change, or with the users who will be working within the changed organization.

Meanwhile, systems development in a broad sense is undergoing change. Many companies used to have their IT systems developed from scratch by their own internal IT departments. Many systems development methods appear still to be based on this premise. Today, most companies outsource their IT development to external suppliers, partners, or subsidiaries when it is not a significant aspect of their business. As a result, IT design projects often involve a competitive bidding process. This is the case with all public institutions and companies within the European Union, where IT projects of a certain scale require competitive bidding according to the European Union rules for invitations to tender and award contracts. Moreover, many IT usages are developed by combining and adapting standard systems into an overall solution. Such combining and adapting of components is often quite complicated, requiring both technical and organizational insight.

In other cases, it is necessary to design systems more or less from scratch, because no standard systems exist that meet the company's goals and needs. When preparing to undertake a new IT project, a company needs to compare its requirements for functionality and interaction with existing systems on the market and then determine a strategy for implementing new IT usage. This is where IT design projects come in.

Standard system: A system in the form of a product offered by a supplier to several customers (unlike a customized system, which is specially tailored to a customer). Standard systems may often be substantially modified and are sometimes referred to as generic systems. Standard systems can be adapted, for instance, by installing different preferences and parameters, special functions and tools, or dedicated programming languages.

Definition 1.11 Standard system

Many systems development methods involve initial activities resembling IT design projects and often use similar terms, such as survey, pre-analysis, or preliminary study. However, such methods rarely operate with a call for tenders, since they implicitly require the IT system to be developed from scratch. Furthermore, many systems development methods reflect a far better established understanding of needs and requirements for IT usage than we encounter when starting an IT design project. An IT design project could conceivably be conducted using the MUST method, while the subsequent implementation project would employ other methods. Such methods, which primarily target development of new products or customized systems, include Modern Structured Analysis and Design, Object-Oriented Analysis and Design, Rapid Application Development, Dynamic Systems Development Method, Prototyping, and Agile methods. Or they could incorporate methods that more directly integrate a call for tenders and customer-supplier relations into their project model, such as the Euromethod and Performance-Based Procurement.

We have chosen to use the term *IT design project* to highlight that analytical as well as design-oriented activities are involved. We consider a design project to be an independent activity upon which a decision can be based to issue a call for tenders with the aim of realizing visions developed in the design project. An IT design project is carried out at a company with the aim of designing sustainable IT usage in response to a more or less specified problem within the company.

We use the broad term, *IT usage*—rather than IT systems— because an IT design project also needs to focus on the organization of the work which the IT systems will support and on the required user qualifications. The results of a design project are summed up in a report and possibly supplemented by prototypes, which create the foundation for a call for tenders and a decision to undertake an implementation project. The report will highlight the business goals and user needs that dictated the design's premise. It will include one or more visions for new IT usage, as well as an evaluation of the extent to which they accommodate the designated goals and needs. Finally, the report will include a strategy, plan, and financial estimate for realizing the design visions.

An IT design project is more comprehensive than traditional pre-analysis and preliminary studies. In our experience, an IT design project is a sensible investment as a step in determining an IT project's goals, content, scope, ambition level, and so forth. A design project typically lasts from one to six months and will, at a minimum, involve resources corresponding to one to two man-months. In a large project where we participated in the upfront design activities, described in section 1.6.2, the IT design project accounted for 1 percent of the total costs. In other projects where the implementation projects are less expensive, the IT design project may account for 5 percent of the total costs. An IT design project must be sufficiently comprehensive to develop knowledge that enables fundamental design decisions to be made before an implementation project begins. It often turns out to be very important if fundamental decisions—for instance, regarding the overall design of an IT system—are changed in the course of implementing the system. On the other hand, a design project should not be confused with the overall IT project. After the IT design project is completed, there is still a need for analysis and design activities, but the overall framework is in place.

Some might argue that, in light of rapidly evolving business needs and opportunities, there is no time to undertake an IT design project. According to this argument, once a problem has been resolved—once there is clear agreement about it and clear relations to outlines of possible IT usage answering the problem—there is no need for a design project. In such cases, it may seem expedient to go straight to an implementation project. However, we have seen many IT projects that, in retrospect, turned out not to be in that situation after all. Likewise, it is important to pause occasionally and examine closely the relations among individual projects, the company's business goals, and problems experienced by the users in their everyday work—another reason why an IT design project is the most sensible choice.

1.4 Organizing and Managing IT Design Projects

Throughout this book, we generally describe the MUST method based on a structure that includes a project group led by a project manager and a steering committee headed by a chairman. We have settled on this model because it is the most common. An IT design project following the MUST method may, of course, be organized according to another model—for instance, one featuring a sponsor, requisitioner, and project group.

Perhaps the presentation of the four phases and the decision-making sequence they imply may seem to imply that an IT design project can be planned and carried out as an entirely rational and unequivocal process. It cannot. IT design projects are marked by too high a degree of uncertainty for that. The uncertainty of IT design projects is due to four factors:

- High complexity: Many variables are not given in advance—they first need to be identified—and they are also often hard to isolate because they are interdependent.
- High mutability: The problem is not clearly defined from the outset and changes occur during the design process. New requirements may emerge and new possible solutions appear.
- High situation-dependency: Although an IT design project may have features in common with past projects, the project group always has to plan and manage the process according to the specific conditions at hand.
- High risk of value conflicts: Various parties involved in the IT design project, or those affected by its course and results, often have conflicting interests.

Accordingly, detailed insight into the goals, progress, status, and plans of the design project is necessary so a design team can step in and regulate the process when unforeseen events occur. Project management must be performed in close accordance with the project group's other activities.

Project management is about planning, evaluation, and regulation. Planning involves laying out the IT design project based on an understanding of the conditions for the project:

for instance, activities that must be performed and techniques and representation tools that shared be used. Evaluation involves comparing the planned process and the planned products with what has actually been accomplished. When significant variation between the current status of a project and its plans occurs, regulation involves making the necessary adjustments to the plans or ambition level.

Project management is concerned with the division of work in the project group and the distribution of competencies between the project group and its surroundings, while also overseeing quality assurance and conflicts. Project management can be defined as establishing, maintaining, and overseeing the mutual commitments that make the project what it is.

The project manager should have experience in IT projects and how to handle them. He or she will typically be a person with an IT background or a middle manager with the company who has general competencies in organizational change. The project manager is responsible for planning the IT design project and, together with the steering committee, for continually assessing whether the plan is being followed. The project manager and project group as a whole will produce guidelines for the steering committee. However, for the project to run efficiently, the project manager and project group should also be able to make decisions on their own between steering committee meetings. Thus, significant competency must be delegated to the project manager. For an IT design project to run efficiently, the project manager must have a level of decision-making competency that enables him or her to act without having to consult with the steering committee too frequently. Within certain guidelines, the project manager should personally be able to regulate the plan, the project conditions, and the expectations of others involved in the project. Beyond these guidelines, he or she is responsible for creating a foundation for the steering committee to perform such regulation.

The function of the steering committee is—based on proposals by the project group and in accordance with the company's strategies—to make the required decisions, handle possible conflicts, guarantee the forward progress of the design project, and make sure that it leads to the desired outcome. Of course, due to the uncertainty inherent in a design project, the steering committee must continually revise its expectations for the outcome. The steering committee, moreover, holds overall financial responsibility for the IT project, as well as responsibility for coordinating with other projects, either other IT projects or initiatives that may relate to the ongoing project. The steering committee chairman should be a manager from the department that is most affected by the project, in order to guarantee the project's anchoring with the company's management and ensure that the project leads to the desired changes.

If a project runs into problems—for instance, by exceeding its timetable or budget—it may be because insufficient time has been spent on project management. In our experience, a realistic calculation calls for 15–25 percent of the project group's total time to be spent on project management because of the high degree of uncertainty involved. Experience shows that much time is spent discussing, planning, and deciding how to organize the project and adjust it on an ongoing basis. In addition, time is spent following up on whether various products meet expectations and, not least, maintaining the values, agreements, and obligations on which the project builds.

The MUST method is thus structured to make it possible to address the underlying causes of uncertainty and risk in the design project. The project group gathers and continually processes information that forms the basis for decision making. If new information so dictates, decisions must be assessed, regulated, or reformulated entirely. For instance, it may be necessary to rethink the basis for the project if the in-line analysis phase uncovers new relations between business goals and the goals of the ongoing design project or gaps that necessitate reformulating the scope of the project. Likewise, additional studies of certain work domains may be required, if, for instance, a vision turns out to have an impact on domains that have not been sufficiently analyzed. If this happens, the innovation phase is expanded to include such activities. The whole point of insisting on a relatively extensive design project before the implementation project is because it is possible (and much cheaper) to remake decisions during the course of the design project than during the implementation project, because of the increase in knowledge produced by the design project. Moreover, project management activities such as baseline planning, risk management, and reviews ensure that a design project can be planned, assessed, and regulated in response to specific uncertainties at hand.

Finally, the MUST method suggests a high level of user participation, emphasizing an anchoring with the relevant parties regarding the processing of the project group's intermediate and end products. Here, the various parties involved can point out errors or shortcomings and protect their interests. This input may then be incorporated into the further efforts of the project group and the steering committee. We recommend that the project group spend resources to ensure that those who will be making the decisions about the design of the system, those who will implement the system, and those who will have to live with its consequences are all informed about the project group's work and empowered to influence it.

Having made all these qualifications, it should be stressed that the MUST method aims for design projects to be organized and conducted in ways that support rational decision making. The concept of rationality in this context should be understood as "good sense," allowing solutions to be shaped and implemented with a clear link to identified goals, problems, and needs.

1.5 Relating to Other Methods

The issues and concerns dealt with by the MUST method are also addressed by other current methods. However, there are significant differences between the MUST method and other methods. The central differences are outlined in this section.

Compared to traditional waterfall models and evolutionary models, MUST is designed to incorporate the best—and avoid the worst—aspects of these approaches. Even though

MUST is divided into four phases, which are suggested to be separated from implementation by a rather extensive decision process, we recommend iteration between analysis and design activities within and among the phases—including development and testing of prototypes and mock-ups. Thus MUST relies on a different concept of phases (see definition 1.6) than is the case with the waterfall model. In the waterfall model, each phase consists of similar activities, and therefore the result of the analysis phase does not really produce a qualified basis for deciding on how to proceed. In MUST, each phase, and the concerted four phases, is designed to allow the project group to produce a sustainable foundation—from which management and users are able to decide how to proceed.

On the other hand, evolutionary models like prototyping are recommended by the MUST method as part of an IT design project. But unlike prototyping, MUST stresses the importance of clarifying the relations between the current project and business strategies as well as the relation to the work processes and organizational context in which the new IT system will operate. All too often, prototyping approaches—and waterfall models for that matter—either neglect such issues or presuppose that they have been taken care of by others.

Other contemporary methods or approaches have also abandoned the traditional phase model. Rapid Application Development or "agile" methods, like Extreme Programming, focus on fast deliveries of potentially operative systems and incremental development, relying on project models with strong iterative elements controlled along the time dimension by time boxes. These approaches differ in various ways, but they share a strong focus on programming and implementation aspects. A basic assumption for a project following these approaches is that a decision to build a system of a particular kind has already been made. These methods are not intended for larger projects involving multiple systems, some of which are customized systems integrated within an existing system portfolio.

These methods, like modern object-oriented software engineering methods such as Rational Unified Process (RUP), focus on building systems from scratch. RUP, in turn, does incorporate early design activities—in the inception and elaboration phases. These activities are integrated into a software engineering method with a strong focus on modeling, specifications, and implementation, striving for the classic virtues of robustness and maintainability.

Contextual Design (CD), as formulated by Beyer and Holtzblatt (1998), has a scope similar to MUST, which its proponents refer to as front-end design, requirement engineering, or systems analysis. However, CD does not deal with project management and seems to expect the design team itself to be in charge. Quite possibly related to this, CD does not distinguish between the users—those that will interact directly with the systems—and the customers—those that order and pay. In addition, the method does not suggest ways of handling potential conflicting interests. MUST acknowledges that an IT design project may involve politics and is explicit about the different roles and competencies in organizational life in general and in IT design projects in particular.

While a CD process aims at specifications meant for developers or coders, including detailed OO-models of the system functionality and structure, MUST argues for a separate design activity where such specifications are deferred until a decision has been made on what to build or buy. In this way, MUST is inscribed in an overall project model where it is assumed that not all IT systems are built from scratch and where the implementation of customized systems will most likely be outsourced. The rationale of CD seems to be that the same group of people proceed all the way to implementation, in which case this type of detailed description is valuable. Instead, we hold the point of view that detailed technical descriptions are superfluous for those systems that the company in question decides to buy as standard systems, those that are outsourced for a vendor to deliver, and those that are not to be pursued any further.

Business Process Reengineering (BPR), in its original form as proposed by Hammer and Champy (1993), has the same scope as the MUST method. They both address the early analysis and design activities in an IT design project as well as project management. They aim at formulating one or more visions for the future use of IT, while the technical and organizational implementation is considered outside the scope of these methods. BPR and MUST consider the relations between a design project and an organization's business and IT strategies, which are either neglected or considered outside the scope of many current methods—with potentially damaging results.

While radical change, including downsizing, is a major part of the rationale of BPR, it does not deal with ethical or practical issues in relation to users. MUST states explicitly that if management aims at job cuts and / or other drastic changes, this should be announced up front. If users know and accept these objectives, MUST still recommends a participatory approach. Instead BPR suggests an expert strategy, neglecting the knowledge, experience, and interests of users, thereby risking that the visions developed do not meet real needs.

BPR orients its deliverables primarily toward management, offering no help in understanding, developing, or presenting relations between IT and users' work practices. The content and the form of the reports and prototypes resulting from a MUST process are meant for management to prioritize further directions for the subsequent implementation activities. They also allow users to understand the consequences—as to their work practices—of the proposed coherent visions for change.

1.6 Five Examples of IT Design Projects

To illustrate how different IT design projects can be, we conclude this chapter with five examples showing the range of design projects, with an emphasis on describing their aims, process, and results. These examples are all based on design projects that were conducted using the MUST method:

- Example 1 is an IT design project with a specific, organizationally defined premise. As overlapping tasks between two departments involved were quickly clarified, the design project was able to concentrate on specifying two solution models, which led to a choice between two suppliers' products.

- Example 2 describes a rather extensive IT design project. A lot of people and resources were involved in the project. The subsequent implementation was central to the company's strategic development, since it involved a fundamental technological switch and a restructured work organization.
- Example 3 shows how suppliers of standard systems can use a design project and the MUST method when assessing the potential of their IT solution with a customer.
- Example 4 describes an IT design project where the initial system idea turned out to be unsustainable, and the design project as a whole took on a significant element of strategic clarification.
- Example 5 involves a medium-sized department of a big corporation. Here, the IT design project resulted not in detailed descriptions of IT systems, but in an outline of possible IT usage linked to various forecasts for the department's future tasks and function within the corporation.

Examples 1, 2, 4, and 5 all describe ways of carrying out an IT design within a Business organization. The design project is conducted by IT designers (who may be employees of the company or external consultants) in cooperation with the management and staff of the affected parts of the company. Example 3 describes how IT design projects can be handled by development organizations, which then assume the function of the supplier, with the business organization represented as the supplier's customer.

Business organization: The (part of the) company where the IT design project is carried out and where the design project's visions will be realized.

Development organization: The company (supplier) that develops and supplies the IT systems involved in an implementation project.

Definition 1.12 Business organization and development organization

1.6.1 Example 1: A Focused Project in a Small Business

A small contract manufacturer with five employees in a joint warehouse and shipping department (referred to here as "the warehouse") had long been needing to replace its inventory management system. Annual inventories showed substantial variation between actual stocks and the system's data. The warehouse manager had explored the market and come up with three suppliers that he thought would meet the warehouse's needs. From executive meetings, he knew that the order department also used the old inventory system and was not satisfied with it either. At an executive meeting, a decision was made to establish a project group, including someone from the warehouse and someone from the order department. Together with an IT designer, they would examine the departments' needs and come up with proposals for a new IT system. The warehouse manager and the head of the order department made up the steering committee.

The project group started out by developing a project charter, which was then adopted by the steering committee. This charter stated that the project group would investigate opportunities for streamlining interaction between the two departments. The group would also assess whether the three standard systems that the warehouse manager had come up with would be able to support this interaction or whether they only applied to warehouse work. Finally, the group would make a recommendation to the steering committee on the main initiatives needed to solve the problem of the inventory management system. The project group had three months to handle the assignment, and the warehouse representative was named project manager, with the IT designer in support. The project manager was allocated two days a week to work on the project, while the other group member was allowed half a day a week. The IT designer was paid for one workday a week during this period.

On the IT designer's recommendation, the project group began the in-depth analysis phase by developing two models, each capturing different aspects of the work in the two departments. One focused on the flow of an order, from receiving through shipping to receipt of payment. This model focused on who did what in the two departments and what data was involved. The accounting department was originally not among the departments examined. However, at a brief meeting with the steering committee, the project manager argued in favor of including the accounting department. This was approved, since all it involved was the head of accounting evaluating the accuracy of the data received by the accounting department from the two other departments and noting any problems that the accounting department had in obtaining correct data from the other departments. Internal accounting department procedures were not examined.

The second model focused on the flow of communication between the three departments: who communicated with whom, what was communicated, by what means (forms, telephone, electronic), and what could go wrong in this communication?

These models, in simplified form, were submitted to the steering committee in an analysis report describing the problems and needs, with an emphasis on which problems were due to inexpedient workflows and which were caused by the old IT system. The steering committee prioritized the problems and needs it considered most urgent. The IT designer also recommended that the steering committee indicate which of the uncovered problems it would like to see resolved, if they could be handled easily and cheaply by a future IT usage, and which problems should not be part of the project group's further efforts. Following a steering committee meeting, the project group and steering committee jointly presented the staff of the three departments with the prioritized conditions that needed visions to be developed. Management made on-the-spot decisions about which staff reactions to incorporate into the project group's further efforts.

The design project then entered the innovation phase. The IT designer started by describing the functionality of the three standard systems with regard to which of the departments' tasks they were able to support or automate. After a couple of project group meetings, one of the three systems was rejected—although it covered the warehouse needs, it was unable to support order-receiving tasks. The project group now received demonstrations of the two systems, one with a supplier, the other by way of a visit with a company of the IT designer's acquaintance. Here, they were able to see the system at work and hear about the staff's experiences with it. The two staff members in the project group then developed proposals using each of the two systems for new work practices within and between the departments of their company. This provided an opportunity to further specify the requirements for the systems' functionality and interface with regard to meeting prioritized problems and needs.

For each of the two adapted standard systems, the project group outlined a scenario describing an order's flow through the company, including which department would handle which tasks and which would be automated. Although only minor changes were involved in terms of task distribution, the project group still left it to the steering committee to decide whether these tasks would be handled by the order department or the warehouse, as the project group did not feel competent to make such decisions. For each of the two systems and related work organization, moreover, the IT design report included an evaluation of how each department contributed to correct inventory information and which of the documented communication problems between departments would be remedied. For both systems, the project group described the content and level of the training that would be necessary for the staff to be able to handle its tasks. Finally, the report included a plan for implementing the visions and a proposal for prioritizing them. Settling on one of the visions, the steering committee placed an order for the involved IT system with the supplier, which would also oversee the staff's training. The steering committee would personally organize the restructuring of workflows between the warehouse and the order department. Three months after the IT design project concluded, the new system had been implemented as planned.

1.6.2 Example 2: An Ambitious Project in a Big Company

A major radio station decided that its departments should take on a greater share of responsibility for their future IT systems. The station was faced with replacing its technical platform and IT systems. This involved what was broadly labeled "office systems" (from mainframe-based systems to client-server solutions), as well as equipment used for the production and broadcast of radio programs (from analogue to digital technology, as well as multimedia workstations within a network). To that end, a new IT manager at the station had conducted a series of seminars for the heads of the various departments. Lengthy efforts were in motion on the executive level to outline the station's business and IT strategies. Apart from the technological switch, the strategies called for producing more radio for less money and a requirement that the new technology could be used to facilitate a new division of work among journalists, technicians, and administrative staff. Following the IT strategy, a supplier was found for the new technical platform and computer systems for some of the office systems, while other systems were put out to competitive bidding. In addition, a decision was made to conduct an IT design project in order to develop visions for future IT usage. The focus was on program production, while management and administrative aims would be affected only to the extent that program-related activities generated information relevant to these aims.

In accordance with the departments' newly gained responsibility for their own IT systems, the head of the selected department was made chairman of the steering committee, which also comprised the rest of the department management and the IT manager. A middle manager was named project manager. The project group also included two journalists, a technician, and two external IT designers. The project manager was assigned to the project full time, while the users were each allocated one day a week to work on the project. The IT designers combined would perform what amounted to the work of one person for the five months that the project was scheduled to run.

To gain an initial impression of the complexity of the work that went on at the radio station, the IT designers carried out a full-day observation of an editorial unit's work in preparing, broadcasting, and reporting on a program. They also interviewed a radio host, a journalist, a technician, and an administrative staff member. One of the IT designers helped the project manager write a draft of the project charter, specifying the scope of the IT design project and including a project plan emphasizing the alignment and in-depth analysis phases. At a meeting of the project and steering committees, the project charter was approved with a few corrections and submitted as a proposed department briefing.

Over the next couple of weeks, the project manager, the steering committee chairman, and the two IT designers worked on the in-line analysis phase, developing the department's own business and IT strategy. Apart from the overall strategies for the station, which were specified in relation to the department, the strategy mainly built on the following elements:

- A fusion of the technical platforms used for (journalists') office work and for the production of radio programs
- A selective call for tenders regarding procurement and development of equipment and IT systems
- Procurement of standard systems taking precedence over new development
- Using IT as a strategic tool to reach the right listeners with the right programs at the right time and to blur job demarcations between the department's three personnel groups
- Management and staff becoming active in the initiation and implementation of new IT usage

During the strategic planning, the IT designers read a number of reports and interviewed the department management about their ideas for the project. The next step, the in-line analysis phase, resulted in a brief strategic alignment report that specified the department's business and IT strategies and identified which work domains the in-depth analysis phase would focus on regarding the production aspects of the department's radio programs.

Over the next eight weeks, the project group concentrated on the in-depth analysis phase. The work involved interviewing or observing a third of the department's 150 employees or having them participate in thinking-aloud experiments. Recordings were made, and the employees approved the summary transcripts produced by the project group after each session. The project group gathered and analyzed the various documents and materials involved in the production of radio programs. Some of the project group's own meetings were held as workshops where the collected material was shaped into graphic representations of the work. The project group subsequently wrote an analytical report to the steering committee based on the project's strategic goals, comparing these to the identified needs and various possible groupings within the department, including management as well as single- or multiple-person editorial units. The report also contained a plan for the innovation phase. Once the steering committee had approved a plan that prioritized the goals, needs, and possibilities to be worked on in the next phase, a department meeting was held to discuss the report. The steering committee chairman decided that the project group should work some of the comments from the meeting into the report, while judging that the report did not need to be resubmitted to the steering committee for approval.

The innovation phase was scheduled to last ten weeks. The project group first went on a fact-finding mission to another radio station which had recently switched to digital technology. Management and staff at this station were interviewed, their radio-production process was observed, and everything was recorded on video. Later, this material was analyzed and summarized in a note about the other station's experiences with broadcast quality, personnel cuts, blurring of job lines and training requirements, along with any significant experience gained in the process during and immediately after the systems had been installed. The IT designers then organized a series of design workshops. At one of these, the project group listed all the goals and needs that had been prioritized in the previous phase, along with any other design ideas that had been conceived (including a few from the fact-finding mission), and wrote them down on colored adhesive notes. The notes were stuck on a wall and grouped together to link goals and needs to design ideas. This procedure revealed gaps in the project group's knowledge about how some of the editorial units worked, so a few additional interviews were conducted.

Most of the design ideas needed to be developed and combined into suggestions for IT systems and work organization. This was accomplished at a workshop, as the project group outlined typical production processes on large rolls of paper. Here, functionality that was familiar from already elected IT systems was outlined in the context of the work organization that management had demanded and supplemented by knowledge of staff preferences. This led to an articulation of the requirements for modifying elected systems and integrating them with a series of new systems, whose functionality and interfaces were described by the IT designers. The new functionality, including electronic editing and broadcast capabilities, implied a broad potential for journalists to take over large parts of the technicians' work. The sketches focused on the relations between the IT systems' functionality and interfaces, on the one hand, and the new roles to be performed by the staff, on the other.

On this basis, the IT designers developed a computer model covering the entire radio-production process. The computer model served as the basis for developing a series of prototypes, programmed by the IT designers in cooperation with users from the project group. When the prototypes had been tested by a few editorial units, the project group concluded its work by writing a final project report to the steering committee. Relations between goals, needs, and suggested IT systems were presented and assessed in table form. Each new IT system was described and illustrated with figures. Scenarios illustrated the relations between the IT systems and the new work-organization proposals. This enabled the group to specify the content and scope of the required staff training and work out a cost estimate for purchasing and adapting multimedia workstations, servers, networks, and standard systems, as well as for new development and integration of the IT systems. The report concluded with a strategy for introducing and operating the various IT systems and a plan for implementing the technical and organizational changes during a first stage.

The steering committee opted to submit the report to a hearing among the staff and called a meeting to discuss it before making a decision. The meeting produced a number of suggested changes, which the project group incorporated. Then, the steering committee voted to roll out the first stage of the plan. Roughly two years later, most of the design project's recommendations had been implemented. By then, the total cost of the IT project amounted to about $14 million.

1.6.3 Example 3: A Supplier Investigates the Feasibility of a Standard System

Over a period of years, an IT supplier had been developing an extensive and specialized system for Computer Integrated Manufacturing (CIM), targeting certain kinds of manufacturing companies. The CIM standard system is sold to companies worldwide. It can be tailored to the individual client, and this process is a relatively large aspect of the whole IT project. Furthermore, the standard system is developed gradually: if a customer has a need that the system cannot support and this need is judged to be "general," the supplier develops a new module for the system in the course of implementing the system with this customer. This module then becomes a feature of the overall standard system and is offered to existing and new customers.

When the supplier contacts a new potential customer, it is rarely completely clear at first, either to the supplier or the customer, how the customer's needs relate to the system's functionality. First, it needs to be clarified whether the customer is "interesting"—that is, if the customer actually needs major parts of the system or if the customer provides a good opportunity for further developing parts of the system that the supplier expects will have a broader market. In the supplier's experience, the customer's technological "maturity," as well as cultural aspects of the customer's nationality, are important factors here. In other words, the extent of the common interests between the supplier and the customer needs to be clarified—whether there is sufficient overlap between the customer's needs and the standard system's present and projected functionality.

The supplier offers to perform such clarification free of charge in the form an IT design project conducted by the supplier with the customer. Since it is free for the customer, the project is organized as a "MUST lite" project—a brief but effective process. The project is carried out by two experienced IT designers with in-depth knowledge of the production process of this particular kind of company gained from past IT projects with other customers. The design project, lasting two to three months, involves a total of three visits with the customer and costs the supplier around two man-months of resources plus travel expenses. The outcome is a clarification of the customer's problems and needs, including which modules of the standard system are immediately relevant, required adaptations, which newly developed standard modules or specially developed system parts are needed, financial estimates, and an implementation strategy.

This type of design project was undertaken at a promising large company in Hungary. In advance, a sales manager had paid a visit to the company to demonstrate the supplier's CIM solution. The two IT designers assigned to the project had a couple of initial meetings with the sales manager, who filled them in on the company. Then, the first visit with the company was scheduled. The IT designers devised a preliminary plan for this two-day visit and submitted a proposal to the company's management that informed the staff about the visit. The IT designers asked the company to make a number of representatives of the various personnel groups available during their visit. A week or so before their visit, they also submitted a draft of a project charter and a design project plan.

The visit kicked off with a half-day meeting of the IT designers and eight management representatives from the company, including the CEO, CFO, IT manager, and five production managers. The IT designers made a presentation describing what the design project would involve and thoroughly went over the outlined project charter and plan. A large portion of the meeting was spent discussing which work domains to focus on in the project. The CEO and the CFO put a priority on production planning and management information, while several of the production managers also wanted to see a focus on the subsequent production processes. The discussion ended with the CEO stepping in and deciding that the design project would focus on production planning and that IT support for subsequent processes would only be considered to the extent necessary to provide data for the planning. A number of comments for the design project and plan were taken down, and the IT designers promised to go over a new draft with the CEO before leaving the next day. This meeting had thus taken care of both the initiation and the in-line analysis phases, and the in-depth analysis phase could now be undertaken.

The IT designers also interviewed eight employees who broadly represented the entire production process. All interviews were recorded. That evening at the hotel, the IT designers revised the project charter and plan and discussed the day's events. A meeting was held with the IT manager who went over the company's present production systems, and the IT designers received a volume of documentation for these systems and their databases.

Upon returning from Hungary, the IT designers listened to all the recorded interviews and scrutinized the documents they had received (brochures, strategy plans, systems documentation, descriptions of production processes, and so forth). In the process, they made notes of their observations using keywords. At a full-day workshop, with the participation of the sales manager, all the keywords from the interviews and the document studies were reviewed, discussed, and scribbled on to colored adhesive notes. These were organized in diagnostic maps under the headings of "needs," "problems," "causes," "consequences," and "ideas for solutions." The results of this workshop served as a starting point for the second visit with the customer.

The second visit, which lasted two days as well, concluded the in-depth analysis phase. The first day was organized as a full-day workshop with the eight management representatives. Here, the IT designers reviewed the diagnostic maps they had developed. The maps were commented on, corrected, and rephrased. The workshop acquainted the company's management with the prioritized problems and needs, as well as with the potential computer-based solutions presented in the workshop's diagnostic maps. The remainder of the visit was spent conducting four follow-up interviews and in an extended meeting with the IT manager and the company's database administrator, discussing possible connections to the CIM system.

In the period leading up to the third and last visit with the customer, the IT designers prepared a final project report based on the prioritized ideas for computer-based solutions produced by the mapping activity of the in-depth analysis phase. The report graphically outlined the full IT solution, describing the functionality of the recommended CIM-system modules and its relations to the company's existing systems and databases. The report included three scenarios, each describing how the system would be used by the CEO, a production manager, and a shop foreman. Finally, the reported contained a proposed implementation strategy, which included recommendations for subproject divisions, integrated adaptations, and training processes.

The project report was presented at the third visit with the customer and reviewed by the eight management representatives. The visit and meeting were scheduled to last four hours but ended up taking nearly seven hours. The report presentation was supplemented by a demonstration of selected aspects of the CIM system. The meeting was extended to allow for a discussion of possible alternative implementation strategies. The IT manager, in particular, questioned whether the CIM system would be able to deliver on its promises. In turn, the IT designers proposed a strategy of an initial "proof-of-concept" pilot project involving a test run of the CIM system with the customer, using sample data partially transferred from the company's own databases. The pilot project was successfully completed four months later. During the follow-up process, the customer visited a company in England that had been using the CIM system for a while. A contract was then signed, which included the implementation of most of the supplier's standard CIM system.

1.6.4 Example 4: Focus on Strategic Alignment

The management of a company with seventy employees and three departments had decided to reprioritize the resources in the customer service department. The company had two types of customers, personal and corporate. The customer service staff was divided into two groups, each handling one type of customer. The idea was to service a greater number of personal customers via a network of middlemen who already dealt with such customers. The company already had a budding partnership with these middlemen. The staff, freed from dealing with personal customers, would participate in an intensified drive for corporate customers. This would be accomplished while the company's old computer system, which was used only in personal customer service, was being replaced. Corporate customer service would be affected by the planned change only inasmuch as their efforts were to be enhanced. The company commissioned an IT designer to conduct a design project. The aim was to outline a new computer system to be used both by the middlemen and the remaining staff in personal customer service that handled the customers who were expected to continue contacting the company directly. The computer system was to be outlined in a way that would allow it to serve as a basis for various suppliers to tender bids.

The IT designer had two initial meetings with the CEO and the head of the customer service department to specify the company's market situation and the goals of the project. The department head relayed the concerns that some of her employees—who had previously serviced personal customers based on phone or written inquiries—had about possibly needing to deal with corporate customers. In addition to demanding new professional and personal qualifications, this kind of work also required more outreach activities (mainly taking place at trade fairs and conferences) and involved using a different computer system. However, the CEO ensured these staff members that provisions had been made for these changes. These employees would take supplementary training courses and would initially act only as "trainees" under the guidance of an experienced co-worker.

The IT designer, who had been named project manager, prepared a draft of the project charter that specified the scope of the design project. It was decided that the IT designer would work the equivalent of two hundred man-hours over two months. Together with a staff member from customer services, the IT designer would suggest uses of IT in personal-customer services. The IT designer also requested that he be authorized to assess whether the workflows of customer inquiries in the middlemen's organization matched the company's in-house procedures. The CEO was surprised by this initiative, but immediately called up a couple of the middlemen and obtained their consent. The IT designer's project organization proposal was also accepted. The proposal called for forming a project group of himself and the staff member from customer service, who was assigned ten hours a week for the task. The CEO and the department head would comprise the steering committee.

The IT designer interviewed three staff members in the customer service department and observed five situations where customers called in to inquire about the company's products or to place orders. The project group reviewed the work practices involved in the processing of three written inquiries by personal customers. They described the relations between the data in the company's customer and product systems and the data to be generated by order receiving and processing. On this basis, the IT designer outlined a first draft of a computer model, listed the system's functions, and made a few freehand sketches of a user interface. The staff member suggested a few corrections, and together they proposed a pair of reports with statistics showing relations between the company's product selection and inquiries by personal customers. The steering committee in turn approved these proposals as adequately covering the company's projected need.

The IT designer next paid his first visit to a middleman, whose chief also approved the proposal as adequately covering their needs. However, a subsequent meeting with a staff member from the middleman's organization revealed that the work practices for handling customer inquiries varied substantially, depending on whether the inquiry involved the company's products or the middleman's own products. For instance, the middleman received far fewer inquiries about the company's products. The customers seemed not to be aware that they could purchase them there. In addition, the company's products could not be handled by the middlemen's new joint computer system, requiring them to switch to another system to handle this type of inquiry. This was confirmed by the IT designer's visit with a second middleman.

The IT designer examined the middlemen's joint computer system and concluded that major investments would be required to enable this system to handle the company's products or to enable the company's new computer system to communicate with the middlemen's system. Moreover, he realized that transferring the company's personal customers to the middlemen would require some sort of advertising campaign. The IT designer wrote a brief report describing his impressions from visiting the middlemen and called a meeting of the steering committee.

The CEO distributed the report to the entire steering committee, who were all asked to attend the meeting. Here, they agreed that the original goal of the design project—the need to make a drive for corporate customers—was still valid. However, they had apparently chosen the wrong approach. The IT designer instead suggested developing a self-service system for personal customers, an online solution with a Web-based interface to the company's product system. In a new transitional phase, customers would be made aware of this option when they made inquiries to the company and a brief introduction to the service could be enclosed when billing orders. Moreover, based on the project group's work to date, the IT designer assessed that the old computer system, if treated to a bit of "artificial respiration," could be kept running for another year or so. At that point, the success of the self-service system could be assessed, as well as which way to go from there.

The IT designer's proposal was adopted and a new project charter was developed. The designer set to work examining the computer systems and order patterns of personal customers in the home, along with their use of online services. He developed a prototype for an ordering system, which he tested on five personal customers. On this basis, he wrote a design report that was approved by the steering committee. Three Web design agencies were then invited to bid on the contract and one was picked to carry out the implementation.

1.6.5 Example 5: Clarifying Organizational Potentials

The personnel training department of a large Danish manufacturer, whose products rely on continual product development, carried out a design project with the goal of enabling IT support for interdisciplinary tasks, such as internal communication and coordination among the department's twenty employees. The department tasks involved included managing supplementary training for the many production and office workers, overseeing course participation (including IT courses) for staff in the research and development departments, as well as executive training.

Internally, the department was divided into three aspects:

- A technical-vocational aspect, managing supplementary training in production, communications, and office work
- An executive aspect, developing and conducting executive training courses
- Informatics, which includes developing and conducting IT courses

Each aspect involved three types of staff: consultants, with an academic background, in charge of the content and organization of the courses; specialist instructors, often with a vocational background and years of experience in production, handling a large part of the many training activities; and administrative assistants, overseeing course participation, course advertising, and so forth.

The department, which had started as an office for supervising employee participation in external courses, had slowly obtained its present size and responsibilities. During the last three years, however, the department had grown considerably: training activities had doubled and the staff had increased by one-third.

The department was physically located around newly built classrooms on two floors. The offices with all the administrative assistants and management (head and deputy head) were located on the ground floor, while the rest of the staff were on the second floor. The department's growing pains—aggravated by the physical situation—were the specific reason for the design project. There was a major need to strengthen cross-task communication and coordination of various tasks. Furthermore, the consultants had many activities outside the department, such as meetings and external courses, whereas the tasks of the specialist instructors and administrative assistants were physically tied to the department's rooms. The offices thus performed numerous functions as a kind of command center for messages to and from the consultants. But this was impeded by the physical organization, since consultants on the second floor did not pass by the administrative offices on the ground floor. In the department's own words, they wanted a design project to "clarify how department staff could make better use of one another and IT usage." Moreover, via their contacts, the consultants had formed the impression that the company generally and to a greater degree needed to develop in parallel IT, the work organization, and users' qualifications.

The scope and content of the design project were set down in the project charter. The design project would be conducted by two IT designers in cooperation with a "contact group" consisting of three department staff members, an administrative assistant, and two consultants. The contact group would critique the proposals and furnish the contact to other workers in the department. The members of the contact group were each assigned to the project for two hours a week for the four-month course of the project. Moreover, two IT designers were on the project with resources equal to one workday a week.

A decision was made for the design project to continue with an in-depth analysis phase and an innovation phase. During the in-depth analysis phase, the IT designers conducted interviews with the three members of the contact group, the department head, the deputy head, and roughly a third of the other staff. The focus of these interviews was on understanding each employee's task and gathering opinions on the needs for better communication, coordination, and any other ideas for IT usage. The efforts were documented in an analysis report describing three possible prioritized subjects for an innovation phase.

In consultation with the IT designers, the department decided to prioritize the subject of "management in developing and using modern IT" for the innovation phase. The IT designers would also study management communication, and coordinating tasks. Next, in-depth interviews with management and selected staff were conducted, along with observations in the administrative offices. Workshops were held, featuring demonstrations for department staff of a series of new cooperation-supporting technologies and discussions of how the department could use these technologies. The workshops confirmed the interest in technologies for supporting communication and coordination, while also revealing that such technologies required greater experience with electronic communication than the department had at the time.

Accordingly, the IT designer planned an experiment in which the department would make use of a structure for expanded communication in electronic form over a period of time. A prototype in the form of a "low-tech" conference system was developed for the experiment. However, since a management vacuum was opening up (due to an upcoming executive change) and there was general uncertainty about the department's future tasks, the experiment was called off before it began. Consequently, the final design report outlined a limited number of visions for the department's tasks, linked to a large number of ideas for advanced IT usage and an action plan setting out an approach for further progress. A central element of the action plan was a proposal to conduct experience-generating experiments before choosing a specific IT usage.

1.6.6 Summary

Certain differences exist among the five IT design examples described in this chapter. Different premises may apply to a design project, independent of the nature of its content. A company may have decided always to work with standard systems that are adapted. Even so, a design project may reveal that (parts of) a company's computer systems require specialized development in order to meet goals and needs. A company policy or the scope of the project may prescribe a basic model that always involves a competitive bidding process for supply of the development project in whole or in part. In other instances, a company may have signed strategic deals with one or more partners supplying the equipment and IT systems that the company needs. Of course, the design project must then be organized to accommodate the premises.

Likewise, the desired degree of specificity or detail of the design project's results may vary. For instance, a company may request a design project in the form of general consulting on the potentials of using different types of IT systems. In such cases, the design report will list the company's different development options and identify and discuss appropriate IT usage on a general level. If a company is able to indicate more specifically what aspects of its business need changing, the design report can indicate various relevant IT usages, weigh them against each other and the premise, lay out alternative implementation strategies and plans, and suggest paths for further progress.

Finally, the scope of a design project may vary depending on the number of corporate departments involved, their size, and the complexity of tasks handled by the involved units.

Naturally, situations that call for a design project have a number of features in common, as do the possible project planning procedures. A significant common feature may be a lack of clarity or agreement in the premise on the nature of the problem or the choice of IT usage. Second, design projects should be constructed so that their progress supports incremental decision making. The project is planned based on an open problem formulation using baselines and milestones, with a focus that is gradually sharpened and prioritized.

Third, the ideal for all decisions made during the design project is the presence of clear relations to their basis. Arguments for or against aspects of the design project should be explicit. For instance, there should be a clear idea of the link between the proposed visions and the company's goals, problems, and needs.

2
Principles of the Method

The MUST method builds on four principles, according to which a project group should think and act when planning and conducting an IT design project. The principles indicate how to plan and carry out a design project as a process, as well as the nature and content of products resulting from the design project. The principles express the essence of the method. This chapter reviews what each principle means and in which phases they require special attention. Moreover, examples are provided of methodical guidelines for supporting the practical implementation of these principles. Implementation of the principles is reviewed in greater detail under the description of the four phases in part II of this book, as well as in part III, which describes the techniques and representation tools referred to throughout this book.

2.1 The Principle of a Coherent Vision for Change

A company's primary resources are its staff members, with their qualifications and experiences, plus its financial foundation and technology (including computer systems). A design project is carried out at a company with the aim of designing sustainable IT usage that accommodates the company's current goals and needs, without jeopardizing its future development potential. Accordingly, IT usage should contribute to a balance in the development, use, and protection of a company's resources. For instance, the IT systems should enable staff members to utilize and continue to develop their qualifications when handling their tasks. Likewise, the cost of implementing a design project's visions should be weighed against other measures that could benefit the company.

> **Sustainability:** A company's primary resources are its employees (with their qualifications and experiences), its financial foundation, IT systems, and other technology. Accordingly, IT usage is regarded sustainable to the extent that it contributes to a balance in the development, use, and protection of a company's resources. This should be done in ways that accommodate the company's existing goals and needs, without jeopardizing its future development potentials.

Definition 2.1 Sustainability

One way to ensure sustainable IT usage is to think in terms of a coherent vision. A coherent vision comprises suggestions for IT systems and work organization, as well as mapping the qualifications users will need to perform their work within the new organization using the new IT systems (see figure 2.1). The different elements should be weighed individually, according to the scope and nature of the overall change.

Thinking and acting according to the principle of a coherent vision can help safeguard a company and its employees against many of the problems that traditionally arise from IT projects: expected improvements that never materialize, substantial budget and time overruns, plus difficulties for the staff in performing their tasks using the new IT systems or in drawing on and developing their experience and qualifications.

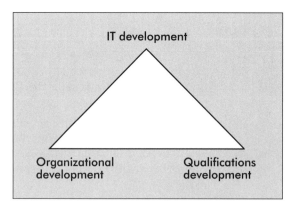

Figure 2.1 Three elements of a coherent vision

Many IT project designers underplay—or completely ignore—such problems due to their blind faith in technological progress. However, the whole idea of running a design project is, on account of its incremental decision-making process, safeguarding the company against such problems. Each of the four phases of the MUST method are designed to produce a decision-making foundation enabling management to assess whether the project is moving in the right direction. Likewise, continual information efforts by the project group and the steering committee enable employees and other stakeholders to make their own evaluations, which may then be integrated into the final design proposal.

IT projects often focus exclusively on technology, which may cause the systems not to be used in the way they were designed to be used. If this results in unanticipated problems and expenditures in the organizational implementation, it is because the project group failed to produce a viable foundation for decision making.

Of course, opposing interests may be at work in assessing a project's results. Evaluations may vary, for instance, between staff and management, as well as between different departments and personnel groups. The point is to insist on openness about expected consequences and offer the various stakeholders in the design project the best possible decision-making foundation in relation to the company's internal decision-making structures and procedures. Accordingly, the final design project report should contain an evaluation of the expected pros and cons of implementing a vision. When possible, the report should also outline measures for fixing the problems. The project group, when presenting a decision-making foundation, should consider the IT systems, the work organization, and the required qualifications. We will return to this subject later on in this section.

The project group should keep the principle of a coherent vision in mind when developing visions, especially during the innovation phase. However, the principle also warrants attention during the initiation and in-line analysis phases, as it is there that the foundation for the vision is clarified and decided.

> **Vision:** The result of a design project is one or more coherent visions for meeting the goals, needs, and potentials underlying a company's business and IT strategies. Visions describe future IT usage, including the IT systems' function, interfaces, ways of interaction, and technical platform. A vision also accounts for the work organization and required staff qualifications.

Definition 2.2 Vision

For the steering committee and the design project's stakeholders, it is sufficient to maintain a focus on the principle of a coherent vision at steering committee meetings and by the various forms of evaluation. Such evaluation, for instance by way of hearings, affords the project group and the steering committee opportunities to be made aware of factors that they may have overlooked and include such factors in their continuing efforts.

Some IT projects are undertaken because management wants changes in relation to new business goals or the work organization, and it views technology as the engine for change. Such changes may involve requirements for a system's functionality, ways of interaction and interfaces, as well as new user qualifications. In the process, an exploration of technological options can pave the way for advisable changes in the company. For that reason, the design project must run on parallel levels in developing the three elements of the vision and the relations among them.

With regard to IT systems, the design project should develop visions for functionality, ways of interaction, and interfaces with other systems. Regarding the work organization, the project should develop visions for future ways of organizing the work based on coherent business procedures. Rather than thinking in terms of individual tasks, this involves taking a survey across existing departments, even companies. Only then will the potential for fundamental innovation be fulfilled. Mapping the need for development of qualifications is about both enabling staff members to better utilize the systems' potentials and ascertaining whether they might have to perform new tasks within a new work organization.

Integrating the three elements of a vision often requires shifting the focus back and forth between these three elements. If, for instance, the premise involves an idea for a new work organization, the project group can derive visions for IT systems and qualification requirements from the new work organization. If these requirements cannot be met or will have undesired consequences, it is necessary to adjust the premise.

Experiments demonstrating how the three elements can support each other may lead to scenarios, useful prototypes, or the testing of IT systems in realistic settings. Other techniques include future workshops and mapping. Such techniques (and their resulting representations) are especially well suited for alternating between the three elements of a vision, and thus can contribute to realizing the principle of a coherent vision.

The project group is responsible for developing visions for all three elements and relations between them. However, it is important—by using a baseline to assess the results of a phase and consulting with the steering committee—to present the results to the company in order to get feedback. Drawing in people other than the members of the steering committee and the project group contributes to realizing the anchoring principle (this principle will be covered in section 2.4).

The many textbook cases of failed IT projects, which occasionally make it into the press, were what initially inspired the research project that produced the MUST method. Our own studies, supported by volumes of other research, revealed that one of the most significant causes of failure is a lack of attention toward integrating IT systems and work organization. Likewise, management may often be surprised by the need for staff training. However, businesses that have employed the MUST method all clearly identify the concept of working with a coherent vision as one of the method's great strengths.

2.2 The Principle of Genuine User Participation

The principle of genuine user participation calls for the active participation in the project group's efforts by representatives of staff members who are directly affected. There are both pragmatic and political arguments for such user participation.

The pragmatic arguments rest on the need for mutual learning between users and IT designers: IT designers need knowledge about the work environment that make up the design project's object field, and users need knowledge about technological options. That end is most effectively attained by organizing activities that enable the two groups to learn from one another. Such a mutual learning process also supports developing a shared understanding of the problems that the design project aims to solve and helps anchor the proposed solutions in the business organization (see section 2.4). It is our experience that users can contribute innovative and constructive suggestions for change when they have the right conditions for doing so. We will return to this mutual-learning perspective later on in this section.

The political arguments revolve around the users' right to influence their own working conditions, which are often significantly affected by IT projects. Many managers also regard staff members' influence on their own working conditions as an element in establishing and maintaining a good working environment and, as such, a strategy for attracting and keeping the staff members they consider central. Moreover, as regards participation, some staff may have an interest beyond the ongoing current project: knowledge about IT projects can be a valuable competency for an individual to further his or her own career.

In stressing user participation as a principle, we have two goals. Initially, user participation increases the potential of visions produced by a design project to reflect the users' true situation and needs. Later, user participation increases the potentials of the systems to be used according to their intentions. However, the principle of genuine user participation does not imply, as the examples in chapter 1 demonstrate, that IT designers will always be working alongside users. First, users may not be exempted from their day-to-day work to participate in the IT design process; second, IT designers handle certain tasks on their own.

Experientially, the aims of user participation may vary widely, just as the ways in which users actually participate in IT projects may vary. Sometimes, users may be involved only as informants for IT designers, who then analyze and present the results on their own. That is not what this book means by "genuine user participation." If users' participation is limited to serving as informant, for instance, in interviews about their work functions and IT needs, or to taking part in systems testing, the resulting systems may not cover the users' actual needs. Possible reasons for this may be that the wrong users participated or that the focus of user participation was too narrow. Often, participation is limited to middle managers or executives, who may excel at representing the company's overarching goals for the project. They typically express how they think the work should be performed under ideal conditions. However, they rarely have insight into day-to-day routines, including what factors may be complicating the work or what useful alternatives could be.

In many IT projects, the aim and focus of user participation are unclear. This may be the case where IT designers are mostly concerned about specifying IT systems while users and managers are primarily focused on the new products and services that the systems may enable. As a result, participation may be handled in ways that do not afford users opportunities to develop and express their needs, ideas, and visions for IT usage.

Management is responsible for allotting the time and information resources necessary for making user participation happen. Furthermore, it is up to management to delegate decision-making competency and clarify the types of decisions it will entrust to the project group. Once the decision-making competency has been established, the project group is responsible for organizing the design project to make for genuine user participation. It is a good idea to clarify both the aim and the focus of user participation during the initiation phase (see chapter 4).

How user participation actually progresses depends on how the users are situated in relation to the design project. Their influence may extend to the results of the design project or to planning and managing the course of the design project. As is further discussed in sections 2.4 and 2.5, conflicts may exist—or emerge—around an IT project. For that reason, it is important that there are forums for resolving such conflicts. Beyond their representation in the project group, users may sometimes also serve on the steering committee. Depending on the company's corporate culture or the nature of the design project, shop stewards or employee representatives on management-and-union committees may be steering committee candidates.

To aid the project group's efforts, other staff members can be drawn in via interviews and various forms of workshops. They may also be included when the project group updates the staff members about the status of the project and the products, offering them opportunities for feedback and dialogue. Both procedures help prepare them for changes that will result from the project. This is part of what we call "anchoring." Accordingly, accommodations should be made to allow staff members and affected parties to keep tabs on the design project and comment on its products.

As users in the project group cannot be expected to possess any knowledge about how to go about a design project, it is the IT designers' job to develop project proposals, which are discussed in the project group before being submitted to the steering committee for a decision. Moreover, users in the project group are key persons in developing an understanding of the selected work domains and in assessing the visions for overall change.

During the initiation phase, it is decided which users will participate in the project group's work. Whether the employees themselves or the managers make the selection depends on the corporate culture. We recommend including two to three users in the project group. These users should have knowledge of the involved work domains and professional respect among their co-workers. Another more pragmatic criterion often is who has enough time to participate in the project. But the more important the project is to the company, the more important it is to accommodate the first two criteria.

Users in the project group will participate over the entire course of the design project. This includes participation in project group meetings, information gathering and analysis, and possibly in developing the design project's products. Users may be assigned autonomous tasks in the design project or may work together with an IT designer, depending on their familiarity with the tasks in question.

A common practical problem involves handling the differences that often arise between the users in the project group and other staff members. Users involved in the project group often gain greater understanding of, and insight into, the project and its ends and means. They typically develop a stronger commitment to the project than their fellow workers. Accordingly, it is necessary to continually consult other staff members about goals, problems, needs, as well as generated visions for solutions.

2.2.1 Mutual Learning Process

The view of the design project as a mutual learning process primarily focuses on the users and IT designers in the project group. But the principle can also be employed to guide the project group's interaction with other cooperating actors. A design project generates knowledge about present work practices. Together with the company's business goals, this knowledge makes up a basis for developing visions of new IT usage. The aim of the design project is to establish a viable foundation for the subsequent technical and organizational implementation. This requires that people of different backgrounds enter into fruitful dialogue.

In the project group, central staff groups and competencies are represented by the users and the IT designers. The users have been selected because of their knowledge of the involved work domains. Often, their experience with past reform measures is an asset. If the users do not cover the entire operation, the project group should draw in other users in its information-gathering efforts. IT designers have experience with IT projects and their relations to organizational change. Such experience includes knowledge of methods. More knowledge than that cannot generally be demanded at the onset of a design project. Since IT design is about manufacturing a decision-making foundation for judging how new IT systems and work-organizational realignment may combine to promote the implementation of desired changes, cooperation between designers and users in knowledge generation is required. Such cooperation is most effectively realized by setting up mutual learning processes, where involved parties articulate their concerns and visions of the design project can be generated. Mutual learning processes require direct communication between the parties as well as the ability and willingness to listen.

Figure 2.2 shows the three areas where the project group needs to generate knowledge: users' present work practices, new IT usage, and technological options. The knowledge will be gained in two ways: by concrete experiences (direct firsthand experience of the area in question) and as abstract knowledge (expressed via descriptions and models of the respective area of knowledge).

Knowledge about the users' present work practices includes
- products and services supplied;
- why and how the various tasks are performed, plus any problems involved;
- obstacles to the business goals that the design project is intended to promote;
- management strategies and style;
- use of IT systems and other technology;
- relations to other staff members, customers, and suppliers.

	Users' present work practices	New IT usage	Technological options
Abstract knowledge	Relevant descriptions of users' present work practices	Visions and design proposals	Overview of technological options
Concrete experience	Concrete experience with the users' present work practice	Concrete experience with the new IT usage	Concrete experience with the technological options

Figure 2.2 The six areas of knowledge in a design project

Knowledge about the new use of IT comprises
- IT systems and other technology;
- ways of organizing work within the company;
- possible needs for new user qualifications.

Finally, technological options include
- general knowledge about IT, including relevant standard systems;
- possible ways of organizing the work in relation to different types of IT systems;
- concrete experience with the above conditions from past IT projects.

Knowledge of these three areas must be gained on both the concrete and abstract levels. Regarding the area of "new IT usage," prototyping has long been recognized as an effective way of supplementing—and assessing the relevance of—abstract design representations. Prototypes give users concrete, hands-on experience of how a system can support their work. Likewise, IT designers need to have concrete experience with the users' present work practices. This enables them to develop relevant abstract descriptions of goals, needs, and potentials, as well as to understand and judge the relevance of the oral and written abstract descriptions they get from management and users.

A user's abstract representation of his or her present work practices is, of course, relevant for assessing design proposals. However, it may not be sufficient in terms of the agenda for change that characterizes IT design. The same goes for the abstract knowledge expressed in users' written work descriptions. It is ultimately the project group's responsibility to produce abstract descriptions of central and defined aspects of the users' present work practices as they relate to the goals and focus of the design project.

Finally, users and IT designers need both abstract knowledge about and concrete experience with potential IT usage. Concrete experience with IT usage is a precondition for understanding and assessing the relevance of abstract descriptions presented by materials describing potential IT systems.

Figure 2.2 can be used as a starting point for planning the project group's activities to ensure that all six areas of abstract and concrete knowledge are covered. Moreover, the figure can be used to select the techniques and representation tools that will aid the generation of knowledge about the respective areas. We return to the use of figure 2.2 in part III.

Figure 2.2 is not a process model. Accordingly, it says nothing about the sequence in which the project group should generate the six types of knowledge, merely that three different areas (current work practices, new IT usage, and technological options) and two different levels (abstract and concrete) are involved. The project group can alternate between the two levels and shift between the three areas, to generate the knowledge necessary for the design project.

Knowledge generation as a mutual learning process is especially relevant to the project group's activities in the in-depth analysis and innovation phases. The mutual learning process is important when the project group is focused on creating common understanding of problems and needs relating to the business goals for the relevant work domains and working to develop visions of overall change. Here, the combination of different staff groups and competencies becomes essential for the success of the project. Accordingly, the project group's meetings, workshops, and other attempts to gather and analyze information must be organized to enable mutual learning.

When has the project group learned enough about the relevant work domains? When have the visions of coherent change been sufficiently analyzed to provide the project group an adequate understanding of the nature and scope of the change? When have the design visions been presented in a way that allows them to serve as a foundation for the deliberations and actions of the other actors involved in the project? The pragmatic answer to these questions is: when the time scheduled for such activities has passed. Generally, it is not possible or necessary to map all work domains in detail, nor is it possible to present all alternative visions for change. The ideal answer to these questions is: It is time to stop when the project group gets the sense that it is not gaining any significant new knowledge from its information gathering and analysis and when the group and other actors involved believe that the desired results have been sufficiently captured in the design proposals. If this conflicts with the allotted time, the project group should present arguments to the steering committee for adjusting the scope or timetable of the project, since the project group is responsible for securing a sustainable foundation for the steering committee's decision making.

When planning the design project, experience from past projects should be incorporated into creating a timetable. When the project group regulates the plan by using baselines, the answers to the preceding questions will depend on whether the project group gets the response it needs and whether the steering committee is able to make the necessary decisions.

Finally, it is important not to confuse the design project with the entire IT project. There is a need for mutual learning after the design project, as well. A significant, practical task exists in making sure that knowledge generated during the design project is not lost during the subsequent implementation when new actors enter the stage. We will return to this issue in the discussion of the anchoring principle in section 2.4.

2.3 The Principle of Firsthand Experience with Work Practices

There are three different ways, basically, of obtaining new insight into subjects relevant to a design project. You can read up on the subject, you can ask someone to tell you what they know about the subject and, finally, you can put yourself in a situation where you experience the subject firsthand. The first two ways are the most commonly used in design projects and in systems development in general. They are recommended for many of the activities under the MUST method, including such techniques as document analysis and interviews. This section focuses on the third way as an effective means of gaining concrete experience with users' present work practices, one of the areas of knowledge discussed in the previous section.

The principle of firsthand experience specifically targets IT designers and is mainly realized by observation, as the designers experience the work practice(s) they are in the process of changing. In utilizing this principle, users in the project group also gain new knowledge about their co-workers' work practices. It is especially important to be aware of this principle during the in-depth analysis phase.

The principle that work practices need to be experienced firsthand builds on the proposition that to understand any phenomenon one needs to experience it firsthand. IT designers can achieve this through three different methods: observation, in situ interviews, and thinking-aloud experiments. All three techniques are followed by systematic analysis and presentation of the gathered information (described in part III). Later in this section, we focus on observation. However, we first need to stress the necessity of alternating between information gathering using such techniques as document analysis and interviews, on the one hand, and by the techniques of observation, in situ interviews, and thinking-aloud experiments, on the other. This will heighten awareness of what is called "the say/do problem." The say/do problem highlights the difference between what people say they do (e.g., in written work descriptions and what an outsider may observe them actually doing (see figure 2.3). For instance, we once encountered a group of users requesting a system that would provide everyone access to the same information. However, by observation, we learned that these users consciously kept some information to themselves. For the vision of information sharing to be viable, they needed to discuss and change this practice or the system would have to be abandoned. Examples of say/do problems can thus be used to confront the people involved with such apparent contradictions and uncover their causes, before the project group works out the final design proposals.

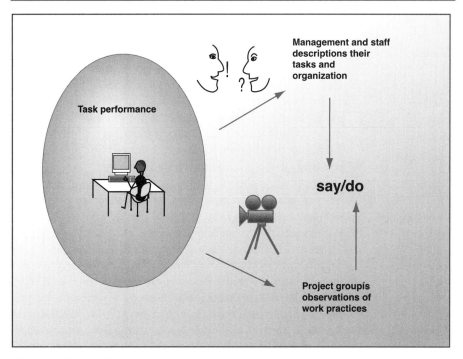

Figure 2.3 The say/do problem

Some phenomena can only be understood when one attempts to change them. For that reason, the MUST method operates with two different types of measures for change centered on the IT designer's experience with the users. First, change can be sought solely in whatever abstract thoughts and conceptions the participants have in the course of a design project. Second, one can conduct specific experience-producing experiments aimed at change in the real world.

Changes solely in the participants' thoughts and perceptions may be accomplished when the project group presents visions of change in a future workshop, develops scenarios, discusses ideas with the steering committee, or presents ideas at a hearing. Here, one can work with ideas and proposals, discuss their consequences, and make changes and additions in order to maintain advantages and limit or eliminate drawbacks. Or an idea may be completely rejected and it becomes necessary for the project group to start over. Such efforts, set in an abstract world, may be supported by scenarios, drawings, and diagnostic maps.

At times, these more abstract measures are insufficient for testing the viability of an idea or proposal. Then, the project group needs to operate with specific, experience-generating experiments, typically involving prototypes or new ways of organizing the work. In our experience, ideas involving new cooperation patterns need to be tested in practice, for instance, by experiments with prototypes. In developing and testing prototypes, subjects or requirements that had not previously been uncovered will typically surface.

Likewise, certain fundamental conditions of the business organization may be so implicit or hidden that they show up only when one tries to change them. However, there are many conditions that the project group either cannot change or are too costly to change. In these circumstances, we recommend adjusting the ambition level of the reform measure based on an understanding of the company's readiness for change, which can be gained via observation, interviews, and document analysis.

After carrying out a reform measure, further studies may be necessary to expand the project group's understanding of conditions uncovered by the measure. This involves getting a handle on an area in order to develop relevant design proposals, which help point out conditions that need to be understood more clearly. Alternating between change and understanding, as discussed in the review of the six areas of knowledge in figure 2.2, is necessary for generating and documenting the knowledge that is the desired goal of a design project. Such iterations also facilitate insight into (or "measure") a company's readiness for change at an early stage, affording the project group time to regulate and adapt its proposals for the company at very little cost.

We now return to the issue of observation. Observation, together with an analysis and presentation of the information it produces, operates along four guidelines:
1. Observation involves gaining firsthand experience of the area one wishes to understand.

2. It produces relevant and comprehensible descriptions that the observed subjects can evaluate. Thus, it must be based on their conceptuality.
3. Observation aims to describe, not prescribe. Accordingly, it is about uncovering how things are really done rather than how they ought to be done.
4. Observation is about studying and describing situations from the perspective of the observed subjects. Thus, the goal is to produce descriptions that document the work process as it is experienced by those involved, capturing their understanding of what works and what does not.

In terms of figure 2.2, observation is relevant in generating knowledge about users' present work practices on the concrete level (point 1), while descriptions made based on the observations contribute on the abstract level (points 2, 3, and 4). This applies to gaining understanding of problems and potentials, as well as to developing ideas for improvements.

The understanding and the descriptions produced by observation are used to comprehend present work practices, including the need and potential for change. They form a basis for suggesting changes or innovations that no one within the business organization may have brought attention to in interviews. Such descriptions should not be confused with the highly detailed descriptions that certain conventional systems development methods recommend. The issue is one of finding the right level of abstraction while maintaining the design project's focus, in order for the descriptions to capture the relevant work domains—both to document needs and potentials and to serve as a starting point for vision development.

The four guidelines for observation, as well as analysis and presentation of the information produced by observation, are useful and relevant in IT design. However, design projects are commonly subjected to resource restrictions, which require an awareness of the scope and situation of activities that the first two guidelines address. In IT design projects, there is rarely enough time to gain firsthand experiences of all aspects of the users' work practices. Moreover, the descriptions will mainly be read by the project group and the steering committee. A realistic distribution calls for spending a third of the total design project time in gathering, analyzing, and presenting information about present work practices, including how and why the work is performed the way it is—and here observation serves an important function. Though it may not sound like much, it pays to bear in mind that in the course of such efforts, many ideas surface that are later included in the vision development. Furthermore, the generated information makes it easier to link visions to uncovered needs.

There is another important question regarding observation: who and what to observe? If a small business or department is involved, most of the staff members and managers may be observed as they go about their day-to-day work. When a bigger company is involved and the in-line analysis phase has pointed out a work domain that goes across several departments, it becomes necessary to make choices. The main criterion for selecting the subjects to observe is that they should reflect the diversity and complexity of the work practice under investigation, while also making sure that the various staff groups and interests are represented. Representativeness and generality can then be tested by inviting others to comment on the results of the observation and analysis.

Who in the project group will perform the observation and analysis depends on the extent that user representatives have been assigned to the design project. We have had positive experiences with IT designers and users working closely together. A user is quickly able to clear up misunderstandings and obscure points, while an IT designer will typically be better at asking the obvious "stupid" questions. If users are assigned to the project for a limited time only, the IT designer can conduct the observation alone, while the users should focus on assessing the IT designer's analyses.

2.4 The Principle of Anchoring Visions

The anchoring principle involves informing a target group about the design project's goals, visions, and plans. In the process, the design team is attempting to gain wider support for its proposal. The target group includes every-one not directly participating in the design project who can contribute to, and will be affected by, its implementation.

The principle of genuine user participation—and the view of a design project as a mutual learning process—involves project group participants gaining a good, common understanding of the results produced by the design project. The principle of a coherent vision states that the vision should include technical, organizational, and qualificational aspects. However, management, staff members, and those who will be implementing the design project's visions will not all be directly involved in the project. The project group may then run the risk of developing what may at times amount to "insider reasoning" informing the study's results. Accordingly, the anchoring principle is about why and how the project group relates to other actors in the project.

Proposed changes will only be realized when they are anchored with

- the steering committee (and other management) with de-cision-making competency regarding the recommendations and results of the design project;
- staff and stakeholders who will be using the envisioned IT systems or who will be affected by them;
- the people in charge of further technical and organizational implementation of the design project's visions.

Figure 2.3 illustrates the responsibilities involved in the different elements of anchoring. The responsibility for anchoring should be located with the project manager in charge of securing anchoring with the steering committee and other management. The steering committee chairman is responsible for securing anchoring with staff members and stakeholders, as well as with those in charge of the technical and organizational implementation of the design visions. Figure 2.4 indicates the focus of the various anchoring responsibilities.

Target group	Steering committee and other management (decision-making competency)	Staff and stakeholders affected by the vision	The people handling the technical and organizational implementation of the visions
Responsibility	Project manager	Steering committee chairman	Steering committee chairman
Focus	Assessing results and making decisions about baselines	Sharing results, gathering comments	Coordinating ongoing results; informing affected parties about the reasoning behind visions; cooperation between the business and development organizations
Activities	Steering committee meetings and meetings with other management Meetings between the steering committee chairman and the project manager	Evaluation with staff members and stakeholders Informing stakeholders	Meetings with the people overseeing the technical implementation Meetings with the people overseeing the organizational implementation

Figure 2.4 Target group, parties responsible for anchoring, main focus, and possible anchoring activities

Anchoring is not something done only to cap off a design project—it is not about "selling" the project group's solution proposals. Rather, it is a principle that should help guide all the phases of the project. During the initiation and in-line analysis phases, the scope of the design project is established and business goals clarified with regard to the selected work domains. The in-depth analysis phase generates understanding of problems and needs, as well as their relation to the business goals. The innovation phase develops visions of future IT usage. Only when these results are effectively communicated to the groups involved in the project has a sustainable foundation been laid for subsequent implementation and use.

The anchoring principle thus targets what may be called "proactive technology evaluation." That is, it enables the groups involved in the project to assess the consequences of a given design in the course of the project, allowing the project group to accommodate their feedback in the final design proposal. It also makes it easier to foster realistic expectations of what the various actors have to gain—or lose—by the design, thus counteracting disappointment and irritation during and after implementation.

All change takes time and mental readjustment. Anchoring may help introduce the proposed organizational change at an early point in the design project, which improves the potential for acceptance of, and backing for, the project group's final design proposal.

In a design project, the project group develops various representations of the existing situation and visions of the desired changes. Such representations are perceived and interpreted individually and differently by the people to whom they are presented. An important means of anchoring is to communicate representations that provide the truest image of the existing situation, as interpreted by the project group. This can be achieved by the project group systematically discerning among the information it has gathered and the assumptions and hypotheses it has made.

The project group's view of the company's existing situation builds on gathered information (registered in documents), observed events, statements from interviews, and so forth. Such information is indisputable in the sense that it "exists"—for instance, in the form of quotes from past reports on business strategy, from statistics on the frequency of errors in a business procedure, from observation of information imparted on slips of paper, from interview statements that the interviewees do not know "what becomes of" all the information they have to enter in a system, and so forth.

Using the collected information, members of the project group piece together a general image of the existing situation and problems that have been identified. Designers, who have a lot of experience in the work domains on which the design project is focused, sometimes need only a little information—for instance, from a short series of interviews—to be able to piece together a convincing generalization of the situation and identify relevant problem domains.

In both cases, the generalization is information-based, but is tied together by a string of assumptions and hypotheses generalizing the information to cover the situation as a whole. Assumptions and hypotheses are often implicit and typically take the shape of patterns of explanation and interpretation of the gathered information.

For example, at a steering committee meeting, a project group presents the results of the in-depth analysis and points out a problem identified by the analysis. A member of the steering committee may deny the problem or claim that it has been misinterpreted. He or she might say, "We don't do that at all" or "You must be mistaking this for something else." The project group then explains that three interviewees mentioned the phenomenon and characterized it as a problem. Someone, then, indisputably is performing the work procedures that way and consider it a problem. The steering committee meeting can now concentrate on discussing the causes of why these work procedures are performed the way they are, the possible consequences, whether the problems experienced apply generally to other staff, and so forth.

Similar considerations may apply to representations of the design visions and plans for implementing the visions. A reader will use a representation of a vision to form an image of what the future will look like from his or her specific perspective. This image builds on this person's interpretation of the project group's representation of the vision—an interpretation that correspondingly builds on that person's assumptions and hypotheses of how a coherent vision will work in practice. Here, an important element of anchoring is for the project group to present its assumptions. This may be done by explaining why the group considers the vision relevant—that is, what business goals it meets, as well as what problems and needs will be addressed by the proposed IT usage. This may be done by the project group explaining how it envisions the IT systems to be used in practice, as viewed from the various actors' perspectives.

In presenting the products of a design project, the project group should focus on getting feedback on the information it has gathered and its assumptions. Accordingly, this also means confirming or rejecting the assumptions and hypotheses upon which the project group has built its representations of the existing or future situation.

The project group achieves firm anchoring for the results of the design project by, in its internal work and in the submitted products, adhering to three basic anchoring rules:

1. The group must separate its suppositions (assumptions and hypotheses) from the information gathered. It should be aware of what can be traced back to various documents, audio or video recordings, and notes from interviews and observations, on the one hand, and the project group's suppositions, on the other.

2. The group needs to test its considerations, assumptions, and hypotheses, not just its conclusions. It should be open to all suppositions, while bearing in mind the importance of challenging and testing them. The group should visualize the considerations by forging a coherent argument from problem identification through to solution proposals. To that end, techniques such as diagnostic and virtual mapping may be used.

3. The group must give the design visions a usage-oriented perspective and visualize them in relation to usage situations. Scenarios may be used to describe the relation between IT systems and work organization. Also, the group should describe the design visions in relation to business goals, enabling management to discern if and how the goals are met.

Anchoring is closely linked to understanding how the design project should be managed and, thus, to clarifying the distribution of competencies between the project group and the steering committee, as discussed in section 1.4.

2.5 Conflicts and Dilemmas in IT Design

So far, this presentation may have given the impression that if the project group follows the MUST principles, then no problems will occur. Of course, this is not the case. This section discusses some of the conflicts and dilemmas that may arise in the course of a design project.

Since IT design takes place in an organizational context, any number of political aspects may give rise to conflict. Many people think of conflict as something negative that should be avoided. We think of conflict as closely linked to different interests and power, and thus as something to be expected in companies. Conflicts may be manifest—that is, acknowledged and visible. Or they may be latent—that is, they are hidden at the moment but may become manifest over time, perhaps as a consequence of a design project laying bare and disrupting different interests and power relations. A design project may tip the power balance between two departments, revealing conflicts between a department manager and staff, or between different personnel groups. In such cases, the design project may cause conflicts to become manifest. A company and its employees' trade organizations have developed structures for handling certain types of conflict, such as salary and working conditions. Some conflicts are solved by talks between the directly involved parties, while others are solved by management intervention.

We think of companies as frameworks for both consensus-based cooperation and conflicts. Individuals, personnel groups, and managers may have common or competing goals and interests. Accordingly, IT designers should be prepared for certain conditions that they were not aware of or did not consider important may suddenly cause reactions in the company that at first seem out of proportion. It is not the IT designers' job to cover up or try to solve political conflicts that surface during a design project. However, it is their job to develop different design visions and assess their consequences for the affected parties. The involved interest groups should resolve conflicts themselves in relevant forums. This may sound simple, but such is not always the case. It is far from certain that conditions exist for producing several design visions and describing their consequences in equal detail for all parties. In what follows, we discuss some of the moral or ethical dilemmas that an IT designer has to face in such situations.

Like other fact-finding efforts, a design project may have an ulterior motive for legitimizing decisions that have already been made. When this occurs, the IT designers should clarify that fact and assess whether it will prohibit or complicate honest fact-finding efforts. If so, the problem should be taken to the steering committee or other management. If this fails to remedy the problem, each IT designer should clarify his or her attitude toward continuing to be a member of the project team.

In projects involving user participation, there is an important ethical condition. If management is aiming for downsizing, layoffs, or other drastic changes, this should be openly stated as part of the project agenda. If this kind of agenda is more or less kept secret, a central ethical principle is broken when staff members are invited to participate in the project. Serious conflicts may arise and user participation in any future project will be the object of deep distrust. This is not to say that drastic changes cannot be achieved in projects that build on a strategy of user participation. We have carried out successful design projects at companies where broad job cuts had been made just before the project began or where drastic changes were an explicit goal of the project, and where staff members were familiar with—and accepted—the terms and goals of the project.

IT design is also a political process. Accordingly, participants and other affected parties may have different opinions on a subject and actively try to have their interests accommodated within the design project. The question is whether an IT designer can take a stand in conflicts triggered by such differences in opinion. It is hard to offer any surefire rules on this issue, but we will make a few general suggestions.

First, it is important to bear in mind that different opinions and interests do not necessarily clash, although the actors initially may see it that way. An IT designer may encounter a situation where the different parties stress different aspects of a design proposal because they are situated differently in relation to the project's focus and may be talking past one another. The task then becomes one of
- understanding the reasoning behind the different positions;
- clarifying how they relate to each other;
- designing and presenting a solution that accommodates the affected parties;

- describing the consequences of the solution according to the interests of the different parties, providing them with a basis for discussion.

However, if the actors already are (or become) aware of each other's positions, and they have (or develop) opposing interests regarding the design project, it can make life hard for the IT designers and the users in the project group. For instance, some may prefer a standard solution while others want the design project to lead to development of a customized system tailored to how the users want the work to be organized. In addition, different interests may be at work concerning how the work should be organized—for instance, regarding the distribution of responsibilities between two departments or among different staff groups. Finally, some personnel groups may see their working conditions negatively affected or, in the most extreme scenario, may lose their jobs.

Companies are used to handling conflicts by cooperation negotiation with the proportional strength of the parties deciding the outcome. It is not the IT designer's job to take sides in such political processes. The designers have their professionally founded opinion based on the pros and cons of various solutions—and this is what they have been hired to argue. However, since it is the other parties in the design project who will have to live with the consequences of the various solutions, they will have to make the decisions. This decision-making process falls outside the IT designer's job description. In the necessary clarification process that enables choices to be made, it is the IT designer's job to illustrate, as clearly as possible, the consequences of the different options. This process involves

- understanding the reasoning behind the different positions;
- clarifying how they relate to each other;
- designing and documenting several alternative solutions in such cases that accommodate the different parties' needs;
- enabling the parties to assess the consequences of the different solutions themselves, according to their own interests.

After the design team has done these things, the involved parties in the company will have to make the decisions themselves in the proper forums to handle such conflicts.

Still, IT designers may encounter situations where their work has been used to further certain interests to the detriment of others. Moral dilemmas may arise if, for instance, some staff members end up with less interesting work or perhaps even become superfluous and, consequently, are reassigned or fired. What to do in such situations is a personal choice. Some IT designers reason that they did what was necessary, and if they had not, someone else would. Others decide, after a number of such experiences, to seek other work (in IT or other industries) where moral dilemmas are fewer or easier to handle. Some convince themselves that the profit to the company, perhaps even to society, outweighs difficulties for some people that emerge from a design project.

II
Phases of the Method

3
Phases, Decisions, and Contexts

This part of the book, consisting of chapters 3–7, reviews the four phases of the MUST method. The four phases are the method's suggestions for the overall organization of a design project. They are not phases in the conventional sense—as seen in waterfall models, for instance, where a phase consists of only one type of activity, such as analysis or programming. Instead, we use the same phase concept as in baseline planning. Here, a phase is the period between two baselines, comprising activities that will take the project from one assessable situation to the next and often include different types of activities. The MUST method recommends organizing a design project by baselines, with four general decision-making situations supported by intermediate and end products produced in each phase.

The four phases of the method can be outlined in a baseline plan, as in figure 3.1. The "baseline planning" technique is described in greater detail in section 9.1. In terms of figure 3.1, the most important characteristics can be summed up as follows:

- The design project moves chronologically from left to right.
- The design project is divided into four phases: initiation, in-line analysis, in-depth analysis, and innovation.
- A phase is the period between two baselines. The baselines are illustrated by the vertical lines in the figure.
- A baseline is a well-defined state in the course of a project. This state is assessed by the planned intermediate and end products generated in the phase. These products are represented by the boxes on the baselines. The products for phases 1–3 are sometimes called intermediate products, and the products for phase 4 are sometimes called end products.
- A baseline constitutes a decision-making point in the design project. The baseline's products constitute a foundation for the decisions that need to be made.

- Between the baselines, activities leading to a baseline's products are performed. Activities are represented by oval balloons. An activity is a defined work process with a specific aim. An activity may be supported by selected techniques and representation tools. Some activities are interrelated and performed in parallel or in extension of each other. This phenomenon is shown by partially overlapping oval balloons.
- A planned baseline has been achieved when the predefined criteria for its product have been met. The act of assessing whether a baseline has been achieved is not shown as an independent activity. Such evaluation, typically accomplished by a meeting of the steering committee, should be considered part of the baseline.

The four phases suggested for organizing a design project support four general decision-making situations.

1. The initiation phase is based on a decision to carry out a design project that is set down in a mandate. It produces a project charter and a plan for the design project. These two intermediate products support decisions about the premise and scope of a design project—including such factors as time, content, financing, and participants.
2. The in-line analysis phase produces a strategic alignment report. This intermediate product supports clarifi-

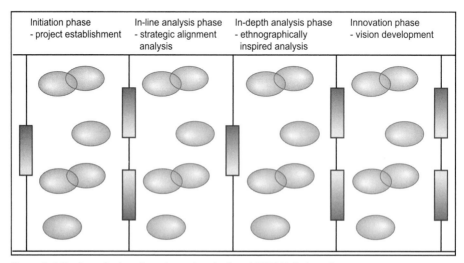

Figure 3.1 Outline of a baseline plan using the four MUST IT design phases

cation of the relation of the design project's objective to the company's business and IT strategies, as well as to other ongoing IT projects. Moreover, the report supports a decision about what work domains should be the focus of the future course of the design project.

3. The in-depth analysis phase produces an analysis report. This intermediate product supports a decision about which goals, problems, and needs to prioritize, as well as what ideas for IT support need to be designed in greater detail. The analysis report may be supplemented by descriptions of work practices in the work domains studied.

4. The innovation phase produces a final design project report. This end product supports a decision about what design visions to realize and how to realize them. The design project report may be supplemented by mockups and prototypes.

This organization and its incremental decision-making process (a central aspect of the method's risk management) take account of the fact that IT design projects are generally marked by a large measure of uncertainty. It may at times be necessary to divide a phase into several subphases, whose intermediate products reflect a priority among the project's risk factors. In chapter 4, we return to the considerations involved in handling a design project's risk elements. Chapter 8 describes specific techniques for handling risk.

The priority that should be assigned to the individual phases depends on the specific situation of the design project, as illustrated by the five project examples in chapter 1. Of course, a design project involving IT systems within a budget framework of $100,000 is different from a design project initiating a multi-million-dollar IT project. The situation should be assessed at the start of each of the four phases, and the scope and ambition of each phase adjusted accordingly. In some cases, the in-line analysis phase can be reduced to a single activity under the initiation phase. That may be the case when a design project's focus can be clearly defined in its premise.

The content of each of the four phases may profitably be planned in terms of products to be generated in each phase.

For the design project to produce coherent visions (see section 2.1), it is important that all intermediate and end products relate to the different contexts—here termed the project context, the usage context, and the technical context. These contexts constitute a framework within which the actions and statements acquire meaning. When a design team becomes aware of these contexts and adapts them according to its interpretations of the current situation, these contexts may profitably support the team's reflections on efforts to generate coherent visions.

For instance, when a design proposal is discussed at a steering committee meeting, the IT manager's statement will likely reflect the extent to which the proposal falls within the company's IT strategy. The head of a user department will emphasize the extent to which the proposal promotes the changes he or she desires for his or her department. A staff representative will inquire about how the proposal will affect the work organization and potential shifts of responsibility among staff groups. Finally, the project manager will attempt to get the steering committee to make any number of decisions to ensure the project's momentum. These are all legitimate concerns that may be compatible. The design team's task is to ensure that these aspects are studied and prioritized, and their consequences integrated into the further course of the project.

IT design and systems development generally take place within what we will here define as the *project context*. An IT designer's job in a design project is to produce intermediate and end products addressing the project context, as well as what we will here define as the *usage context* and the *technical context*. All three contexts can be divided into two aspects.

The *project context* concerns the IT project as a temporal process—that is, it runs for a constrained period of time. The project context involves a network of different actors: IT designers, managers, users, and external partners, as well as various internal and external suppliers of products and services. All of these actors have a responsibility to their permanent organizational context. We divide the project context according to our IT project model into two aspects (see figure 1.1):

- The design project, that is, the context of other related projects. The relations may involve content or reflect the fact that the design project's actors are also committed to other ongoing projects. This applies to all aspects of managing, steering, coordinating, and planning a design project.
- The implementation project, that is, the context of the process of the subsequent implementation project. A design project's visions should be assessed in the light of the project's scope (goals, timetable, budget, and so forth), according to the strategies and plans to be realized in the implementation project and in relation to other ongoing or planned projects.

The *usage context* involves the organizational context of the business organization (or the part of the business organization) involved in the design project. The usage context is divided into two aspects:

- Business strategy: A coherent vision must be viewed within the context of the business strategy that IT usage will support. The business strategy represents a company's overall business goals and its plans for meeting them.
- Work practice: An IT system (or collection of IT systems) constituting the technical component of a coherent vision should be viewed in the context of the work practice of its planned use. Work practice is a collective term for everything involving the users' work—including work as function, task, and process (the why, what, and how). Work practice also includes work organization—that is, how the work is divided and organized, the products or services supplied, and the tools and materials used.

The *technical context* involves integrating the envisioned IT systems with the company's existing technical framework. This ties in closely with the company's IT strategy. We distinguish between a business-based IT strategy (choosing and prioritizing planned IT systems, such as portfolios or product suites of IT systems) and a technical IT strategy (choosing and prioritizing hardware platforms, networks, operating systems, development environments, and so forth). Accordingly, we divide this context into two aspects:

- IT systems: An IT system that is part of a proposed vision should be viewed in the context of existing IT systems and the company's business-based IT strategy, as well as in the context of other IT systems included in the vision.
- IT platforms: An IT system or collection of systems should be viewed in the context of the company's technical IT strategy in which they will function.

The six aspects of the MUST system (IT design project, implementation project, business strategy, work practice, IT systems, and IT platform) are presented here as stand-alone elements, but in IT design they naturally interact. Figure 3.2 illustrates the relevance of these six aspects in terms of the intermediate and end products to be produced by the four MUST phases.

The next four chapters review the four phases of an IT design project. The representations of the phases are uniformly handled. Our description of each phase includes six elements:

- The objective of the phase
- The motivation for carrying out the phase
- Situations and ambitions for the phase (typical situations that can be used as starting points for planning the activities of a phase are listed)
- Examples (typical examples of the phase, corresponding to the above-mentioned, typical situations)

Context	Aspect	Initiation phase	In-line analysis phase	In-depth analysis phase	Innovation phase
Project context	IT design project	●	○	○	-
	Implementation project	○	-	-	●
Usage context	Business strategy	○	●	-	○
	Work practice	○	●	●	●
Technical context	IT systems	○	-	○	●
	IT platform	○	-	-	○

Figure 3.2 Relevance of the phases' products to the six aspects of an IT design project: (●) indicates primary relevance; (○) indicates secondary relevance; (-) indicates that this aspect is relevant to the phase only in certain cases

- Possible activities of the phase (the process aspects of the phase, which describe all activities that may potentially be performed between the baselines for the phase)
- Possible results of the phase. This section reviews (the product aspects of the phase, which provides a checklist of all the results that may potentially be produced in the phase)

In this chapter, we have described the contexts of which a design project is part. The most important terms in operation here are project context, usage context, and technical context. These terms and their content are summarized in definitions 3.1, 3.2, and 3.3.

Project context: the IT project viewed as a defined period of time. The project context involves a network of different actors: IT designers, managers, users, external partners, and various internal and external suppliers of products and services. *IT project* is the overall term for the design project and its subsequent implementation.

Design project: carrying out an IT design.

Implementation project: realizing the visions of the design project.

Definition 3.1 Project context, design project, and implementation project

---

Usage context: the organizational context in the business organization (or part of the business organization) involved in the design project. Usage context concerns business strategy and work practice.

Business strategy: the company's visions for the future, plus a definition of the means for realizing the visions.

Work practice: a collective term for everything involved in the users' work, including work as function, task, and process (the why, what, and how). As a subset, work practice includes work organization—the way the work is divided and organized, the products or services supplied, and the tools and materials used.

Definition 3.2 Usage context, business strategy, and work practice

> **Technical context:** integrating the envisioned IT systems within the company's existing technical framework and conditions. Closely linked to the company's IT strategy.
>
> **IT strategy:** the company's usage of IT for achieving its business strategy. The IT strategy can be divided into a business-based IT strategy and a technical IT strategy.
>
> **Business-based IT strategy:** setting goals for—and choosing and prioritizing among—projected IT systems, for instance, represented as a portfolio or product suite of projected IT systems.
>
> **Technical IT strategy:** setting goals for—and choosing and prioritizing among—platforms of hardware, networks, operating systems, and development environments.

Definition 3.3 Technical context, IT strategy, business-based IT strategy, and technical IT strategy

4
Initiation Phase: Project Establishment

The initiation phase involves clarifying and agreeing on the scope of the design project. What will the assignment involve? What conditions apply to solving it? How should the project group approach the assignment? We recommend that a design project always start with the project group and the steering committee spending some time to agree on issues such as objective, level of ambition, financial and technical conditions, project management, and steering. Moreover, we recommend setting down such agreements in a project charter—an elaboration, systematization, and specification of the design project's premise, as well as a plan for carrying out the design project.

The idea or need for an IT design project may come about in various ways. The incentive may be a new management initiative, originate with a single person or department, or be caused by a preceding activity, such as an evaluation of the company's other initiatives, projects, or strategic concerns.

The reason for undertaking a design project is always the result of someone designating a goal, expressing a need, or experiencing a problem regarding IT, or the emergence of new ideas for IT systems or usages. These goals, needs, problems, or ideas for IT may be unclear initially. They typically spring from new business goals or organizational changes. When such a reason for a design project has been noted and a decision has been made to do something about it, the initiation phase can begin. The initiation phase "breaks ground" on a number of issues relevant to the whole design project.

4.1 Objective

The objective of the initiation phase is clarifying and fostering a commitment for the premise and conditions of the design project in which resources will be invested. The objective includes six elements:

- Clarifying the design project's level of ambition as well as the involved company's existing organizational, financial, and technical conditions. In brief, what are one's aims and capabilities?
- Specifying the assignment that the design project as a whole will solve. This also involves limiting the project—for instance, by identifying areas not to be included in the project.
- Organizing the project. This includes distributing tasks and decision-making competencies between the project group and steering committee, appointing management and members for the group and committee, plus clarifying the relationship between the project group and its stakeholders.
- Planning how to conduct the project within the given scope. This involves organizing the subsequent phases and identifying relevant activities, techniques, and representation tools that might be used.
- Increasing—by discussion and negotiation—all involved parties' understanding of the premise determining the course of the design project.
- Writing a project charter and plan for the design project, coherently specifying the premise and further course of the project. This charter constitutes the project group's contract with the steering committee and serves as a reference guide for the further development of the project. The project group and steering committee may return to this charter later in the project and, if necessary, renegotiate it.

4.2 Motivation

In systems development, it has long been a well-known fact that it pays to invest in thorough project establishment. This applies to IT design as well. Launching a project on very loosely defined terms may quickly give rise to misunderstandings, which can be time-consuming and difficult, and demotivating to have to adjust. Thorough preparation is especially relevant in design projects involving user participation: As the premise generally applies to an uncertain situation, specifying challenges, problems, and needs is part of the assignment. In such situations, moreover, user participation requires openness and dialogue about the premise and objective of the project. Accordingly, the initiation phase is always relevant—although, of course, the scope of the phase depends on the specific situation and the company's experience and routines in carrying out design projects. We have gathered some of the arguments for conducting a well-organized and systematic initiation phase in figure 4.1.

> • Initiation makes for a realistic premise.
> • It clarifies uncertainties and risks in the project.
> • It provides fixed points for steering the further course of the project.
> • It bolsters the project group's internal chemistry, forging team spirit and consensus about the design project's goals.
> • It clarifies the division of labor between the project group and its stakeholders.
> • The project charter promotes shared understanding of the scope of the project and provides a basis for clarifying potential internal and external conflicts.
> • Initiation does not consume a lot of resources, and the resources it does consume are quickly made back.

Figure 4.1 Arguments for carrying out a systematic initiation phase

4.3 Situations and Ambitions

At the outset, a design project is typically marked by a high level of uncertainty and, consequently, an openness to many different interpretations and approaches to handling the situation. An effect of the initiation phase is setting down a strategy for reducing uncertainty and risk in the project with regard to both product and process—that is, what results the design project will deliver and how to conduct it. The greater the uncertainty of the initial situation, the more it pays to spend resources on the initiation phase. In addition, the relevance of the initiation phase is not dependent on the scope of the design project: Thorough initiation is equally profitable in less extensive design projects.

The situation for an initiation phase depends on the number of stakeholders to be included in negotiations, their experiences with IT design and the company, as well as on whether the phase progresses in a "hand-in-hand" fashion or whether the project is troublesome and the cause of conflicts. Figure 4.2 describes three typical situations for the initiation phase, as detailed in section 4.4.

Situation 1 typically has relatively few people involved in the design project. The company has experience with design projects, and the IT designers have experience with the company. The process of writing a project charter is routine. The issue is exclusively one of defining the assignment for the design project. Other issues, such as the project's organization, stakeholders, critical factors, and so forth, require no major discussion and analysis, since they are partially familiar to the involved parties from previous projects. The initiation phase can then be handled by one or a few meetings where the project group and the steering committee discuss drafts of the project charter and plan.

Situation 2 is one where many people across the company are affected by—and should be involved in—the design project. This situation may also arise when the company has no experience with IT design. Finally, situation 2 may

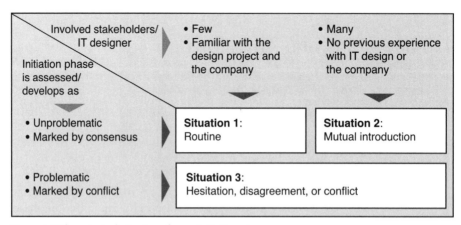

Figure 4.2 Three typical situations for an initiation phase

involve IT designers who have no past experience with the company—perhaps they are external consultants. The IT designers then need an introduction to the company, and the company needs to be introduced to the IT designers—as well as, perhaps, the IT design concept and method. All the issues of the project charter need to be introduced, analyzed, and discussed.

The initiation phase may typically start when the IT designers obtain an overview of the company via document analysis, meetings, and possible interviews. It may involve a visit and an introduction of the IT designers to staff members at the company. The IT designers and the project group submit their plans for the project to the steering committee, which is then asked to prioritize among them and define a number of possible tasks and activities. The project is presented to the company, for instance, in staff meetings, through internal news information, and the like. It may also be relevant to submit a draft of the project charter to a meeting among selected stakeholders. The initiation phase may last from a few days up to a few weeks, depending on the resources and scope.

Situation 3 may start out like situation 2, or even situation 1. However, the project group in situation 3 encounters a drawn-out process, and there may be disagreement or direct conflict over the design project's focus and priorities. The initiation phase may then lead to a political process, as the parties within the company negotiate the agenda and focus of the design project.

The IT designers may support the negotiations by helping to bring disagreements and conflicts into the open. To that end, the initiation phase can be supplemented by interviews with the various stakeholders, freehand drawings focusing on disagreements and conflicts, or analyses and presentations of different stakeholder perspectives by diagnostic or virtual mapping techniques.

Hesitation in realizing the project may also be symptomatic of a lack of motivation or executive support, or of uncertainty among staff members who fear hidden agendas—for instance, that the project will be used to legitimize unpopular restructuring or job cuts.

If the hesitation, resistance, and conflict persist, it may be impossible to obtain satisfactory results from the initiation phase. A situation may then ensue that allows the project charter to be described only in very vague, general terms, and where management or participating staff are not especially motivated or committed to the project. Finally, a decision will have to be made about whether to continue the project on an unsatisfactory basis (with the implied risk of failure), to postpone it, or to abandon it altogether.

4.4 Examples of Initiation Phases

The following section outlines three different situations along with their potential related activities (see figure 4.2).

4.4.1 Situation 1: Routine

A chain of retail stores has outsourced the development and operation of its IT systems to a software company. The two parties have agreed on a business-based IT strategy. In this instance, the retail chain was faced with replacing its payroll system. The software company's IT designer on the account consequently requested a meeting with the head of the payroll office and the vice-president, who was in charge of IT in the company.

At the meeting, the IT designer recommended conducting the project according to the usual model. This meant starting with an initiation phase. She had brought along the standard draft of a project charter that her company usually implemented. The people at the meeting used this charter as an agenda to clarify what was laid down in advance as a link in the business-based IT strategy—mainly, that they needed to obtain a standard payroll system. She also recommended working with the usual project organization of a project group and a steering committee. The steering committee ended up consisting of the head of the payroll office and the vice-president. They predicted that the project would mainly be marked by consensus. Since the payroll system would be used both at the general office and in all the stores (where it also needed to be integrated with the shift-scheduling system), the project group included an outlet manager and a staff member from the payroll office, along with the IT designer.

They scheduled a new meeting to include the whole project group. Before this meeting, they made an attempt to establish what each person considered to be the conditions needing clarification before a decision to buy a payroll system could be made. For her part, the IT designer promised to have a draft of the project charter and a proposed baseline plan ready for the next meeting.

At the next meeting, the outlet manager and the payroll office staff member went over the problems with the old payroll system and why they needed a new one. The IT designer also asked the participants to state what they considered to be critical factors for a good payroll system and whether any other special conditions applied to this project.

The members of the group subsequently reviewed the IT designer's proposals for a project charter and plan. Each point of the project charter was considered, with the IT designer integrating agreed changes and additions on the spot. Proposals by the outlet manager and the payroll office staff member caused a few extra activities to be added to the plan. These involved clarifying and potentially redesigning workflows between the outlets and the central office regarding the reporting of hours to the payroll system. The meeting lasted three hours and concluded with the project group and steering committee signing the project charter and adopting the plan.

4.4.2 Situation 2: Mutual Introduction

A law office had undergone rapid expansion in recent years, and the three partners had decided to scrap the old paper-based filing system in favor of an electronic case management system. "In the old days," when they were just three lawyers, each had a secretary to file and locate cases. Now four paralegals and another secretary had been added to the staff and organized into a joint pool with the other secretaries. The secretaries had now (in principle) been relieved of managing the case files. The idea was for the lawyers and paralegals themselves to be able to write, file, and locate their cases using a computer system, which the secretaries would also use in their work.

One of the partners commissioned a consulting firm to help locate the right case-management system. The IT designer who came to the law office had solved similar tasks before, though never at a law office. Accordingly, he suggested that he be given an opportunity to obtain an overview of the company before devising a plan. The lawyer filled him in on their case processing, what types of documents were involved, and the process by which case files were located. He then called the entire staff together and told them about the project. The IT designer, in turn, related how he usually conducted a design project.

Over the next few weeks, the IT designer made three visits to the law office. Selecting both a current and a closed case, he asked a lawyer, a paralegal, and a secretary to describe specific case processing, focusing on problems with the existing system and what potentials they saw with the new system. On that basis, he drafted a project charter that addressed the issues he had become familiar with so far and left the rest blank.

The partner asked a paralegal and a secretary to participate at the next meeting, as he wanted the three of them to form a project group together with the IT designer. The three partners would make up the steering committee. At this meeting, the project group discussed the IT designer's draft charter, which was revised, expanded, and finally adopted. The IT designer outlined a plan for the overall design project, specifying how much time the project group should expect to spend on its efforts. After some discussion, the plan was adopted and the staff was called together for orientation. The project group then started conducting the planned activities.

4.4.3 Situation 3: Hesitation, Disagreement, or Conflict

The owner of a contract manufacturing company commissioned an external IT designer to carry out a design project with the aim of revealing what new production management system would best benefit the company. Customers had repeatedly complained about products not being delivered on time or turning out to be too expensive because the raw materials had to be delivered express and in small quantities. The owner asked the IT designer to talk with the warehouse manager and the production manager, recommending that they be included in a project group together with the IT designer. The designer quickly realized that there were problems with the management philosophy. The warehouse manager controlled the stocks of raw materials, while the production manager assumed that the warehouse would always be able to provide the necessary materials.

Moreover, the IT designer got the distinct impression that the two managers were not on good terms. Joint meetings were repeatedly postponed, and the IT designer had not managed to get the owner to intervene. The IT designer decided to temporarily abandon the formation of a project group. Instead, he conducted a number of interviews with the two managers and the sales manager, who was in direct touch with the customers. The designer represented the results of these interviews in a series of freehand drawings and diagnostic maps focusing on both the company's existing financial and its organizational conditions.

The IT designer asked the owner to call an executive meeting and presented his freehand drawings and diagnostic maps. The IT designer outlined the situation and explained that, in his opinion, it would be a waste of money to introduce a new production management system as long as the company's management philosophy had not been clarified. He also asserted that he had the support of his boss to pull out of the project, since he did not want to be co-responsible for the project under the present circumstances. At the same time, however, his firm was offering to take part in clarifying what management philosophy would best serve the company before going on to explore the market for IT systems. Such a project needed anchoring with the owner.

No decision was made at that meeting, but a week later the owner got back to the IT designer and told him that he was ready to continue. He had decided to shut down the warehouse function and rely on sub-suppliers instead. He still needed a production management system, but now with an additional requirement of enabling contract bidding and follow-up.

4.5 Possible Phase Activities

This section reviews the possible activities included under the initiation phase. Sections 4.5.1–4.5.12 provide a maximum list of potentially relevant activities in carrying out an initiation phase. Figure 4.3 is a survey of phase activities. The initiation phase starts with a more or less specifically worded mandate for the design project. This mandate may be oral or written. After an initial discussion of what will be involved in the project, one or more persons are assigned to initiate the design project.

4.5.1 Planning the Initiation Phase

The aim of the initiation phase is to obtain a decision-making foundation for shaping a coherent design project in the form of a project charter and plan for the entire design project. The content of the project charter may provide guidelines for conducting the initiation phase. Those assigned to undertake the initiation phase may profitably start by writing a first draft of the project charter. This first draft

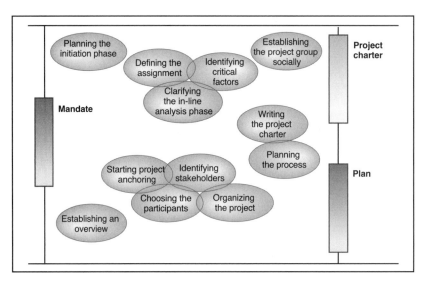

Figure 4.3 Products and activities potentially included in the initiation phase

will make it clear what sections need clarification or elaboration and, accordingly, which activities to perform during the phase. We generally recommend planning by the technique of baselines. Figure 4.3 shows an outline of a baseline plan. It is not always relevant to spend a lot of time on every activity in the figure—that depends on the specific project. However, we do recommend considering the relevance of every activity in the figure.

4.5.2 Establishing an Overview

Many situations first require the IT designers to gain an overview of the company and the activities that broadly make up the design project's object field. An adequate overview is a requirement for planning the initiation phase in any detail.

Establishing an overview as an independent activity may be necessary if, for instance, the IT designers are external consultants. As a part of this process, the IT designers are introduced to the company at initial meetings and interviews. Document analysis and freehand drawings may also be used. The document analysis may involve the company's own documents, such as marketing and promotional materials, annual reports, bylaws, agreements, and business and IT strategies. Freehand drawings attempt to establish an overview—for instance, of the work organization involved in a specific business process. They may be used individually—as a step in internal discussions by the project group—or as preparation for, and follow-up to, initial meetings with the company's managers and staff. If the design project is to extend to large parts of the company, and if many different staff members need to be included, we recommend making a round of introductions to the company's various departments and units. Here, the project group will be introduced to the departments' staff, who will get the real impression that a project is underway. It also provides an occasion for the project group to present the underlying idea, objective, and plan for the design project. Comments and questions from staff members will give the project group concrete impressions of how the project is perceived within the company.

4.5.3 Defining the Assignment

One of the most significant activities is defining the assignment based on the available mandate at the start of the initiation phase. Because the premise of a design project usually involves a situation with wide potential for interpretation, clearly defining the assignment and its objective is an important activity.

As a step in the design project, we recommend making room for critically examining the staff's own definitions of problems and solution proposals. It has often been our experience that managers and staff initially have detailed ideas for the IT systems they need. However, during the design project, it becomes clear that IT designers have not sufficiently analyzed the staff's initial ideas. In some instances, seemingly relevant IT systems were rejected completely or, in other cases, substantially revised. The IT designers are responsible for critically examining such existing interpretations of problems and solution proposals— and the initiation phase provides the first opportunity to challenge and assess them.

Defining the assignment means clarifying why particular problems need to be solved and what is involved, without going into great detail about how to solve them. Although one might assume this is something all involved parties understand, we still recommend always presenting convincing arguments for the goal of, and need for, the design project. To guarantee the highest possible authority and commitment, the steering committee should specify and articulate these arguments or approve the project group's suggested description for the goal of the design project.

The assignment is mainly defined via discussions and negotiations at various meetings with a few key persons who are involved mainly in executive functions. Diagnostic mapping can be used at these meetings. A few key persons, mainly in executive functions, may be interviewed.

4.5.4 Identifying Critical Factors

IT designers should identify and closely monitor critical factors—risky conditions that imperil the project and its implementation. A distinction can be made between two types of critical factors:

- Critical success factors: conditions and goals for the assignment that are requirements for success—that is, the project will fail if these conditions are not addressed or the goals not achieved. Critical success factors are often measurable, making it possible to ascertain whether the project has achieved its goals. They include requirements for higher efficiency and new types of tasks that need to be solved.
- Critical preconditions: fundamental premises for the project that, if negatively affected or eliminated, put the project in a difficult/perilous situation. Critical preconditions may involve resources, the attitude of management and staff toward the project, supplies and services required by project, coordination with other projects and suppliers, and so forth.

Specifying the critical factors for a project heightens awareness of possible future deviations. The IT team can refer to these critical factors if disagreement, conflict, or problems occur among the stakeholders (including the steering committee). If the project significantly deviates from the premise, the project charter and plan should be renegotiated.

Critical factors often surface during the activities that define the assignment, but the project group will also benefit from identifying factors in a brainstorming session. Analyzing critical factors may be supported by the technique of SWOT (Strengths, Weaknesses, Opportunities, and Threats) analysis.

4.5.5 Clarifying the In-Line Analysis Phase

The scope and nature of the in-line analysis phase should be clarified during the initiation phase. The in-line analysis phase may vary in scope according to the situation. It could involve only a single meeting under the initiation phase or it may constitute the main goal and assignment of the entire design project (see chapter 5).

The scope and relevance of this activity depends on two conditions:

- How clear is the company's business strategy and possible business-based IT strategy, and how clearly can the design project's objective be defined and linked to these overall strategies?
- How specifically can the work domains on which the design will focus be defined?

The more uncertain these conditions seem, the more ambitious and detailed the planning of the in-line analysis phase should be. Then again, the in-line analysis phase can be reduced to a single activity under the initiation phase if the conditions are clear to the participants or are covered by other projects or organizational units. In the latter case, the project charter should clearly state procedures and responsibilities for coordinating the design project.

The plan for the in-line analysis phase is thus clarified as part of this activity. For help in analyzing how much weight to assign to the in-line analysis phase, refer to the description of the situations and ambitions of the in-line analysis phase in section 5.3.

4.5.6 Organizing the Project

Regardless of its scope, the design project should be organized in a way that makes it clear to everyone involved who is responsible for what. As mentioned in chapter 1, we generally describe the method based on an organization into a project group (led by a project manager) and a steering committee (led by a chairman). Other organizing principles may, of course, be employed—for instance, organizing with a sponsor, requisitioner, and project group.

As mentioned in section 1.4, the project manager should be provided with a high degree of decision-making competency. The project manager and the project group develop proposals for planning the design project, indicating the results to be produced for the selected baselines. The project group carries out project activities and presents the results of the design project to the steering committee. It is not the project group's job to try to solve potential political controversies. However, the project group should make sure that conflicts are taken up for discussion in relevant forums, including the steering committee.

The steering committee decides which products the design project should generate and evaluates them at the planned baselines. It also makes decisions based on the project group's proposals (while considering business and IT strategies). The steering committee should also be ready to advise the project group on how to deal with latent and manifest conflicts. We recommend making it the steering committee's job to handle conflicts that arise over the course of a design project.

We recommend the project group and the steering committee coordinate with significant stakeholders as much as possible—for instance, by informal contacts or actual hearings (see figure 2.3). Stakeholders may be organized into reference groups and granted special opportunities for tracking and influencing the project.

4.5.7 Choosing the Participants

A fixed activity of any initiation phase is choosing the people to participate in the design project. We distinguish among four categories of persons in a design project: IT designers, users, management, and other stakeholders.

Managers assign participants to the steering committee and the project group. The IT designers can (and should) participate in this process, but the final decision rests with management.

We recommend putting the steering committee under the direction of the top executive for the part of the company that is involved in the design project. Other steering committee participants should include management representatives from the affected organizational units—what textbooks refer to as owners *business-process* or *problem owners*—as well as the head of the company's IT department (if one exists). At times, partnership and technology agreements will also require users to be represented on the steering committee.

The project group comprises a combination of IT designers and users. Usually, an IT designer with expertise in IT design serves as manager of the group. The IT designer should have competencies in IT design and management, experience in IT projects, and good communication skills. If the project manager is not an IT designer, but someone from within the business organization, he or she should, apart from leadership qualifications, possess experience from similar projects where significant changes were implemented.

Often, it is quite accidental which users are chosen for a project group. The selection may depend on who took the initiative for the design project, who participated in the initial meetings, whose calendar is not overbooked at the start of the project, and so forth. Experience has shown that it is very important which users are chosen for the project group. We recommend selecting users according to the following criteria:

- They should possess a good overview of the work domain concerned. In other words, they should have experience and broad insight into this work domain, not just narrow knowledge of their personal work domain. The ideal user occupies a central position in the business organization and has substantial insight into daily operations, an overview of business processes, and a capacity for seeing the effects the potential IT systems could have on present work practices.
- They should enjoy broad respect and confidence among their co-workers, as they will be important sources of information and central actors in anchoring the results of the design project. They should enjoy both professional respect and "political" backing.
- They should be committed to the project. It will not be productive if they were pressured into participating. The users' commitment should be maintained throughout the project. If not, the project manager and the IT designers are responsible for opening a discussion about why their commitment is waning.
- They should be neither technology freaks nor technophobes.

Smooth collaboration between users and IT designers is, of course, a precondition for an effective design project. It is important to give participants in the project group the time necessary for participation. Management should support excusing them from their day-to-day routines in order to support the project. However, this is often a problem: As a rule, project participation leads to overtime. We have often witnessed that agreements regarding relief or exemption from day-to-day tasks could not be practically accomplished or were simply not kept.

4.5.8 Identifying Stakeholders

Stakeholders are individuals and groups of people, organizational units within the company, customers, suppliers and strategic partners who have an interest in the design project's progress and results, or for whom the project group has a particular need. Stakeholders may have official—or more hidden—interests to maintain by the design project and, accordingly, may want to keep tabs on the project and be able to influence its progress and results. Stakeholders typically include staff members who may be affected by the design project's results—even if they will not be using the envisioned IT systems directly. The project group may also require, or even directly depend on, stakeholders delivering services or products during the course of the design project. These may be actual project resources, such as programming aid in prototype development, or various studies and reviews upon which the design project will build, such as the results of a study of the company's customers.

Identifying stakeholders is necessary for clarifying mutual requirements and needs for information, supplies, coordination, and cooperation.

Figure 4.4 presents a list of potential stakeholders. Such a list is generated during the initiation phase—typically by

- Indirect users of IT systems
- System administrators and other IT managers
- People in charge of the technical and organizational implementation of the IT project
- Interest and trade organizations
- Departments and projects within the company
- Trade groups within the company
- Suppliers and strategic partners
- Customers

Figure 4.4 Some potential stakeholders

interviews, meetings, or brainstorming sessions among the project group.

Identifying stakeholders should answer certain questions, such as:
- Who will be affected by the envisioned IT systems? What are their interests in the design project?
- On whom does the project group depend? What services and products require outside supply?

At a minimum, the project charter should name all stakeholders and their interests in the design project or specify the project group's needs and requirements.

Furthermore, the process of identifying stakeholders should include considerations of how to link to stakeholders (see figure 4.5). Decisions regarding the design project's relations to stakeholders should be documented in the project charter.

4.5.9 Starting Project Anchoring

Considerations regarding anchoring (see section 2.4) should be made in continuation of the stakeholder analysis. Firm anchoring requires allocating time and resources to inform all involved stakeholders and discussing intermediate products and visions of the design project. Anchoring should thus be ensured already in the initiation phase, since the project charter and plan are the first intermediate products of the design project. Accordingly, it is important to inform all relevant stakeholders about the products and gather comments on drafts of the project charter and plan before they are approved.

- Informal information
- Communication via meeting minutes, newsletters, the Internet, and the like
- Participation in a reference group
- Observer status
- Hearings
- Agreements on coordination and cooperation
- Agreements on negotiations
- Reviews or testing of prototypes
- Approval of intermediate products
- Contracts for the supply of specific services and products

Figure 4.5 Possible relations to stakeholders

In many cases, the stakeholders are already included in the project via meetings between the project group and the steering committee. But in some cases, the project involves considerably more people than are represented at such meetings—for instance, if the envisioned systems will be widely used by many staff members. In those cases, we recommend strengthening the anchoring by submitting the project charter to a hearing. Written comments can subsequently be gathered at a staff meeting, lunchroom meeting, or similar event.

The steering committee should decide in advance how the project will deal with comments. It may have a decidedly negative effect if staff and stakeholders find that their comments are not being heard. Informing staff and stakeholders about management proposals for the design project is preferable.

4.5.10 Establishing the Project Group Socially

The project group will be the setting for the smooth advancement of project efforts—both professionally and socially. This requires convincing the project's participants to share the efforts, an activity also known as team building. If the project's participants know each other in advance and the design project is short or of limited scope, such socialization is usually trouble-free and requires no special steps. However, if the design project involves a greater effort or the project's participants do not know each other in advance, it pays to plan the social establishment of the project group. In our experience, it is rare that much is made of establishing the project group socially. At times, it may also present a challenge if some participants consider team building to be too personal. However, the effect of planned social establishment is generally very positive. Apart from offering the project's participants an opportunity to get to know each other better, it adds to a sense of security and responsibility within the project group, while potentially nipping future causes of misunderstanding or irritation in the bud.

An enjoyable and informal way of establishing the project group may be to ask all project participants out to dinner rather than simply having meetings. A more ambitious option is to take everyone on a cruise or organize a retreat as part of the initiation phase. Regardless of the approach, we recommend giving all project participants the opportunity to express their motivation for participating, along with what they expect of and would like to achieve by the project—socially, professionally, educationally, or personally.

4.5.11 Writing the Project Charter

The project charter, along with the plan for the design project, makes up the foundation for decision making that is the product of the initiation phase. The project charter specifies the design project's mandate and includes written documentation for all significant decisions made during the initiation phase. It is recommended that writing the project charter start early in the initiation phase. Section 4.6 gives a checklist of possible subjects to include in the project charter. Figure 4.6 shows a suggested outline of a project charter.

4.5.12 Planning the Process

The project charter is written by the project group and approved by the steering committee. We have experienced

```
1. Premise
    1.1 Background
    1.2 Assignment and objective
    1.3 Financial and technical framework
    1.4 Critical factors

2. Organization
    2.1 Project organization
    2.2 Resources
    2.3 Stakeholders
    2.4 Agreements and coordination

3. Method
    3.1 Overall approach
    3.2 Plan
    3.3 Techniques and representation tools
    3.4 Working procedures

4. Signatures
```

Figure 4.6 Suggested outline of a project charter

positive effects when the project group and the steering committee sign a project charter: It guarantees a thorough reading of the project charter and a high level of commitment.

In addition to the project charter, a plan for the design process must be drawn up. The plan ought to be read and approved at the same time as, or shortly after, the project charter. The plan should visualize and review the planned design project. The purpose of the plan is both to provide fixed points for managing the further course of the project and to clarify its progress, scope, and ambitions.

We recommend using baselines as a planning technique, supplemented by risk management. The planning should reflect risk-management considerations, in the number and position of baselines as well as in the priority among, and analysis of, identified critical factors.

It is neither desirable nor possible to plan the entire design project in detail. During the initiation phase, the steering committee needs an overall plan for the initial part of the process, while the project group also needs a more detailed plan part of the process. The steering committee's planning should only involve a division into main activities leading to baselines and intermediate products for the steering committee to consider. The project group itself can plan the first part of the plan in greater detail, such as the process leading to the next baseline. The plan may be based on the four phases of the MUST design process and their affiliated baselines, while referring to the overviews of activities and products for each phase in figures 4.3, 5.2, 6.2, and 7.2.

4.6 Possible Results of the Phase

The results of the initiation phase are a project charter and a plan for the further design project. The project charter documents the premise and scope of the entire design project. Together with the plan, it constitutes a contract for the project between the project group and the steering committee. The charter should be limited to ten pages. The plan may well be attached to the project charter, as it will often be modified over the course of the design project. If the terms of the design project change significantly, it may be necessary to re-negotiate the project charter at a later stage.

The initiation phase mainly focuses on the design project. However, in clarifying the scope of the project, it also aims to examine aspects of a subsequent implementation project and the usage and technical contexts (see figure 4.7).

The rest of this chapter outlines all the potential results of the initiation phase in terms of the six aspects described in chapter 3. Accordingly, sections 4.6.1–4.6.6 constitute a maximum list of conditions that may be worth documenting in the initiation phase's project charter and plan.

4.6.1 Results in Terms of the IT Design Project

The main result of the initiation phase is clarifying the design project that is being initiated. This result constitutes the bulk of the project charter and includes several components:

- Examining background and arguments about the need for a design project
- Describing and defining the assignment and its objective, including examples of the types of questions that the design project will attempt to answer
- Clarifying the form of the design project's end products, including a report, drafts of requirement specifications and bidding materials, prototypes, and suggestions for experience-generating experiments

	Aspect	Initiation phase
Project context	IT design project	●
	Implementation project	○
Usage context	Business strategy	○
	Work practice	○
Technical context	IT systems	○
	IT platform( )	○

Figure 4.7 The relevance of the results of the initiation phase in terms of six different aspects: (●) indicates primary relevance; (○) indicates secondary relevance

- Summarizing the financial and technical scope of the design project
- Specifying critical success factors and critical preconditions
- Organizing a steering committee, project group, and possible reference groups
- Describing decision-making competencies and responsibilities of different groups involved in the project
- Determining how much time participants assigned to the project can devote to it
- Drawing up a list of all stakeholders who will be affected by the IT project
- Coordinating with stakeholders as to who will need to be informed or who will be supplying services and products to the design project determining how the project group will cooperate with people in charge of other IT systems and people in charge of the future technical and organizational implementation of the envisioned IT systems coordinating with the people responsible for the company's technical IT strategy (IT platform)
- Outlining an overall approach including significant phases, baselines, activities, and intermediate products relating to the plan
- Providing a list of techniques and representation tools that might be used
- Identifying working procedures in the project group and between the steering committee and the project group
- Obtaining signatures for the project charter

The plan for the design project may be in the form of a baseline plan, including a figure showing the planned progress of the entire design project (for an example, see figure 9.4).

The project charter and plan should both be submitted to selected stakeholders for comment before final approval by the steering committee.

4.6.2 Results in Terms of the Implementation Project

The design project is intended to be followed by an implementation project. Sometimes, clear ideas—as well as a clear scope and conditions—exist for the implementation project. Three conditions may guide the design project and warrant documentation in the project charter:

- A brief description of the goal of the implementation project
- A financial framework and timetable for the implementation project that the design project must respect
- Relations to other initiatives and projects upon which an implementation project depends

4.6.3 Results in Terms of Business Strategy

The ambition level of the in-line analysis phase needs to be clarified and an overall plan for this phase should be determined according to whether the business strategy

- Is identifiable;
- Is immediately linkable to the objective of the design project and the envisioned IT usage;
- Points out the work domains on which the design project will focus.

The project charter should summarize the envisioned IT usage's immediate relations to the business strategy, and the plan should consider their consequences leading into the in-line analysis phase.

4.6.4 Results in Terms of Work Practices

The project charter should explicitly state management's expectations and plans for changes to the company's existing work practices (see section 2.5) and openly account for questions such as:

- Is management expecting moderate organizational realignment or radical change?
- Will there be a need for users/workers to develop new competencies?
- Does the design plan objective imply a redrawing of job lines between specific staff groups?
- Are job cuts a goal and, if so, to what extent?
- Do the changes proposed by the design project have a realistic chance of succeeding considering the corporate culture and the staff's receptivity to change?

4.6.5 Results in Terms of IT Systems

The technical framework and conditions for the design project concern the new IT systems included in the design project's visions. However, the design team will also need to consider how the company's existing systems fit into the project. Sometimes, a company's strategy and plan for IT systems are set down in a business-based IT strategy. Thus, the way in which the envisioned IT systems link into the business-based IT strategy may also be worth documenting in the project charter. The project charter may include five observations:

- An identification of the company's business-based IT strategy and how the envisioned systems link into it
- A brief description of ideas and requirements for the functionality of the design project's envisioned IT systems
- An expected implementation strategy for the envisioned IT systems
- An identification of existing systems that may be supplying or using data (databases, data warehouses, and so forth)
- An identification of existing systems with which the new IT systems are expected to be integrated

4.6.6 Results in Terms of the IT Platform

The scope and conditions for the IT platform may be decisive in determining what types of IT systems design visions are possible. Accordingly, IT platform requirements should be identified as early as possible in the design project. A company's IT platform strategy and plan are sometimes set down in a technical IT strategy. When this is the case, developing the IT platform may include three tasks:

- Identifying the company's technical IT strategy and how the envisioned systems link to it
- Identifying the IT platforms and development environments (including database systems, office-systems package, and programming languages)
- Identifying the technical standards that must be respected (operating systems, communications protocols, and so on)

4.7 Summary and Literature

In this chapter, we have clarified the objective of the initiation phase. We have described the possible activities and results of the phase. Moreover, we have represented three prototypical situations to help a project group organize an initiation phase according to the specific aspects of its project.

The prime inspiration for the content of the initiation phase is the technique of project establishment. Our main source on this topic has been "Professional Systems Development" (Andersen et al. 1990, chap. 4). We have systematically incorporated project establishment in every design project we ourselves have conducted. The descriptions in this chapter are mainly based on experiences gained from those projects.

5
In-Line Analysis Phase:
Strategic Alignment Analysis

In the in-line analysis phase, the project group clarifies and adjusts the design project's goals according to the company's business and IT strategies, in order to identify work domains for the design project to study as candidates for IT support. A result of the in-line analysis phase is selecting the work domains where the IT systems will be used. These work domains typically have a high priority for IT reinforcement in terms of the company's business strategy and business processes. Thus, the in-line analysis phase ties into the company's overall business goals and strategy—as well as to the company's business-based IT strategy, if one has been defined. The in-line analysis phase enables the project and its results to integrate with and be measured by the overall strategic goals. The phase is largely conducted in dialogue with the company's management.

The in-line analysis phase will clarify the potential of the company investing in IT, while identifying the goals, needs, and conditions involved. This includes fostering an understanding of the company's environment and what areas within the company need to be strengthened by new IT usage. The in-line analysis phase involves identifying and analyzing the company's environment, including its customers, suppliers, and competitors. The result of the in-line analysis phase is a strategic alignment report identifying and prioritizing work domains to include in the further design project and to focus on in the subsequent in-depth analysis phase.

5.1 Objective

In the in-line analysis phase, the project manager assumes responsibility for clarifying and adjusting the design project's objective in terms of the company's business and IT strategies, in order to identify what work domains to focus on in the in-depth analysis phase. The phase is not aimed at developing new business or IT strategies, but at clarifying existing strategies and critically examining the planned IT usage for advancing those strategies. If the company has no IT strategy, the project manager may encourage the development of one, and in special cases the ongoing design project may have to wait for this to happen. The objective of the in-line analysis phase includes several goals:

- Identifying and clarifying the company's overall situation, environment, and business strategy
- Clarifying the company's possible IT strategy, especially concerning the choices and priorities of this strategy in terms of planned IT usage
- Clarifying how management and other involved parties understand the alignment of the company's IT usage and overall business strategy
- Ensuring that the scope of the design project's IT usage harmonizes with the company's business and IT strategies, and if not, being prepared to critique the goals of the project or their strategic backdrop
- Developing a foundation for decision making regarding the continued focus of the design project—that is, identifying the work domains upon which the in-depth analysis should focus, based on the company's overall strategies

5.2 Motivation

It should not merely be up to the top management to identify IT projects to match the company's business and IT strategies. Responsibility for doing so must be shared by the managers of the design project and the subsequent implementation of the project. Harmonizing with the company's overall strategies should, in principle, be part of any IT project. When the design project manager takes on responsibility for doing so, it ensures that the results can be assessed in terms of the company's business situation and goals. This process leads to four important developments:

- The design project avoids recommending the prioritization of the wrong solutions for the present situation. In other words, the design project avoids recommending perfect technical and organizational solutions to the wrong problems and needs.

- IT usage is designed according to clear business goals and can be assessed according to these goals.
- The design project gains in efficiency. The next phase (the in-depth analysis phase) will be able to explicitly focus on the candidate work domains for IT support and avoid resource-consuming studies of "irrelevant" work domains.
- Solutions developed in the innovation phase are viewed against the backdrop of the company's strategic situation, its conditions for potential reform, and readiness for change.

5.3 Situations and Ambitions

The design project's situation was already assessed in the initiation phase, where a plan and ambition level for the in-line analysis phase were also determined (see section 4.5.5). The scope and ambition level of the in-line analysis phase depend on how clearly the objective of the specific design project can be defined. Some companies have already determined an IT strategy that identifies certain types of IT systems according to business concerns. Such a business-based IT strategy will often, directly or indirectly, be able to identify the work domains where the planned IT systems will be used.

Whether an IT strategy exists or not, the work domains on which the design project will focus need to be selected during the in-line analysis phase. In addition, it is necessary to assess the alignment of the design project's objectives and the company's business strategy. The alignment may take two forms:

- Highly significant—that is, it is vital to the whole project, highly problematic, or marked by disagreement and conflict
- Partly insignificant to the design project—that is, it is completely clarified, unproblematic, or marked by agreement and consensus

Together, these factors mark a range of four typical situations by which the in-line analysis phase can be planned (see figure 5.1). Section 5.4 provides examples of the four situations.

In situation 1, the in-line analysis phase is omitted. The reason for doing so may briefly be summarized in the project charter. Strategic and management-oriented literature—especially the normative and method-prescribing parts of it—often describes ideal situations, where companies have a clear business strategy and a related IT strategy, providing a rational and clearly defined premise for the proposed IT projects. Such a premise, reflecting an ideal situation, rarely exists in real life.

In situation 2, the in-line analysis phase is reduced to an activity under the initiation phase. This activity involves the project group gaining information about the degree of alignment between the company's business strategy and the goals of the design project, familiarizing itself with the com-

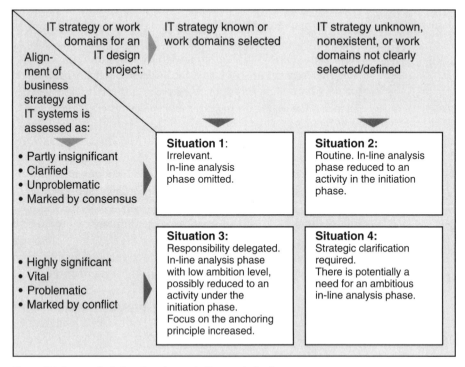

Figure 5.1 Four typical situations for an in-line analysis phase

pany's IT strategy (if one exists), and identifying work domains needing IT support.

In situations 3 and 4, aligning the company's business strategy and the goals of the design project are assessed as vital, problematic, or marked by conflict. Situation 3 occurs if the company has delegated responsibility for the IT strategy to a specialized organizational unit. In such cases, the design project manager needs to ensure a high degree of cooperation with that unit. Responsibility and coordination regarding the tasks involved in such cooperation should be clarified as an activity under the initiation phase.

Situation 3 also includes cases where management has selected the work domains that will be IT supported in advance and where further analysis of the alignment of envisioned IT usage and the company's business strategy is not desired. Sometimes, it is impossible for the project manager to gain support for including an in-line analysis phase in the design project. Management may have formed the opinion—perhaps from previous experience—that "IT people" should not meddle in overall strategic discussions.

If the situation is marked by disagreement and conflict, there is further occasion to increase the focus on the anchoring principle (see section 2.4) and on the project group's recourses in case of conflict (see section 2.5.) This will typically be the case in situations involving substantial organizational restructuring when many staff members face an uncertain future. Under these circumstances, the task of selecting and defining the work domains for the design project may be a simple one, but the project may be marked by conflict, power struggles, and uncertainty among the staff.

In situation 4, it is crucial to ensure a qualified alignment of the company's strategies and the design project's goals, even though it may not be entirely clear how to go about doing so. Three scenarios may arise:
• The work domains on which the design project will focus cannot readily be selected and defined.

- The goal of the design project calls for strategic IT systems—that is, systems vital to the company's competitiveness or very expensive ones.
- The company has no IT strategy and does not want one or, an IT strategy exists, but does not include the design project.

In some cases, the in-line analysis phase may yield a result that entails suspending the design project—where the project must wait for a clarification and consideration of the company's strategic position.

While carefully assessing the situation is an important element in planning the in-line analysis phase, it offers no guarantee that the plan may not later need to be adjusted or entirely rejected. We have witnessed cases that initially resembled situation 1, but where the alignment of the business strategy and the design project's goals later became more unclear, and the resulting situation called for reconsidering the candidate work domains. In figure 5.1, this scenario corresponds with an evaluation of the design project changing from situation 1 to situation 3 or 4. Ultimately, the design project charter and plan may need to be completely revised.

5.4 Examples of In-Line Analysis Phases

This section presents four examples of how the strategic analysis in an in-line analysis phase may proceed. The four examples illustrate the four situations listed in figure 5.1. In the first three examples, as figure 5.1 indicates, the in-line analysis phase is reduced to an activity under the initiation phase.

5.4.1 Situation 1: The In-Line Analysis Phase Is Irrelevant

An insurance company was facing new IT investments in its life insurance department. The year before, a large international consulting agency had performed a comprehensive strategic analysis of the company. This analysis resulted in partial revision of the company's overall business strategies. An IT strategy was established in the process, which identified and prioritized the company's total portfolio of IT investments over the next five years.

The life insurance department was marked by a high degree of stability. The market was predictable and the customers were faithful, expecting the careful, "traditional" service they had come to expect from the company. For instance, life insurance terms were printed on special paper with watermarks and personal signatures.

Life insurance case processing was marked by a high degree of routine, and no plans existed for significant changes. The IT strategy did, however, prioritize one target area: a case-processing system for supporting filing and follow-up of case-processing paperwork. A design project was subsequently initiated with the aim of acquiring a generic system for filing and case support. Since a current IT strategy was available and the work domain was clearly defined (life insurance case processing), the design project team was able to move straight to the in-depth analysis phase.

5.4.2 Situation 2: Routine

A chain of photo stores decided to have one of its stores test a barcode system for keeping track of films dropped off for processing. The company had commissioned an IT designer for the assignment and selected a store for introducing the system. There was advance interest centering on two systems offering the desired functionality.

During the initiation phase, the IT designer began to wonder whether the chain's management was considering applying the experiment to the other stores in the chain. The first candidate system (PC-based) would work at one store, but might fail if it later had to function across several stores. Furthermore, the designer also anticipated future problems involving integration with other systems—for managing discount plans for film processing, customer files, payment in a cash-register system, and so forth.

The IT designer called a meeting with the chain's management, which also included a representative from the selected store. As it turned out, the meeting was the key to the project's strategic clarification. At the meeting, management presented its business strategy. Feeling the pressure from other photo stores, the chain was preparing an aggressive marketing drive, offering customers very inexpensive plans for film processing. Accordingly, management was predicting a dramatic increase in the volume of processed film. The main concern of the design project was to quickly set up a system enabling the stores to handle a lot of film, one that both satisfied customers and did not require hiring new staff. Thus, the most important consideration was implementing a system quickly. If the system could also be used across the stores (at a possible future date) that would be preferable, but this was not an absolute requirement. Future integration with other systems was also worth considering but did not require a high priority either, since the main problem of film processing needed to be solved immediately the chain's existence could be at stake.

A decision was then made to include two stores, testing the first candidate system at one and the second candidate system at the other store, in order to be able to quickly choose the system with the fewest glitches. The systems testing would emphasize carefully monitoring the store's film-processing work processes to make sure that the system would be able to handle different customer needs smoothly.

5.4.3 Situation 3: Responsibility Is Delegated

This example involved a large international IT company that supplied advanced solutions for tax auditing of private companies. The system, consisting of a series of modules, included all phases of tax auditing, from selecting companies in a pre-audit through to post-audit of individual companies. The IT company was offering potential clients (national or regional tax authorities) a free, limited design project to demonstrate how this IT solution could be adapted to their needs.

One client who requested a free limited design project was the Portuguese tax department based in Lisbon. This design project's initiation phase started with a meeting between the company's IT managers and management from the Portuguese tax department in Lisbon. The IT designers, who had conducted IT projects for a number of national tax authorities, suggested that the design project should extend to the

Portuguese tax-auditing process in a relatively broad sense. Tax department management, however, wanted the design project to focus on pre-audit processes. Its reason for this, as stated at the meeting, was that pre-auditing was the most important factor for efficient use of the tax department's resources. Afterward, however, the IT designers were confidentially informed of another reason: the IT managers in the tax department thought of them as competition and a potential threat. Conversely, many tax department managers considered the IT department's performance unsatisfactory. The choice of the "pre-audit" business process was a compromise that the IT managers had been forced to accept, in part because they had neither planned for nor had the resources to develop systems for that area within the foreseeable future.

Accordingly, the design project would not include an in-line analysis phase, although the company's IT designers did consider the phase relevant. Consequently, the IT designers wrote a passage in the project charter emphasizing that the design project would focus on pre-audit processes in accordance with the client's wishes. They planned the design project to increase attention on the anchoring principle, and the project moved on to the in-depth analysis phase. This phase concluded with a full-day seminar for tax department and IT managers, where the results of interviews made during the phase with managers and staff were presented and discussed using diagnostic maps. The mapping revealed a number of problems and needs, including several relating to aspects of auditing beyond the pre-audit process. Detailed discussions ensued on how the tax department's existing and planned IT systems would be able to address these problems and needs. The client then agreed to pursuing some of these problems in the subsequent innovation phase, as long as they were planned as long-term implementation projects following the immediate implementation of a pre-audit system.

5.4.4 Situation 4: Strategic Clarification Is Required

A few years ago, the education ministry of a Scandinavian country decided it wanted more uniform reporting from the nation's public universities. The ministry wanted standardized information on "a student's progress through the system"—including admissions, exam completions, enrollment in individual programs, course offerings, and so forth. The universities were already reporting all this information to the education ministry, but in such diverse forms that it was practically impossible to compare data from different universities. Moreover, the ministry was concerned about the universities' expenses for possible administrative solutions. All the universities needed IT support for their administration, and several had already begun to develop their own administrative systems. In the ministry's opinion, this strategy was way too expensive. If a common system was developed, the overall cost level was expected to be substantially lower.

Consequently, the education ministry wrote a mandate for a design project concerning the development of a common administrative system for the nation's universities. The system would operate with a shared central database under the administration of the education ministry. Until this system was developed, all the universities would be ordered to halt the development of their "private" IT solutions in this area.

Two IT designers from a respected consulting agency were commissioned to conduct a design project with the aim of producing requirement specifications for the system that could be used in a subsequent call for tenders. During the first meeting at the education ministry, the IT designers pointed out the relevance of carrying out an ambitious in-line analysis phase. First, because the project involved a strategically important system (which would be costly to develop) and, second, because the work domains that would be supported by the system could only be defined in very general terms. The ministry accepted this proposal.

In the in-line analysis phase, the IT designers first conducted a series of interviews with top officials from the education ministry on goals and strategy concerning the IT system. Here, it became clear that a major reason for prioritizing a central system was the minister's political agenda. He wanted a change of policy toward the universities, from "framework management" (allocating resources to universities for meeting various goals), to "detailed management" (enabling the education ministry to specifically prioritize resources among the universities). The system would allow the ministry to compare the graduation rates from specific programs—and possibly decide to discontinue inefficient programs at some universities in order to expand more efficient programs at other universities.

Next, the IT designers visited four selected universities to examine their requirements and conditions for the proposed system. It became clear to the IT designers that the university administrators felt pressured into accepting the ministry's plans. The universities' allocations were generally low in those years, and the better terms they were on with the education minister, the better their yield from the annual allocation negotiations would be. Meanwhile, many universities had an urgent need for administrative IT systems and feared delays if a big, common, "gold-plated" system had to be developed first.

The IT designers not only visited the top administrators at the universities, but also several of the departments overseeing day-to-day administration. The education ministry had given the IT designers a relatively simple image of university administration as a standardized procedure of "admitting students at one end and producing graduates at the other." However, the designers learned that the universities had very different programs and practices. Their administrative procedures varied greatly and needed to be able to handle any number of possible exceptions. In addition, standardized procedures would not go over well in academia, since the universities were historically accustomed to a large measure of autonomy. The outcome could be difficult, drawn-out negotiations on the requirements for the system and an endless list of detailed requirements, entailing a high risk of cost overruns and delays for the IT project. Moreover, there was a major risk that the system supplied would ultimately not be able to satisfactorily handle university administration.

Finally, the IT designers conducted a series of meetings with IT managers from the education ministry and consultants from a major database supplier. They then developed an idea for an alternative IT strategy that did not require the development of a common university administration system. Instead, the design project would focus on the ministry's requirements for data from the universities. A database customized to the ministry would be built, to which the universities had an obligation to report their data, regardless of how they chose to administrate their programs and what IT solutions they would end up implementing. Such an IT strategy would comply with the minister's policy and strategy for the universities, without requiring the development of a common IT administration system among all universities.

The IT designers concluded the in-line analysis phase by compiling their recommendations in a strategic alignment report and submitting it to the ministry. The minister and certain officials initially hesitated to follow the recommendation for an alternative IT strategy. First, they thought it should not be such a big problem to standardize and simplify the universities' administrative procedures; second, they expected large savings to be gained by developing a single, common system. A few months later, however, another ministry made headlines in a major IT scandal. In this instance, a big IT project had been significantly delayed and costs had more than tripled over the original budget. Shortly after, the education minister changed his mind and followed the IT designers' suggestions.

5.5 Possible Phase Activities

This section reviews the possible activities included under the in-line analysis phase. Sections 5.5.1–5.5.6 provide a complete list of potentially relevant activities to carry out during the phase. Starting the in-line analysis phase requires that the situation and ambition level for the phase has been assessed (in the initiation phase) and, moreover, that a detailed plan for the phase has been developed (see chapter 4).

Figure 5.2 is an overview of possible activities to be carried out in the in-line analysis phase. Since clarifying a company's strategies is central to this phase, the figure gathers activities to that end under the heading "clarifying strategies." The aim is to critically examine how management understands the company's overall business and IT strategies and how the goals of the design project are seen to be linked to these strategies.

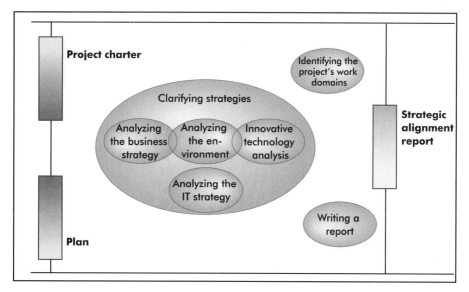

Figure 5.2 Products and activities potentially included in the in-line analysis phase

5.5.1 Analyzing the Environment

Analyzing a company's environment is an important activity in all types of strategic analysis. The environment includes such factors as the company's general market situation; legislation to which the company as well as its products and services are subjected; customers and suppliers; competitors; plus familiar and new technologies (not least as regards IT).

The possible environmental aspects mentioned here should naturally be interpreted in terms of a specific company, whether public or private. The elements of the environment that are relevant to include for further analysis in the design project depends on the company, or part of the company, involved in the design project. If the design project involves the department of a big company, the customers and suppliers may be other company staff members and departments.

The analysis includes identifying the environment and characterizing it in terms of the various potentials, requirements, conditions, and needs, which the company then attempts to influence and accommodate via its business strategy. The analysis may be based on the techniques of document analysis, interviews with environmental representatives (such as selected and representative customers) as well as SWOT and functional analysis.

5.5.2 Analyzing the Business Strategy

In strategic literature, this activity describes a conventional "top-down" analysis. Here, the analysis starts from the company's business strategy. Accordingly, types of IT usage are located that can serve to realize and strengthen the business strategy:

- The company's business strategy is reviewed and clarified based on an understanding of the company's environment (see section 5.5.1) and its internal conditions—including the company's size, organizational culture, structure, management style, and so forth.
- The design team derives the means for maintaining the company's business strategy—that is, the linked business areas and processes, which are mapped to determine problems, bottlenecks, and other weak relations.
- Work domains to be strengthened are located against the backdrop of identified problems and weaknesses. General IT needs, constituting the means to that end, are identified.

The analysis primarily involves document analysis of descriptions of the company's business strategy, along with meetings and interviews with the company's management, possibly supplemented by SWOT and functional analysis.

Occasionally, the company has already had a "top-down" analysis made, typically by an external consulting firm. In such cases, the project group's assignment involves reviewing the results of that analysis and reconstructing the chain of argumentation from business strategy to IT systems.

5.5.3 Analyzing the IT Strategy

Any existing business-based IT strategy, or prioritization among the company's planned IT systems, should be closely analyzed in the in-line analysis phase. An IT strategy—for instance, one that identifies a portfolio or product suite of existing and planned IT systems—is typically the result of a "top-down" analysis (as mentioned in section 5.5.2) and can be viewed as the "result" of that analysis.

The project group should assess whether the company's IT strategy extends to the design project's goals concerning

IT usage. The IT strategy should then be reviewed in order to resolve the IT strategy's alignment with the business strategy—that is, locating work domains to be supported by IT systems, the business areas and processes in which these domains are part, and how the IT strategy promotes the business strategy (see figure 5.3). The main techniques for this review are document analysis of the company's IT strategy descriptions and interviews with the people overseeing its IT strategy.

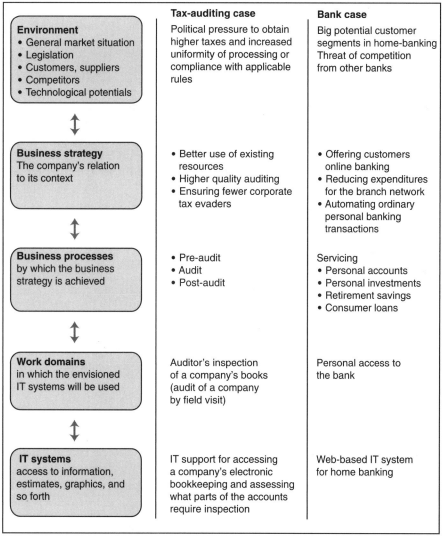

Figure 5.3 Examples of the alignment of environment, business strategy, business processes, work domains, and IT systems

5.5.4 Innovative Technology Analysis

While strategic analysis focuses on how a given business strategy can be supported by IT, innovative technology analysis examines how new technological potentials can radically impact and alter the business strategy, possibly creating whole new business ventures. This type of analysis is familiar from "business process reengineering" (among other things) and what is referred to as "IT-enabled change." The factor here is a new and promising type of IT system that if implemented at the company could lead to major organizational realignment in the form of new production processes, new products, and new markets.

The project group should critically examine such new potentials as the envisioned IT systems propose to provide. The objective here, the same as in analyzing the company's business and IT strategies, is writing (and reconstructing) the chain of argumentation reflected in figure 5.3, in order to identify what existing work domains in the company will be affected by the IT systems. The primary technique to that end is interviews of management and other employees involved in the potential uses of IT. The interviews may be supplemented by SWOT analysis, document analysis of IT systems descriptions, and observation of the IT system in use—at a demonstration with the supplier or with another company using the system.

5.5.5 Identifying the Project's Work Domains

Based on a clarification of the strategies, the project group identifies—that is, it defines, summarizes, and suggests priorities among—the work domains on which the further design project will focus, accounting for their relevance according to their alignment with the company's business strategy. The more clearly these work domains can be defined and specified, the more effectively they can be studied during the in-depth analysis phase. If major uncertainty is involved in defining a work domain, other work domains on the "periphery" should be identified, as they may become relevant for closer analysis at a later stage. There are several criteria for identifying relevant work domains:

- The work domain is central to business areas and business processes under the business strategy.

- It is of major relevance to the company's environment—for instance, to the customers.
- Problems and weaknesses that have been identified within the work domain are important to solve or strengthen in accordance with the business strategy.
- The domain can be supported by IT relatively simply.
- Thorough understanding of the work domain is significant to ensure efficient use of the IT systems—for instance, if the work domain is very complex or managed by staff with a high level of expertise.
- The work domain it holds huge, anticipated efficiency gains—that is, it has significant reform potential.

5.5.6 Writing a Report

The result of the in-line analysis phase is a foundation for decision making in the form of a strategic alignment report (see figure 5.4). The report will serve as a basis for selecting and prioritizing the work domains based on an understanding of the company's overall situation, environment, and business strategy, as well as its possible IT strategy. The report should also be able to argue in favor of the selected work domains according to overall business considerations—in other words, the report should reproduce the chain of argumentation linking the business strategy to the technological options generated by the design project (see figure 5.3). The report thus clarifies the potential for IT investments, outlining the project's overall organizational and technical implications.

In special cases, the outcome of an in-line analysis phase may also include a problematization of the premise for the entire design project, possibly involving a critique of existing business and IT strategies.

1. Environment
   1.1 Potentials and needs
   1.2 Requirements and conditions
   1.3 Special conditions

2. Business strategy
   2.1 Goals
   2.2 Business processes
   2.3 Challenges and problems

3. Work domains
   3.1 Definition
   3.2 Characterization
   3.3 Discussion/conclusion

Figure 5.4 Suggested outline of a strategic alignment report

5.6 Possible Results of the Phase

The in-line analysis phase results in a strategic alignment report identifying work domains for the project group to focus on in the subsequent in-depth analysis phase. Work domains for the project are selected from a business perspective—that is, they are judged mainly according to the usage context (see figure 5.5). A significant result of the in-line analysis phase is reproducing the argumentation for the alignment (see figure 5.3).

In this section, all the potential results of the in-line analysis phase are indicated in terms of the six aspects discussed in the introduction to part II. Sections 5.6.1–5.6.6 thus comprise a total list of conditions that may be relevant to document in the strategic alignment report of the in-line analysis phase.

	Aspect	In-line analysis phase
Project context	Design project	O
	Implementation project	-
Usage context	Business strategy	●
	Work practices	●
Technical context	IT systems	-
	IT platform	-

Figure 5.5 The relevance of the results of the in-line analysis phase in terms of six different aspects: (●) indicates primary relevance; (O) indicates secondary relevance; (-) indicates that this aspect is relevant only in special cases

5.6.1 Results in Terms of the Design Project

A company's business strategy and technological options are factors that do not necessarily remain stable over time, even over a relatively short period of time. Accordingly, it may be necessary to consider how to continually ensure—for the remainder of the design project—the most expedient alignment with the business strategy (see figure 5.3). Moreover, considerations regarding the design project should include anchoring for the results of the phase and possibly a revised plan for further progress. Results of the in-line analysis phase may include three elements:

- A plan for following up on (and continually guaranteeing) optimum alignment with the design project's goals and the company's business strategy, including making agreements with the managers of the business and IT strategies regarding information and coordination
- A possible, revised baseline plan for the further design project, especially considering the in-depth analysis phase
- Informing stakeholders and documenting their comments

5.6.2 Results in Terms of the Implementation Project

The results here may involve new or changed requirements and conditions for the implementation project deriving from the in-line analysis phase. This corresponds to a revision of the potential results set down in the project charter, see section 4.6.2.

5.6.3 Results in Terms of Business Strategy

The business strategy, with which the objective of the design project must be aligned, needs to be identified and clarified, including the business strategy's alignment with the company's environment, as well as to business areas and processes by which the business strategy is achieved. This process involves several steps:

- Describing the company's business strategy;
- Identifying the company's environment, or the environment of the part of the company where the design project is taking place. The environment may here include the general market situation, competitors, legislation, customers and suppliers (external and internal), other related units or departments in the company, and so forth;
- Characterizing the environment—that is, its significant potentials, requirements, conditions, and needs in terms of the design project's goals. Characterizing the environment should also extend to requirements and conditions that one cannot or does not wish to change, as well as those one might or should affect. The characterization may also include special conditions—for instance, concerning customers, about whom a high degree of knowledge should be maintained.
- Identifying and characterizing business areas and business processes necessary for achieving the business strategy. The characterization should include the goals, challenges, and general problems that the new IT usage seeks to address.
- Business goals for IT usage, possibly including a list of quantifiable factors by which use of the IT systems can be measured and assessed

5.6.4 Results in Terms of Work Practices

The work domains where the new IT systems will be used need to be identified, characterized, and defined. These domains can be described in terms of the business strategy, business areas, and business processes. This may involve several types of classification:

- Describing and prioritizing work domains for the design project to focus on during the in-depth analysis phase

- Identifying conditions of present work practices which are especially significant for analysis in the in-depth analysis phase
- Possibly specifying goals and requirements for changes to work practices involving automatization, streamlining, flexibility, coordination, and so forth. This step corresponds to revising the potential results set down in the project charter (see section 4.6.4).

5.6.5 Results in Terms of IT Systems

The results of the in-line analysis phase may involve a new or changed scope and conditions for existing and new IT systems. This corresponds to a revision the potential results set down in the project charter (see section 4.6.5) and may involve three things:

- A summary of existing (and possible future) technological options relevant to the business strategy that warrant elaboration in the design project's end product
- A clarification of relations between the company's business-based IT strategy and the IT systems included under the design project
- Elements of a new or changed business-based IT strategy

5.6.6 Results in Terms of the IT platform

The results of the in-line analysis phase may (as in the aspect of IT systems) include a new or changed scope for the IT platform. This corresponds to revising the potential results set down in the project charter (see section 4.6.6).

5.7 Summary and Literature

This chapter initially clarified the objective of the in-line analysis phase. We have described the possible activities and results of the phase accordingly. Furthermore, we have described four prototypical situations to aid a project group in planning the in-line analysis phase according to their specific project.

The most significant inspiration for the content of the in-line analysis phase derives from our own experiences in applying work analysis as formulated by Schmidt (1986, 1988). Our experiences have been thoroughly discussed in Simonsen (1994). In some of the design projects we have conducted, the in-line analysis phase turned out to be of crucial importance to the content of the design project as a whole. These design projects had a number of parallels to the field of IT strategy. Simonsen (1999) provides an overview of relevant literature in this field, along with an example of the progress and results of the in-line analysis phase in a design project. Our sources on IT strategy include Ciborra (1997); Earl (1993); Hammer and Champy (1993); Henderson and Venkatraman (1992); Venkatraman, Henderson, and Oldach (1993); and Lederer and Salmela (1996).

6
In-Depth Analysis Phase:
Ethnographically Inspired Analysis

The in-depth analysis phase thoroughly examines selected work domains. This phase is the primary analysis-oriented part of the design project. Its aim is to establish a thorough understanding of present work practices and the rationales determining their form. Accordingly, it becomes possible to understand the conditions for change in the form of new information technology and possible changes to the work organization. The primary means for gaining such thorough understanding are techniques enabling the project group to experience the users' work practices (see section 2.3), including ethnographically inspired techniques such as observation and in situ interviews, combined with other more intervention-oriented techniques.

The starting point of the in-depth analysis phase is the decision from the in-line analysis phase determining what work domains will be the focus of the design project. The main result of the in-depth analysis phase is a list of goals, problems, and needs in existing work practices, along with ideas for IT support and changes to the work organization. This list, in turn, constitutes the starting point for the subsequent innovation phase.

Knowledge generated by the project group in the in-depth analysis phase may be challenged in the innovation phase. For instance, development and testing of a prototype may produce a new understanding of the current form of the work that needs to be more closely examined.

6.1 Objective

The objective of the in-depth analysis phase is supporting a prioritization of the goals, problems, and needs for which the project group will develop design visions in the innovation phase. This is accomplished by studying the selected work domains and understanding the rationales determining present work practices.

The in-depth analysis phase works according to the principle that work practices need to be experienced firsthand. This includes the design team basing produced representations on concepts and categories employed in the relevant work domains, as well as grounding—and anchoring—analysis in day-to-day work practices. This builds confidence among IT designers, management, and staff, enabling everyone to see how the changes are grounded in an understanding of—and respect for—the company, its culture, and work practices. Establishing and maintaining that confidence is considered an important aspect in and of itself.

The principle of genuine user participation is likewise applied in the in-depth analysis phase. When staff members in the affected work domains participate in the analysis, their knowledge of, and interests in, their own work situation can effectively be incorporated into the design team's efforts. In sections 6.3 and 6.5, we return to considerations that the project group should make regarding these conditions.

6.2 Motivation

In discussions of the in-depth analysis phase, a frequent question is: Why spend so much time studying something that will be changed later anyway? The main argument in favor of the in-depth analysis phase is that good reasons exist for why the day-to-day tasks at a company are performed the way they are and that their underlying rationale is highly relevant to the design—even in those cases when management seeks drastic change. Moreover, certain aspects of a company's day-to-day work practices often are not apparent to management and staff. We think of IT design as connected to both tradition and innovation. The design must build on, and respect, fundamental and sustainable traditions but should also be innovative—that is, it should break with outdated principles and traditions. Good IT design requires knowledge of work practices in order to determine which company traditions are fundamental and sustainable, and which are outdated. Put in a different way, only when a design team has fundamental knowledge of existing work practices can it arrive at what we call a "sustainable design."

The in-depth analysis phase may produce knowledge identifying assets and qualities that the design should preserve or promote, such as certain patterns of cooperation. This phase may also provide important hints about the company's readiness for change (i.e., what scope of change and innovation the company is able to realize), which the design team should respect. This is the only way to avoid gold-plated and costly solutions, which often are flat-out rejected or can only be integrated into day-to-day operations at great cost and with much effort.

6.3 Situations and Ambitions

The scope and ambition level of the in-depth analysis phase varies from one design project to the next. Two significant factors accounting this variation are the complexity of the company and the work domain, on the one hand, and the IT designers' advance knowledge of the selected work domains, on the other. Figure 6.1 shows the range in scope and complexity of the in-depth analysis phase. Section 6.4 provides more detailed examples of the four situations outlined in the figure.

The complexity of the company (and the design project undertaken within it) depends on the size of the company, the number of interest groups, and the complexity of the work domains included in the design project. When a design project (and, in turn, an in-depth analysis phase) is carried out at a small business or a single department of ten to twenty employees, there will typically be only a few interest groups—such as management, professionals, and secretaries. In such situations, an overview and (in most cases) detailed knowledge of the work domains can usually be achieved by involving most of the staff.

IT design performed at big companies with a number of selected work domains that possibly span different depart-

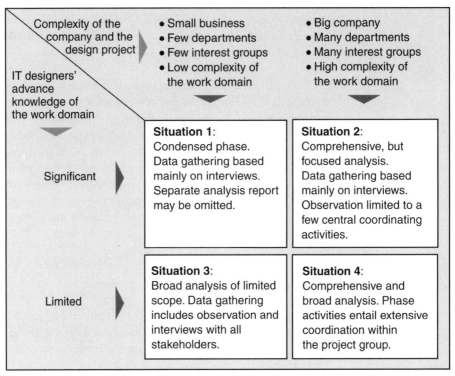

Figure 6.1 Four typical situations for an in-depth analysis phase

ments will by definition involve several interest groups. In such situations, practical concerns rule out gaining an overview by involving all staff. It then becomes necessary to select participants for the in-depth analysis phase. In an in-depth analysis phase, the project group must typically distribute activities such as interviews and observations among its members. This, in turn, entails a higher degree of coordination and information sharing in the project group's efforts.

The IT designers' advance knowledge of a work domain is the other important factor in assessing the scope and ambitions of the in-depth analysis phase. Some design projects are conducted by IT designers with lots of experience in the relevant field from previous projects. Or, the project group may include so many staff members from the work domains involved that the project group can, as a whole, be determined to have substantial advance knowledge of the work domains. Such situations enable the project group to quickly focus the studies based on the advance knowledge. Data gathering can then be mainly interview-based, and observation can concentrate on a few central activities, typically coordination activities, such as meetings and other work situations where even those involved may have a hard time explicitly describing what happens. If the in-depth analysis phase is greatly condensed, a separate analysis report may be omitted. Then, the product for the phase's baseline consists of the developed representations (including problem issues) such as diagnostic maps.

In some situations, the IT designers may have no (or relatively little) advance knowledge of the work domains, and the users in the project group may have no knowledge about the selected work domain. Then, the project group must begin the in-depth analysis phase with an open approach, both when establishing an overview of the domain and when delving into individual problem fields.

6.4 Examples of In-Depth Analysis Phases

The four following sections describe in-depth analysis phases of varying scope, illustrating the range presented in figure 6.1. Thus, a condensed in-depth analysis phase may be conducted making sparing use of techniques for experiencing work practices (situation 1). Or an extensive in-depth analysis phase may be conducted investing many resources in observation, in situ interviews, and thinking-aloud experiments (situation 4).

6.4.1 Situation 1: Condensed In-Depth Analysis Phase

A department of a large consulting firm specializes in supplying adapted generic systems for specific tasks in public administration. The department offers its solutions on the international market and has a lot of experience in conducting quick, efficient design projects to assess the validity of offering a client its (adapted) solutions. These design projects are carried out under significant time restrictions. For one, the department does not wish to spend a lot of resources before it knows if the customer is interested in pursuing the project (since the client does not pay for the design project). Second, the client is not interested in a lot of "disruption" before positively deciding to go with the supplier. The department's experienced consultants are greatly aware of the risk of offering solutions that do not fit the client's needs. Hence, the consultants, despite the time restrictions, aim to conduct a design project that arrives at the closest possible understanding of existing work practices.

To that end, the consultants opt for an approach that may be labeled "MUST lite." Since observation is out of the question (due to lack of resources), knowledge is generated by concrete experience of the work environment via tours and interviews with selected individuals. The interview notes are supported by audio recordings, photos, supplied work documents, and so forth. The "art of it" for the consultants consists in, as specifically as possible, ascertaining these highly selective data, while carefully adhering to the analytical guidelines discussed in section 6.5.3 for anchoring observations and subconclusions in the primary information.

Rather than quickly wrapping up the analysis according to often obvious needs matching the consulting firm's suite of generic systems, the consultants must meticulously construct the "argumentation." Even if the agreement calls for no actual report as a conclusion to the in-depth analysis phase, the designers, to the widest extent possible, involve the client in consideration and analysis of goals, problems, and needs. Moreover, the baseline for the phase is assessed by involving the client in mapping activities based on the project group's results represented by diagnostic maps.

6.4.2 Situation 2: Comprehensive but Focused Analysis

A design project carried out at a big Danish manufacturing company identified a number of potential systems for production planning and management. The company accordingly started implementing the proposals, some of which involved procurement and organizational implementation of generic systems. For other systems, a call for tenders was made. Along with the call for tenders to select a system and supplier, the company decided to carry out design projects in all of its departments in preparation for the organizational and technical implementation.

The design projects were conducted by project groups manned with staff from the departments involved, in consultation with the company's internal IT department and its department of organizational development. In one of the larger departments of about 150 employees, the design project was conducted by a project group of four staff members representing the different competencies within the department. In addition, three task forces were organized to serve as reference groups for the project group on each of three designated focal points: new buildings and rooms, work organization, and systems requirements.

On this basis, the project group elected to conduct the in-depth analysis phase of selected work domains. The overall aim of the analysis was to gain an understanding of problems with the existing work organization and of user qualifications for the new production technology included in the tender documents. Moreover, based on this understanding, the aim was to issue supplementary requirements for future versions of the system. An overview of the department's (roughly 200) production-oriented functions had already been established in the project's initiation phase. Since the project group possessed substantial knowledge of the department's management structure and work organization, the in-depth analysis phase was concentrated on studying selected domains and problems.

Within the area of "new buildings and rooms," the project group decided to examine issues relating to a future organization into open-office sections. As problems emerged in finding sufficient space in the new building, the group's mandate was expanded to examine how many people would be working at the same time in the different sections and the complexity of the existing production forms. The aim of expanding the group's mandate was to evaluate how great a share of the department's services and products could be produced by different configurations of production technology.

The area of "work organization" focused on five issues:
- The physical work organization in terms of noise, office space, and filing (once again, in terms of a possible organization into open-office sections)

- Cooperation between two selected open-office sections
- Social organization (evaluation, recruitment, and coaching)
- Experience with functions or roles as super-users and supporters
- The role of management in concept development, resource planning, and so forth

In terms of "systems requirements," the project group strove to explore the existing use of production equipment, including certain limited experiences with digital production forms and other IT systems. The aim was to examine the complexity of the existing production forms. Data gathering concentrated on testing hypotheses involving the use of different technical facilities. In addition, the project group initiated a fact-finding mission at a similar company that worked with digital production technology.

6.4.3 Situation 3: Broad Analysis of Limited Scope

At a multimedia publisher, a project group of two IT designers and three user representatives carried out a design project to identify IT support for the editorial office. This office receives and processes proposals for multimedia productions and applications for financing. Proposals and applications that receive support are registered and, upon establishment of a contract, the project's progress is monitored in relation to current payments. The publisher's overall work can be described by three business processes: an editorial process, a production process, and a distribution process.

The editorial office, which manages the editorial process, has nine staff members in all: three editors (who receive and process proposals and applications), a consultant (who deals with buying and translating foreign-made productions), three secretaries, a technician, and a production manager. The two IT designers knew nothing about multimedia productions or processing financing applications for these productions. Accordingly, a thorough in-depth analysis phase was necessary. On the other hand, the limited size of the department made it realistic to perform an in-depth analysis phase involving all staff members.

An unstructured interview (lasting one to two hours) was conducted with each of the nine staff members. In addition, thorough document analysis was made of written materials—including pamphlets, production plans, meeting minutes, and documents used in the work. During the first round of interviews, the editors saw no particular need for IT support (beyond word processing). Thus, the second round of interviews included only the secretaries. The interviews were structured as conversations (in situ interviews) about assignments, with the secretaries demonstrating how the various tasks were performed and what information was involved. This process established mutual learning situations between IT designers and staff, enabling relevant representations to be made based on the secretaries' concrete experiences. The results of these interviews were set down in freehand drawings.

The analysis that followed these interviews generated ideas for IT support that focused on production management and the related financial management of sponsored projects. However, the editors' work was less visible in that context—and it was the editors, after all, who were responsible for the creative environment. Accordingly, the challenge in the next round of the in-depth analysis phase was to better understand the editors' function. They were observed working at their offices, visiting multimedia environments for meetings, conducting negotiations on new productions, and participating in weekly production meetings. Some of these observation sessions were video-recorded. Notes from these observations and video reviews comprised the backdrop for a fresh set of interviews with the editors. These studies combined to produce a far richer understanding of the complex interactions between the editors and the multimedia environments—interactions largely taking place prior to, or parallel with, the secretaries' tasks. This knowledge generated ideas for IT support that also extended to the editors' works.

A series of workshops, with the participation of all nine staff members, established and solidified a collective image of the editorial office's work. The work process was modeled on a ten-meter Dead Sea scroll. On the top half of the scroll, workshop participants jotted down descriptions of work activities or functions, indicating the staff members who were responsible for these activites. On the bottom half of the scroll, they listed information connecting to the work activities. This detailed understanding enabled a design of significantly revised visions to be carried out during the innovation phase.

6.4.4 Situation 4: Comprehensive and Broad Analysis

At a big manufacturing company with many single-unit productions, a project group of two IT designers and three user representatives carried out a design project involving a comprehensive in-depth analysis phase. The design project was to explore IT support for production (planning, production, performance, and reporting). The IT designers had superficial knowledge of production, as several of them had previously worked with more administrative aspects of the company. Thus, a thorough in-depth analysis phase was required.

The in-depth analysis phase extended over roughly two months. It included about thirty interviews and observation sessions, as well as a few thinking-aloud experiments. Altogether, this phase involved roughly a third of the 140 workers involved in production at the company. In the process, various work documents were analyzed. Interviews were recorded and transcribed, though not verbatim. Instead, a detailed summary was written for each interview, which was forwarded to the interviewee for comment. The design team's observations were likewise documented in writing, copied, and distributed to everyone in the project group. Documentation of observations was in the form of written summaries, charted timelines (setting down tasks and data in temporal sequence), and communication models. The project group conducted a workshop where the general production work process was outlined on large sheets of paper. This led to an overall thematic division of the process. Subsequently, all interviews, observations, and so forth were compiled in a representation structured according to the selected general themes (productions involving several staff members, one person, management, middle management, or secretaries). Finally, these representations were compiled in a report featuring a problem, list of all noted goals, problems, and needs, along with linked ideas for solutions—including IT-related, organizational, and training proposals.

From activities performed during the phase, the project group gained thorough insight into the tasks involved in planning and production. Moreover, the first ideas for an overall design were developed. In terms of planning, needs for better coordination were identified along with general ideas for answering them on three levels: internally within the individual production group, between the different production groups, and between the individual production group and the overall production management.

A separate report was made of the in-depth analysis phase. The final report listed forty goals, problems, and needs, as well as related ideas for solutions. Based on this report, the steering committee decided which solution proposals to prioritize and more closely examine in the innovation phase.

6.5 Possible Phase Activities

Figure 6.2 is an overview of possible activities to perform in the in-depth analysis phase. This phase starts from the work domains selected in the strategic alignment report. Its final outcome is an analysis report and supplementary descriptions of present work practices. Based on this final analytical report, the steering committee decides which goals, needs, and ideas for IT support or changes to the work organization should be more closely examined during the innovation phase.

Note that figure 6.2—and the following text—describes the sum of the possible activities. It will not always be necessary or expedient to perform the full range of these activities.

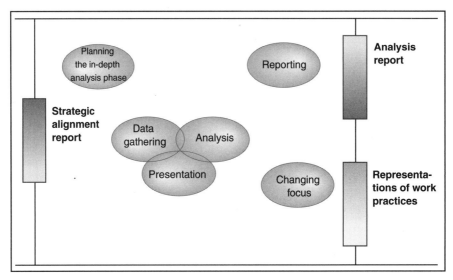

Figure 6.2 Potential products and activities to include in the in-depth analysis phase

6.5.1 Planning the In-Depth Analysis Phase

The aim planning is to clarify the situation for the in-depth analysis phase (possibly based on figure 6.1). The three basic activities of the in-depth analysis phase that follow planning are data gathering, analysis, and presentations. These activities will typically be performed in iteration and in varying degrees of depth and scope.

The planning starts with the reporting from the in-line analysis phase. Based on that reporting, the steering committee has decided what work domains to focus on the in-depth analysis phase.

The in-line analysis phase has established an overview of the design project's work domains and their context. The natural starting point for the in-depth analysis phase is to take things a step further in order to establish a solid overview of all tasks, their interrelationships, and contributions to the company's or the department's services. On this basis, actors and situations can be selected for in-depth study. In big companies with many departments, it is especially important to make these selections carefully in order to ensure representativeness and generality. A decision also needs to be made about how many actors and situations to incorporate into the study. The primary technique for this activity is baseline planning based on the selected work domains and their nature.

6.5.2 Data Gathering

At the core of data gathering is experiencing work practices firsthand in order to gain concrete experience with the selected work domains. The most important technique involved in data gathering is observation. However, because observation is resource-heavy, it is important to first identify those work situations where observation will yield the best results.

Accordingly, we recommend starting by establishing an overview of the overall workflow or business process of the selected work domains. A certain overview has already been established in the initiation and in-line analysis phases. Now, the level of detail needs to be increased, typically by examining how an individual task contributes to the department's overall output.

The techniques that facilitate this process are interviews and document analysis. Knowledge thus gained is set down in summaries and notes. We usually recommend recording the interviews, but only rarely transcribing them. A more obvious course is reviewing the recordings and, combined with notes from the interviews, writing summaries highlighting the most significant aspects. The summaries can be checked by the interviewees (see also section 9.4).

As previously mentioned, the project group may in certain cases possess an advance overview of the work domains. This may be the case if the project group includes participants with concrete experience of the relevant work domains or if the IT designers have wide experience with IT design within the work domains involved. Such advance knowledge should be utilized, of course, but we still recommend remaining skeptical of the project group's advance knowledge and challenging it to see if it sufficiently covers the case in question. We return to this discussion at the end of this section.

The project group's advance knowledge may be incorporated via workshops. At these workshops, the participants can sketch out the workflow on large sheets of paper, outlining the tasks and people involved, as well as the necessary information base—the so-called Dead Sea scrolls (see section 9.10). Or, the project group's knowledge of tasks, the various problems involved, and suggestions for solutions can be systematized and taken up for internal dialogue among the project group by a mapping process involving the joint creation of diagnostic maps (see section 9.12). Both methods are ways for the project group to gain an overview of the work domains. In turn, specific issues can be identified for closer examination via techniques for experiencing work practices—especially observation, in situ interviews, and thinking-aloud experiments.

The focus of the in-depth analysis phase is determined by the overall objective of the design project. The focus will typically be on a client's tasks, roles, and forms and patterns of cooperation or technology use (including its existing systems). At the heart of the issue is identifying goals, problems, and needs for changes regarding IT, the work organization, or user qualifications. Section 8.3 provides a list of possible focal points.

Some cases rule out the use of observation. This typically happens when a company considers it too much of a disruption or when the nature of the work precludes gaining much understanding by observation. The latter scenario applies to companies or departments with engineers or case workers who concentrate for extended periods on work involving drawings or documents. In these cases, techniques such as thinking-aloud experiments or prompted reflection may be used. When the issue involves understanding problems relating to the use of existing systems, thinking-aloud experiments will be suitable. Engineering work can often be analyzed via prompted reflection—where two staff members sit across from one other and tell one another about the work and the problems involved.

Conscious iteration between two different forms of gaining insight is a central element of the MUST method. In the in-depth analysis phase, it is important for the project group to alternate between activities aimed at generating knowledge by concrete experience with the users' present work practices and activities aimed at analyzing the gathered information, and to set down this understanding in the form of representations of the work practice. By alternating between these two forms of knowledge, the project group explicitly addresses the "say/do problem" discussed in section 2.3.

Certain situations call for explicitly putting the say/do problem on the agenda. For instance, it is sometimes necessary to present a person or group with situations where a statement documented in a representation says one thing while an observation documented via notes or video clips says another. This activity can take place within the project group or with a group of interviewees. This may sometimes touch on emotional or highly personal issues if an individual gets the impression that the project group has a lack of faith in his or her statement. If this happens, it is important to stress that the point is not to put someone on the spot by claiming that one statement is more true than another, but to develop representations describing the structures underlying both statements in which both statements are considered equally valid and relevant.

6.5.3 Analysis

Analysis activities of the in-depth analysis phase are based on data gathering and processing. The material may be in the form of audio recordings of interviews, video clips, photos, personal notes, or thoughts. The aim is to process the data into a form that enables them to be used by the project group and, ultimately, for broader communication (e.g., with the steering committee or with a third party involved in anchoring activities). Analysis representations are an important means in this regard, both as tools for generating knowledge and to firmly establish the results. Specific representation tools to that end are described in section 6.5.4 and elaborated in chapter 9.

The results of the phase should be presented in terms of "goals, problems, and needs" as well as "ideas for solutions to be gained by new or changed IT support, work organization, or user qualifications." We recommend the following guidelines for analysis, advancing the anchoring principle (see section 2.4 for more information on the anchoring principle):

- Stick to the primary information. Be careful not to jump to conclusions too quickly, but make time for processing the primary information. The point is to gain insight into (and remain within) "the existing work situation," in order to come up with the clearest possible representations on its terms. Presenting the primary information to the project group, while avoiding premature abstractions and generalizations, enables the company's participants in the project group to ensure anchoring—in analysis as well.
- Make data, considerations, and results visible. In large-size project groups, it is important in and of itself to foster visibility and comprehension regarding the results of analysis. In small-scale projects, this concern mainly applies to the subsequent activities. Roughly speaking, the issue is about "making the calculation process visible"— that is, documenting considerations and immediate results of the project group's reflections.
- Involve the company or department in considerations and reflections, not just conclusions. Involving the company's participants in reflection—such as thinking-aloud experiments or workflow modeling (using freehand drawings made during in situ interviews)—will promote a broader understanding of goals, problems, and needs.

The analysis will both take place "inside the head" of individual members of the project group and via joint activities, such as analytical workshops. Presentation and discussion test the validity of individual evaluations and anchors the results of the analysis with the project group.

Large-scale design projects—with several people from the project group separately studying different issues—automatically involve more work in terms of coordinating, communicating, and compiling the results of all the studies. Two processes may help facilitate analysis within large-scale design projects:

- The project group meets regularly to discuss the preliminary results of the studies on the basis of written summaries distributed beforehand. The project group discusses a structure for compiling the studies. One possibility is reviewing certain typical business processes, personnel categories, or work domains. Within this overall structure, the results may again be divided (e.g., into uncovered problems, needs, and ideas for solutions).

- All the various written summaries are now reread and the material is "cut and pasted" within places where it fits into the compiling structure. The general summary of all the studies is edited and possibly condensed into a brief report providing an overview of the most significant problems, needs, and ideas for solutions (see figure 6.3).

At the conclusion of the in-depth analysis phase, one should explicitly address what in section 6.2 is referred to earlier in this chapter as the "readiness for change." This process involves measuring the distance between the present situation and the desired goals of the project, as well as judging it against experiences from past changes in the company and attitudes toward change among the company's staff. As the ultimate scope of the overall change is not yet known during the in-depth analysis phase (it will not be known until after the innovation phase), this phase includes the task

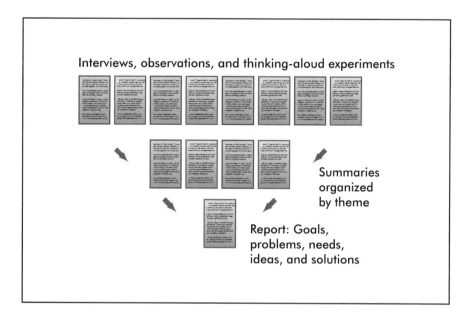

Figure 6.3 Outlined progress of an in-depth analysis phase with related intermediate products and final result

of establishing knowledge about the client's readiness for change and experiences from past reform processes.

6.5.4 Presentation

Presentation involves capturing the products of reflection. However, the various recommended representation tools can also be employed as guides indicating information to be gathered and captured by reflection. Accordingly, the considerations and recommendations in this section are closely linked to the issues discussed in the previous two sections, as well as the aforementioned iteration between such activities.

Presentation comprises everything from notes from the first interviews to the final analysis report. In figure 6.4, the process has been divided into four steps. The progress of the analysis and documentation is left to right.

This section describes the process according to figure 6.4. The listed representation tools, and the techniques they support, are described in greater detail in chapter 9.

The starting point is provided by the primary information gained from data gathering. The primary information is first analyzed individually by the people in the project group who gathered it. Interview recordings, documents, notes from observation, and thinking-aloud experiments are reviewed. Reference may be made to work documents gathered by interviews or observation. Candidates for "goals,

Individual analysis of primary information	1 First joint analysis	2 Overview and contexts	3 Final form
Observation	Summary of main points from individual notes	Diagnostic maps, functional models, role list, communication models, timeline, scenarios, list of ideas for solutions, and virtual maps	Analysis report
Interviews	Affinity diagrams		
Thinking-aloud experiments	Dead Sea scrolls		
Work documents	Freehand drawings and collages		

Figure 6.4 Incremental advance of the analysis and presentation process and its use of representation tools

problems, and needs," plus ideas for solutions to be used in affinity diagramming or mapping, may be noted in key-word form.

Workshops may provide the first common overview of the most significant observations and results—for instance, via affinity diagramming. In affinity diagramming, main points from individual notes are grouped into categories or issues. Representations of workflows may be made in the form of Dead Sea scrolls, freehand drawings, or collages.

Grouping or division into issues in affinity diagrams, plus obvious conflict or breakdown situations identified by free-hand drawings or Dead Sea scrolls, provide input for map-ping. Diagnostic maps help clarify problems, causes, and consequences, as well as the relations between them. Solu-tion proposals, uncovered by data gathering or generated by mapping, are set down on a separate list and may later provide input for design efforts in the innovation phase. Virtual maps, though more design-oriented, may already be used in the in-depth analysis phase to survey pros and cons of specific solution proposals. Maps, as well as freehand drawings and collages, may profitably be reviewed by man-agement and the involved company staff.

Insight from the in-depth analysis phase, focusing on com-munication and cooperation, may also be documented in the form of more focused representations—for instance, a communication model listing the different parties involved in the communication, the media of communication, plus identified problems and breakdowns. A communication model clarifies individual messages and their media. Over-all workflows, such as a dialogue between two groups with-in a work domain, can be modeled on a *timeline*—possibly illustrating how certain dialogues may not need to be repeated when events alter the situation. This enables the extent of the repetition to be assessed, while also making it clear when instances of repetition lead to actual duplication of work.

An alternative analytical tool is describing the different roles of central actors regarding important products or ser-vices within a work domain. Such roles can be documented in the form of a role list. The role list may be used to show how existing IT systems support the different roles. Finally, the work organization can be described by work functions, focusing on tasks performed by the company or department, while the relations between work functions can be illustrated by functional models.

Scenarios are expedient tools for gathering many representations into a whole. Scenarios describe a typical workflow (such as a day's work) and may refer to more specific or detailed representations of selected aspects of the workflow. Typically, scenarios are directly incorporated into the final analysis report.

The analysis and presentation process concludes with a final analysis report. The report essentially consists of the most important of the design team's representations tied together by text. Section 6.5.6 provides suggestions for the content of the report.

6.5.5 Changing Focus

Data gathering, analysis, and presentation may provide insight that requires the design team to reconsider the focus of the in-depth analysis phase. This may be accomplished either by making a specific request to the steering committee or by including new areas that fall outside the designated focus on the list of goals, problems, needs, and possible solutions. It will only be natural to estimate the consequences of including such new conditions for analysis by way of a revised project charter and timetable. Whether to choose one or the other approach depends on how explicitly worded the initial project focus was. The more explicit and specific the initial focus, the greater the need for clarification with the steering committee will be.

6.5.6 Reporting

The result of the in-depth analysis phase is a prioritized list of goals, problems, and needs, plus ideas for IT support, changes to the work organization, and new user qualifications. This list provides the starting point for the innovation phase.

Reporting takes the form of a separate report submitted to the steering committee for a decision on which ideas to prioritize in the innovation phase. Documentation is based on representations developed in the in-depth analysis phase, and the report may profitably be presented together with various representations of work practices—including freehand drawings and diagnostic maps. Figure 6.5 shows an overall outline of an analysis report. As the target group for the report—mainly, the steering committee, but also other affected company staff—have not been following the analysis efforts in any detail, most cases require the various representations to be supplemented by text summarizing the results of the analyses. This text serves three purposes:

- Mapping the backdrop for goals, problems, and needs, as well as the choice of focal points for the in-depth analysis phase
- Gathering and prioritizing goals, problems, and needs, as well as ideas for solutions
- Linking analyses and representations, either by describing relations between goals, problems, and needs or establishing relations between goals, problems, and needs, as well as ideas for solutions

6.6 Possible Results of the Phase

The results of the in-depth analysis phase are an analysis report—summarizing goals, problems, needs, and ideas for

1. Backdrop and focus

2. Significant work practice characteristics

3. Goals, problems, needs, and ideas for solutions

4. Suggested priorities

Figure 6.5 Suggested outline of an analysis report

solutions—as well as a number of different representations of work practices. The report and representations should adhere to a wording and level of formality closely reflecting the language of management and staff.

As for the initiation and in-line analysis phases, all the potential results of the in-depth analysis phase are indicated in terms of the six aspects discussed in chapter 3. Figure 6.6 shows the potential results in terms of these six aspects. Accordingly, sections 6.6.1–6.6.6 constitutes a total list of conditions that may be relevant to document in the in-depth analysis phase.

6.6.1 Results in Terms of the Design Project

The results of the in-depth analysis phase in terms of the design project are usually limited to an anchoring of the results of the phase and possibly a revised plan for the further course of the project. If conditions surface during the phase that occasion renewed considerations regarding the focus of the design project, they should be noted. Accordingly, the results may include three components:

- A revised baseline plan for the further design project— that is, the innovation phase
- An estimate of the consequences of changing the focus, possibly from including new conditions under the design project
- Communicating the changes with stakeholders and documenting their comments

	Aspect	In-depth analysis phase
Project context	Design project	-
	Implementation project	-
Usage context	Business strategy	-
	Work practices	●
Technical context	IT systems	○
	IT platform	-

Figure 6.6 The relevance of the results of the in-depth analysis phase in terms of six different aspects: (●) indicates primary relevance; (○) indicates secondary relevance; while (-) indicates that the aspect is relevant to the phase only in certain cases

6.6.2 Results in Terms of the Implementation Project

The results may include possible specification of new requirements for the implementation project, deriving from the in-depth analysis phase. These may include considerations on choosing a strategy for the implementation project according to the client's present corporate traditions and culture.

6.6.3 Results in Terms of Business Strategy

In terms of the business strategy, specific results likewise are produced only in special cases. Such results may include immediate evaluation of the effects and consequences of proposed solutions on the business strategy. For instance, ideas generated in the in-depth analysis phase might open up opportunities for new products or services.

6.6.4 Results in Terms of Work Practices

There are three primary results of the in-depth analysis phase:

- Representations of present work practices—how the work is actually performed and what information is involved
- Clarification of the rationale behind current work practices—that is, reasons and explanations for the present form of the work practices
- A list of goals, problems, and needs, along with ideas for IT support and changes to the work organization

Representations of present work practices are available both in the forms of notes and summaries of interviews, observations, thinking-aloud experiments, and as representations produced by workshops—including freehand drawings, Dead Sea scrolls, collages, maps, and functional models. These representations (in analyzed form) are attached to the analysis report as appendixes or are used in the presentation of the analysis report. It is not necessary to provide extensive textual descriptions in the report. Text should be limited to describing significant aspects of work practices—including decision-making situations, patterns of cooperation, and coordination aspects, as well as reasons for the high complexity of a given task.

The report should include a list of all identified goals, problems, needs, and ideas for solutions. The list should be accompanied by proposed priorities among them. It is important to reveal the backdrop and reasons for goals, problems, and needs. Likewise, the report should show the relations between goals, problems, and needs, on the one hand, and the proposed solutions, on the other. Any proposed solutions should ideally be substantiated by—and thus be anchored in—business-strategy goals or observed problems and needs. In other words, any questions why a given idea for a solution is relevant should be answerable by reference to (new) business goals or observed conditions of existing work practices.

The report and representations combined should account for the rationales behind the existing work practices. Diagnostic maps offer good support for this, by compiling problems, needs, their causes and consequences, and ideas for solutions (see section 9.12).

6.6.5 Results in Terms of IT Systems

Results in terms of IT systems comprise ideas for IT support as well as an analysis of existing systems. Ideas for IT support may be included on lists mentioned earlier in the section 6.5.4, and can be supplemented by suggestions for lists of required data. In the in-depth analysis phase, it is usually not necessary to perform any type of data modeling, such as ER diagrams. If necessary, this type of data modeling can be produced in the innovation phase as a basis for prototype development.

The design team's analysis of existing systems should extend to the client's central systems, which the envisioned IT systems will replace or in which they will be integrated. There are two primary considerations regarding a client's existing central systems:

- Technical evaluation—including errors, breakdowns, data quality, response times, and so forth
- Usage-oriented evaluation—including problems with navigation, inexpediencies in access rights, missing functions in forms and windows, and so forth

6.6.6 Results in Terms of the IT Platform

The in-depth analysis phase rarely produces results that affect the IT platform. However, it may have an impact on the platform, if analysis of work practices uncovers conditions that could problematize a selected platform—for instance, if there is a need to load specific images and the selected platform for the database only supports text.

6.7 Summary and Literature

In this chapter, we initially clarified the objective of the in-depth analysis phase. Accordingly, we described potential activities and results of the in-depth analysis phase. Moreover, we laid out four prototypical situations to aid a project group in planning an in-depth analysis phase according to their specific design project.

The main inspiration for the in-depth analysis phase activities described in this chapter is positive experience gained by research in Computer Supported Cooperative Work (CSCW) involving ethnographic studies of work practices. This especially applies to our emphasis on gaining firsthand experience of a complex work practice by observation, in situ interviews, thinking-aloud experiments, or prompted reflection. Blomberg et al. (1993), Beyer and Holtzblatt (1998), and others discuss the use of ethnographic techniques in IT projects. Other sources, such as Goguen and Linde (1993), demonstrate the necessity of adapting ethnographic techniques to industrial practice, so that extensive observation is performed only where it will yield good results. We have worked actively with these two aspects in design projects we ourselves have conducted. Simonsen (1994) and Simonsen and Kensing (1997, 1998) discuss issues concerning the use of ethnographic techniques in IT projects, while Bødker and Kensing (1994) and Kensing, Simonsen, and Bødker (1998) provide examples of comprehensive design projects that employ ethnographic techniques.

7
Innovation Phase: Vision Development

The innovation phase is the final part of the design project, in which the project group develops visions for overall change. In all likelihood, various ideas and perhaps detailed requirements for future IT applications have already emerged in the earlier phases. The aim now is to develop one or more coherent visions for meeting the goals, needs, and opportunities identified in the in-depth analysis phase that correspond the company's business and IT strategies. Coherent visions mean visions that encompass the function, interface, and technical platform of the IT systems, as well as work organization and required employee qualifications.

Moreover, the innovation phase includes an evaluation of the advantages, disadvantages, and costs of implementing a design vision for the company as a whole and for different groups of the staff. Consequences of the design visions relate to finances, work organization, training needs, and the company's business and IT strategies. Finally, a strategy and plan for technical and organizational implementation of the visions should be prepared. It is often useful to test ideas in the form of mock-ups or prototypes, since these provide management and employees with a better foundation for decision making than purely paper-based representations, while affording IT designers a clearer view of the context in which the systems will be used. In our experience, both management and staff need such an overall foundation for decision making to be able to make evaluations leading to viable IT applications.

Many projects are concerned solely with specifying a company's IT systems and the technical platform. When receiving the systems the users themselves are often left in charge of organizational implementation. This may be an appropriate strategy when dealing with the implementation of a single or a few simple standard systems that entail no major changes to the company's work practices. However, if a vision includes several IT systems that radically alter the work organization, or if brand new services or products are to be introduced, these parts must be integrated. This can be achieved by arranging the phase as an iterative process where ideas for work organization, services, or products translate into technological requirements, and where technological potentials translate into ideas, new forms of organizing the work, or new services and products.

7.1 Objective

The objective of this phase is to prepare users and management for forthcoming changes and to provide a viable foundation for decision making—in the form of the design project report—prior to a call for tender and purchase or development of new IT systems. Organizational preparation is an important element of design projects, as represented by the anchoring principle (see section 2.4). Referring to the idea of a viable foundation for decision making, we wish to draw attention to the many cases of IT systems that have been implemented according to what later turned out to be a far too optimistic conception of the technology potential to promote change. New technology does not in and of itself lead to better services, better products, or better work organization. The design project report should enable a company's management and stakeholders to welcome the design visions, suggest adjustments to specific elements or to the implementation strategy and plan, or, in extreme cases, reject the proposed visions altogether.

Furthermore, the design project report serves to document the rationale behind the planned changes to those who will be assisting management and staff in the technical and organizational implementation. Specifically, we refer to the people—inside or outside the company—who are responsible for procuring or developing IT systems, employee training, rearranging workflows, and so forth.

The task of the project group thus is to organize a course of development that, in accordance with the scope and ambitions of the project, produces the potential results reviewed in section 7.6. Accordingly, the project group should decide what kind of knowledge should be developed in the phase in order to achieve results. Perhaps the project group already possesses the necessary knowledge for this purpose, perhaps additional qualified staff should be involved, or perhaps it will fall upon the project group to develop this knowledge from scratch. The project group should also agree on how to include or in other ways accommodate the interests revealed in the initiation phase by stakeholder analysis in order to ensure secure anchoring of the design visions. Activities that combine to serve the stated purpose, as well as examples of techniques and representation tools supporting these activities, are described in section 7.5.

7.2 Motivation

There are four reasons why the MUST method includes a phase focused on obtaining synergies between the formulation of requirements for IT systems, redesigning the work organization, and mapping qualification requirements:

- First, integrating these three concerns often proves to be the only way to achieve the quality improvement or streamlining that is the project's objective.
- Second, we have seen a number of projects in which training and work-organizational consequences took both management and staff by surprise. Unforeseen expenses and lengthy introduction processes may result if individuals or staff members themselves adapt workflows to the IT system, if they refrain from using certain parts of the system that they consider to be too difficult, or if "super-users" are frequently interrupted in their work in order to help out co-workers.
- Third, users often have helpful ideas for ways of performing their work that are not supported by the existing technology. Likewise, illustrating the potentials of a specific technology may elicit ideas from users for redesigning the work domain.
- Fourth, the phase leads to decisions about the further course of the IT project. The results of the phase form a foundation for decision making that comprises elements needed by the various stakeholders.

7.3 Situations and Ambitions

The scope and ambitions of the innovation phase will mainly depend on two issues: First, do standard systems that meet the designated requirements exist on the market, should one or several new IT systems be developed, or should a comprehensive integration of standard systems be undertaken? Second, do needs exist for major restructuring of the work organization and performance of new tasks or are only minor adjustments to the work organization involved? Figure 7.1 explores these questions.

Situation 1 is characterized by fairly precise ideas about which standard systems are required. This may, for instance, involve replacing existing systems with new ones that offer the same degree of functionality. The design teams can then focus the rest of the innovation phase on market studies and gathering experiences with usage of the standard systems.

Situation 2 often involves a company that wants to invest in a larger standard system and redesign its work organization and staff qualification profiles to "match" a system's implic-

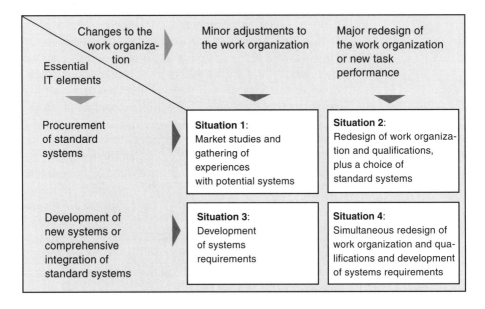

Figure 7.1 Four typical situations encountered in an innovation phase

it models of business procedures. If alternative standard systems are available, the innovation phase in this situation may include experimenting with and evaluating their limitations and adaptability.

In situation 3, no standard system meets the company's stated aims, problems, and needs, or the potential standard systems are assessed as requiring a reorganization of work that is too far-reaching and, thus, unwanted. In this situation, the innovation phase should concentrate on developing requirements for new IT systems that support the existing or desired work organization.

The most ambitious situation for the innovation phase occurs in situation 4. Here, the premise may perhaps set no restrictions on the design visions, and management has decided to use the project to carry out major organizational restructuring, such as task automation, staff cuts, redistribution of tasks and competencies between groups of staff or departments, or to offer entirely new products or services. In this scenario, the project group will alternate between developing the work organization and outlining systems requirements.

In the projects that helped us develop the MUST method, we often found that either management or staff were acquainted with a standard system that they believed would solve their problems. In other words, the situation for the innovation phase had been clarified in the initiation phase. The in-depth analysis phase may also have helped document needs with a quick market study marking one or more standard systems as obvious candidates. Accordingly, determining whether a project team faces situation 1 or situation 3 may depend on the scope of the redesign necessary to adapt the work organization to the system. A project team may find itself in situation 3 when the disadvantages of organizational adaptation to the system are found to be too significant and the company consequently opts for development of a customized system. Finally, a project team may find itself in situation 4 when the company has already decided to use the introduction of new technology to effect major changes.

7.4 Examples of Innovation Phases

We now return to the four situations described in figure 7.1. For each situation, relations between activities will be illustrated in proportion to the complexity of the assignment.

7.4.1 Situation 1: Market Study

A dental clinic was faced with replacing its system for appointment scheduling and managing patient information concerning basic patient data and payments, since the current supplier was discontinuing the old system. The clinic wanted to keep its paper-based case records. The preceding MUST method phases had clarified the clinic's goals and needs, and it had been concluded that the secretarial staff would be most affected by the changes.

The project's IT designer did a study of the market and came up with two systems that both looked promising. Accompanied by a secretary, he visited two clinics that were using these standard systems. The secretary tried her hand at creating a new patient file, scheduling an appointment, and writing out a bill in the system, and she saw how it functioned when patients called the clinic. The IT designer and the secretary interviewed the staff about their experiences with the system's usefulness, the training period, and the supplier service level.

Upon returning to the clinic, the IT designer and the secretary developed scenarios representing the use of each of the two standard systems. The scenarios comprised all the secretaries' tasks and were supplemented by screen shots from the two systems. The IT designer wrote a short design project report reviewing the functionality of the two systems, including the scenarios and an evaluation of the extent to which the systems would satisfy the clinic's goals and requirements revealed in the in-depth analysis phase. For each system, moreover, the report described training classes that the two respective clinics had found satisfactory and included an assessment of necessary supplier service along with a financial estimate of the total cost of purchasing and implementing the two systems.

At a clinic staff meeting, the secretary and IT designer presented the scenarios and described the two clinics' experiences with the respective systems. Based on this information and the report, the three owners selected a system. The IT designer then outlined the clinic's work in converting data from the old system before the chosen supplier took over.

7.4.2 Situation 2: Adapting Work Organization to Standard Systems

A design project at a publishing company had so far resulted in the project group advising the company that the advantages of introducing a standard system would likely compensate for the amount of work involved in changing the company's work organization. The in-line analysis phase had prompted the company's president to argue in favor of a system that the editors could use to gain an overview of the company's past publications for use in assessing new publications and that the warehouse could use to improve inventory management. The director also wanted the warehouse manager to use the system to monitor possible reprinting needs, a task that the sales department had been handling so far (although not satisfactorily). Meanwhile, the editors would still, in collaboration with the president, decide whether a book should be reprinted. During the in-depth analysis phase, the project group had analyzed the editors' and the warehouse's information needs, while creating an estimate of problems and opportunities the warehouse manager would face in taking on the new task of monitoring reprinting needs.

The project group began the innovation phase by undertaking market studies and gathering experiences with the usage of potential systems. It visited another publishing company that had recently acquired a new IT system and a factory where one of the IT designers had assisted in introducing a standard system for handling tasks that she felt resembled those of the publisher. During their visit to the other publishing company, the editors and the warehouse manager were able to try out some of the functions of the new system, and they spoke with the staff about its experiences with the system and possible transitional problems. Prior to the project group's visit to the factory, the IT designer who had worked on the factory's system had explained how some of the factory's business processes could be seen as a metaphor for their own. For example, the factory manager's task of monitoring raw materials and their processing at various machines could be compared to the editors' need to know how far a book had advanced in the production process. The IT designer utilized this metaphor to illustrate how the system could be used to give the editors access to various overviews that she knew had helped the factory manager. One of the editors, who immediately understood the analogy, asked whether the system could be adapted to enable graphic illustration of the information the project team had obtained during the in-depth analysis. The IT designer believed this would be possible, but the supplier would have to provide the final answer, as well as an estimate of the cost involved.

The project group systematized the experiences gained from their visits in a combination of diagnostic and virtual maps. At a meeting with the steering committee, the project group outlined its evaluations using the diagnostic maps and recommended basing further project efforts solely on IT system implemented at the factory. However, the company president, who was also chairman of the steering committee, first wanted to meet with the supplier to hear about its experiences with the publishing industry or similar industries and about its service record. The outcome of his inquiries were positive, and the project group began to develop visions of how to organize the work based on this supplier's system.

At a workshop, the project group used a Dead Sea scroll produced during the in-depth analysis phase (which illustrated the "stages" that a book went through in the publishing process) as its starting point. Then one of the editors gave an account of her work processes and the kind of information she needed for her work. The IT designers, who had collected some screen shots at the factory and a list of the system's functions, supplemented her observations by explaining how the new system would support such tasks. Based on the in-depth analysis, the project group knew that each editor worked in a different way, but that their needs for information were the same. The system prescribed no specific approach to performing the work. However, it would be able to automate certain tasks and was capable of producing overviews for management—a task that until then had taken up a lot of the editors' time. This change would allow editors to intensify their collaboration with authors, a goal that had been formulated during the in-depth analysis phase, but that the system did not need to support. During this process, the project group sketched out some screen shots that illustrated the data needed by the editors at various stages of the publication process. At the meeting, one of the IT designers documented the desired relation between the system and a couple of variations on the editor's work processes. These were later developed into scenarios for inclusion in the design project report.

A scenario was also prepared for the warehouse's use of the IT system. In addition to his usual tasks, the warehouse manager was now responsible for the task of monitoring reprinting needs. The project group had to acknowledge that, during the in-depth analysis phase, it had not fully grasped the true nature of the sales department's problems with this task. Accordingly, the project group now conducted a few interviews with the sales manager and one of his staff members. As it turned out, problems had occurred because the sales department's IT system was not sufficiently integrated with the old inventory system, forcing the department's staff to perform cumbersome manual procedures in order to produce the necessary data for decisions about reprinting. When the project manager brought this to the president's attention, the president replied that he was aware of this situation but that the company could not currently afford to give priority to such integration. Furthermore, he believed that the warehouse manager, by using the new system, would have more time available to solve this task than would the sales department.

In collaboration with the warehouse manager, one of the IT designers examined the potentials of the standard system for producing the required inventory overviews. The sales manager provided them with some data showing when the stock of a given book could indicate the need for a reprint. This decision depended on the type of book, its subject, and the author's past success. For every possible reprint, the warehouse manager would receive this data from the sales department and log them into the system, which would then automatically print out lists to aid the editors and the president in making decisions. The IT designer prepared a specification of this part of the system that, along with the adjustments that the editors called for, was added to the design project report. Mapping the qualification requirements revealed that the supplier's standard training courses were sufficient. Systematic examination of the standard system, incorporating the proposed changes, and the scenarios showed that all the company's goals and needs would be met. The project group wrapped up its assignment by planning the technical and organizational implementation and drawing up a budget for the implementation. The steering committee accordingly decided to award the order to the supplier.

7.4.3 Situation 3: Adapting IT Systems to Work Organization

Prior to the onset of a design project, a large meatpacking plant had carried out a major realignment of its work organization and the interaction between its sales department and production unit in order to improve the relationship between sales campaigns and production capacity. Since the old IT systems were unable to support this relationship and generally needed replacing, the sales manager and the production manager had argued in favor of implementing new IT systems. Management, on the other hand, had undertaken a design project premised on using standard systems as far as possible.

In a combined initiation and in-line analysis phase of this design project, the project group had recommended including the administration department in the design project, since they largely drew on the same data material. In the in-depth analysis phase, the project group illustrated interdepartmental coordination in the form of communication models documenting problems and needs in the exchange of data between departments. The main problem lay in the sales department's insufficient knowledge about fitting production increases resulting from the company's sales campaigns into normal production.

In the innovation phase, the project group began by describing the communication flow in the new work organization, specifying what data the sales department needed and how the production unit would supply them. This produced minor changes in the coordination between these two departments and prompted the department to produce statistics of peak loads in production. The revised work organization was set down in a number of scenarios describing work in each of the three departments and the coordination between them. The project group also suggested that the managers of the sales, production, and administration departments establish a tighter coordination structure, and determine what data should be the focus of their future meetings. The project group made lists of functions that the different departments needed the system to support and sketched out various screen layouts for the different departments. Apart from the aforementioned statistics, the functions involved sales department calculations and production planning. Screen shots showed examples of tables and graphic presentations of such statistics and calculations.

These representations were adjusted at a workshop between the project group and representatives from each of the departments, and the project group completed its work by writing a design project report containing the representations and an evaluation of the relationship between the outlined systems and the work organization. The report's emphasis was on demonstrating that the minor adjustments in the work organization did not constitute a major break with the recent realignment and that the systems would support the desired, improved coordination between departments. One section of the report dealt with affected users, stating that the suppliers' offers should include the required training. The report concluded with a plan for the meatpacking plant's tender, what tasks the company should handle in terms of assessing the received offers, as well as the technical and organizational implementation.

The steering committee discussed the report and determined a fixed margin within which suppliers would make their offers. The material was then put out to tender. One of the IT designers helped the meatpacking plant assess the received offers, one of which was selected.

7.4.4 Situation 4: Simultaneous Development of IT Systems and Work Organization

A medium-sized municipality undertook a design project to find out how to realize the city council's visions for quicker and easier public access to municipal administration. Prior to the onset of the design project, a steering committee made up of the chiefs of administration and the municipal IT director had put the tax administration, social services, and technical services departments in charge of conducting an experiment. During the initiation phase, a project group was formed consisting of an employee from each of the three departments as well as an internal and an external IT designer. In the in-line analysis phase, the group conducted interviews and held a collective brainstorming session with the mayor and the chiefs of administration. This process produced the idea of realizing the city council's objective by establishing a joint group situated in the town hall lobby with three members from each department, which would enable citizens to direct their inquiries to a single administrative body. In addition, a Web site with information for citizens and options for electronic inquiries and reporting was to be created.

The in-depth analysis phase included interviews with, and observations of, citizens during their inquiries with municipal representatives, as well as interviews with administrative staff about typical case flows. The project group also carried out a study of a broad section of the citizens' current and planned Internet access and their expectations of the city's Web sites. The project group categorized citizen inquiries and administrative departments' cases and singled out cases that required cooperation across departments. The group concluded the phase by summing up typical problems, needs, and ideas in an analysis report using diagnostic maps.

As a starting point for the innovation phase, the steering committee prioritized problems, needs, and ideas for the project group to develop. The new joint group had to be able to handle 80 percent of all inquiries, and the website would first offer a few services and then extend its range as citizens and the municipality became familiar with this kind of administration.

The project group planned its work in this phase as an alternation between outlining system requirements and developing the work organization of the new group, on the one hand, and the new group's interaction with the three administrative departments, on the other. It selected a subset of inquiries and cases, roughly corresponding to the proposed 80 percent. For each category, the work processes involved in case flows and public services were sketched out on large rolls of paper. A Dead Sea scroll described the data needed and the data that would be produced. Accordingly, the project group was able to list a number of requirements for the IT systems' functions, user interfaces, and ways of interaction.

The IT designers studied a few Web sites to help develop the municipality's range of services. With the prioritized problems, needs, and ideas in mind, the project group outlined three initial services provided on the Web site:
- Tax information reporting and reply in the form of an advance tax assessment
- An overview of the processing of applications for construction licenses, featuring application forms and listing tax-related consequences of taking out construction loans
- Admission applications and current waiting periods for municipal child care facilities

The IT designers made an outline for each of these services on the Web site, including the interactions it was designed to support. Detailed design, data modeling, and integration with the municipality's present systems would be the responsibility of the supplier that made the best offer and won the order.

The qualification requirements for the new group and the division of labor between it and existing administrative departments were specified by reviewing a number of typical cases and inquiries that the group should be able to solve using the outlined systems. The user representatives in the project group suggested manning the joint group by letting staff from the three administrative departments rotate between the group and their respective departments in order to secure a homogeneous qualification level.

Finally at a workshop, the project group assessed the extent to which the outlined design visions met the steering committee's priorities. The group was able to document that the new group, in all likelihood, would be able to handle the designated 80 percent of citizen inquiries, while it was unable to evaluate the effect of the Web site. Accordingly, it suggested that the chosen supplier develop a series of Web prototypes to be tested by selected citizens. Moreover, the project group's proposed strategy and plan for the technical and organizational implementation called for first integrating the IT systems of the three administrative departments. This could take place while the first team manning the new group went through a training program organized by the municipality. Finally, the project group described the tasks of the administrative departments and the IT department in terms of the tender. The results were summarized in a design project report that the steering committee, adding only minor adjustments, used as the basis for a tender.

7.5 Possible Phase Activities

The innovation phase starts with the results from the in-depth analysis phase. While developing the design visions, it may become necessary for the IT designers to supplement their previous analyses if the visions point to new work domains that were not initially candidates for analysis or were not sufficiently conceptualized in the in-depth analysis phase. All potential activities for the innovation phase are shown in figure 7.2 and further described in sections 7.5.1–7.5.8. Please note that this constitutes a total list of activities that may potentially be relevant in the innovation phase.

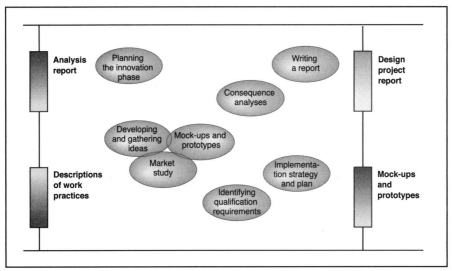

Figure 7.2 Potential products and activities to include in the innovation phase

7.5.1 Planning the Innovation Phase

The innovation phase can be planned by breaking the phase down into a series of activities, as illustrated in figure 7.2. Subsequently, the IT designers decide which techniques and representation tools best support these activities. First, we will offer a description of the objective and content of each of the activities, along with the techniques and description tools that have proven suitable for each activity. Baseline planning is the recommended technique for planning this phase.

7.5.2 Market Study

The aim of a market study is to find out whether standard systems exist that meet a company's needs that are revealed in the in-depth analysis phase. A preliminary survey of the market can be made by reading sales material and reviews or by visiting trade fairs. In addition, members of the project group may be familiar with potential systems. The aim of a market study is to gather and systematize experiences concerning a system's usage and application. This can be done by organizing a company visit to a similar company or one that simply handles the same kinds of tasks.

The next step of a market study is to have potential systems demonstrated or tested in as realistic a setting as possible. Whenever possible, future users should try their hand at performing their everyday tasks using the proposed system and the organization's own data, since this provides a better basis for evaluation. As an alternative, staff representatives may observe how a proposed system is used or try to perform a task using the system, guided by an employee in an organization that already uses the system in day-to-day operations. This may be followed up by sharing experiences about the implementation of the system, problems, advantages, and so forth.

7.5.3 Developing and Gathering Ideas

The aim of this part of the innovation phase is to gather and further develop ideas for new IT systems and work organization uncovered earlier in the process or during interviews specifically focusing on the requirements of management and employees for future technology use. Workshops are a suitable technique for achieving this goal, and the project group may include some of the future users whose tasks it is redesigning.

The starting point may be either ideas and requirements for work organization or ideas and requirements for technology, including requirements for compatibility with other existing or planned IT systems. The choice will depend on whether the organization requires the main part of the design vision to be made up of standard systems (and on how flexible these systems are) or whether there is an opportunity for developing new systems.

If standard systems are to be employed and the market studies point to one or more potential solutions, there will generally be various options for organizing the work. For example, a project group may focus on a temporal division of individual tasks according to the nature of the work— some tasks must necessarily be performed before others—or on a model that reflects who a given group of staff communicates with in performing its tasks. The point is to consider the tasks in context. The focus is on the goals, problems, and needs revealed in the in-depth analysis phase. Questions are then asked along the line of "What if we organized things differently instead?"

Answering such questions incorporates the functionality and interface of the standard systems into a restructuring of the work organization in order to meet the goals, problems, and needs revealed in the in-depth analysis phase. Several techniques and description tools are available to the project group: virtual mapping, drawings, collages, and scenarios. The project group should strive to have an open mind about changing how the work in the company is performed. In this regard, visits to other companies may provide inspiration. This activity may lead to various requirements for adapting the standard systems or to new IT systems that need to be integrated with them. The activity concludes by prioritizing the potential standard systems that best support the desired work organization.

If opportunities exist for developing new IT systems, this activity begins with the project group systematizing and prioritizing the requirements for work organization. Once again, it may prove helpful to review the entire cycle of a task—for instance, by means of a timeline or a communication model. The project group's point of departure is with the goals, problems, and needs uncovered in the in-depth analysis phase, while also bearing in mind the organization's business strategy. Accordingly, the project group can work out a list of requirements for the function and interface of the systems, while respecting the organization's IT strategy in terms of preferred platforms and compatibility with other systems.

To start out, however, it is preferable to be as open-minded as possible. Questions such as "What if we had a system that could . . ." may be one way of letting imagination run free. Other techniques include workshops simulating task performance, focusing on who does what using which information, technologies, or other tools. Subsequently, the project group must judge the visions against any economic or technological limitations and adjust the requirements accordingly. This activity concludes with a description of the desired work organization, possibly including which tasks the system should automate or support and how to bring about these goals. In this situation, the technique of scenario development may profitably be applied.

7.5.4 Mock-Ups and Prototypes

Experimenting with mock-ups and prototypes are very efficient techniques for visualizing and simulating selected elements of envisioned IT systems prior to their implementation. Paper-based mock-ups, outlines of parts of the systems and their functionality on large sheets of paper or transparencies, are an expedient tool to use in a workshop simulating the performance of selected tasks. These kinds of organizational games can be played to develop and test organizational changes brought about by use of the technology. If, for instance, the issue involves systems for supporting a particular workflow, all involved staff may take part in an organizational game simulating an entire workflow for one case while using and referring to mock-ups of the systems. This is one way of surveying complex business processes that allows the involved staff to test design ideas, while discussing and coming to grips with the systems' effects on the work organization.

If the issue involves the development of new systems, design vision representations may be supplemented by making one or more prototypes illustrating the functionality of the proposed IT systems. The prototypes are designed and tested by the project group and representatives of the involved stakeholders. They help the project team evaluate the relationship between technological requirements and demands on the work organization. Prototypes often prove effective when all stakeholders need to be informed of—and have to collectively decide on—the design visions. Finally, prototypes provide the future developers of the systems with an excellent supplement to the descriptions in the design project report.

It is essential to test mock-ups and prototypes in as realistic a context as possible in order to create the most solid basis for evaluation. In other words, the aim is for the project group to organize tests in which future users input their own data to perform their own tasks in their own context.

7.5.5 Identifying Qualification Requirements

The aim of identifying qualification requirements is to ensure that future users acquire the qualifications and skills necessary to use the new technology within the proposed work organization. These skills naturally include operating the IT systems. However, when new tasks need to be performed or when major changes to the work organization are proposed that require a redistribution of roles, it becomes necessary to clarify which staff groups need which kinds of training and education in order for the proposed design visions to lead to the desired changes. Qualification requirements may include courses in using the new systems and the more general level of education required for handling new areas of competency. Whether this activity will be managed by the project group or entrusted to others will depend partly on the scope and complexity of the activity and partly on the corporate practice in this area. In any event, the activity should result in an overall training plan concerning the new IT applications.

7.5.6 Consequence Analyses

The aim of consequence analyses is to identify the advantages and disadvantages that can be predicted to result from implementation of the design visions. This includes consequences to the company as a whole, to individual staff groups, to interdepartmental relations, as well as to relations with customers and suppliers. Such consequences may relate to themes of finances, working conditions, products, and services, and should, of course, be viewed in relation to the overall objectives of the project. The project group should carry out a systematic study of the proposed design visions with regard to the stakeholders and themes involved in order to provide the organization with the best possible foundation for decision making. When forming its evaluation, the project group may start from the representations of proposed systems and the scenarios for their use produced by the previous activities. This may be supplemented by the SWOT technique if necessary.

Normally, identifying the advantages offered by proposed systems is a relatively uncomplicated task, since these advantages have been discussed throughout the design process. Identifying the disadvantages involved is a more complicated task, however. As the project group has created these visions themselves, they are the group's "babies," and it is difficult for the project group to genuinely critique them. Tests of mock-ups and prototypes and reviews of scenarios by stakeholders outside the project group are techniques to help reveal drawbacks of certain design visions. Use of new technology always entails certain disadvantages, and if the design project report does not describe any disadvantages, it is a sign that the project group is unable to critique its own solutions.

At this point, the consequence analysis may incorporate two obvious areas where disadvantages may arise:

- *Problems in the organizational implementation of the design visions, changes to the work organization, and work practices.* Job cuts, attrition, and other kinds of staff reorganization are always problematic. Disadvantages may also show up elsewhere, however—as duplication of work and other resource-intensive transitional measures; as training in new routines, new roles, distribution of competencies and patterns of responsibility; changes to organizational structures; increased recording and monitoring of work routines; and so forth.
- *New routines in using proposed systems that present no immediate advantages to the user.* If using a system forces the user to perform tasks or routines for which he or she is not immediately motivated and the advantage of which escapes him or her, this is generally considered a disadvantage. Often, certain users need to enter data into the IT systems so that others can benefit from it. A classic example is the use of electronic calendars, requiring all employees to record meetings and other such activities in order to enable others, such as managers and secretaries, to use the data in a common calendar to schedule meetings, and other events. Generally speaking, logging data into IT systems for use in statistics and other kinds of management information entails extra hours—the advantages and purpose of which may not be apparent to users.

7.5.7 Implementation Strategy and Plan

The final element of a company's decision-making foundation is a strategy plan for the technical and organizational implementation of the design visions. Strategies—such as the overall approach or method of the implementation project, the scope of the activities it comprises, and the finances involved—may be decisive in determining whether visions are realized in full, in part, or even rejected altogether. Such considerations are typically made throughout the entire design project, especially by the project manager and the steering committee. The project group should devote at least one meeting to systematically reviewing the conditions and possible strategies for the implementation project and assessing the pros and cons of alternative strategies.

The best strategy for the implementation project depends on the nature of the proposed IT systems as well as on their scope and complexity. This can include several issues:
- Whether the project involves standard systems or customized solutions
- Organizational factors, such as the overall situation of the entire IT project, as analyzed in the in-line analysis phase
- A company's readiness for change
- A company's traditions and experiences with past IT projects
- A company's management style
- A company's corporate culture

Risk management is an important element of the strategy for an implementation project. Major implementation projects can be divided into subprojects, and the strategies for such subprojects should accommodate for their interdependency and interaction. When risks are assessed as high and time is not of the essence, it may be appropriate to opt for an incremental strategy in which the design visions are gradually realized, the experiences continually evaluated, and the further course of the project adjusted accordingly. If, for instance, a company is about to invest in a sophisticated and costly standard system and has concerns about how to achieve the efficiency of this system, it may attempt to persuade the supplier to take part in a pilot project. In such a pilot project, part of the system is installed at the company for a short period of time, enabling selected aspects of its functionality to be tested. Organizational changes can be tested according to a similar strategy, where experience is generated through experimentation or a test that runs over a limited period of time and where evaluation criteria and procedures are agreed upon in advance.

Incremental strategies can be realized either by introducing a subset of the visions broadly across the organization or by introducing the entire design vision into a subset of the organization, with a selected group of users "leading the way" for other parts of the company.

When a company is pressed for time—for instance, if heightened competition threatens its survival—the strategy may involve instant or rapid implementation of radical changes, as familiar from BPR (Business Process Reengineering). Of course, this entails a considerably greater risk of the IT project failing. Still, it outweighs the dangers of remaining inactive for too long.

Strategies are followed up by a general plan for activities to be carried out under the company's implementation project. The potential overall activities of the implementation project can be modeled in a baseline plan. This plan includes activities that the organization must perform itself and those that may be outsourced, since managing external supplies may prove a particularly demanding task. Candidates for implementation activities include preparing tender materials, assessing offers, contract negotiations, gathering experience through experiments and pilot projects, supply management, internal development and adaptation of IT systems, training and education, implementation of a new work organization, converting and integrating old and new systems, and user tests.

7.5.8 Writing a Design Project Report

The results of the previous activities are compiled into a design project report, which is submitted to the project's steering committee. Figure 7.3 shows a suggestion for the contents of such a report. Based on the report, as well as on comments from the stakeholders and discussions with the project group, the steering committee should be able to decide which parts of the design visions to realize. The report sums up the background of the design project and the results of the initiation, in-line analysis, and in-depth analysis phases. It presents a vision for overall change, while proposing an order of priority among them. It also includes an analysis of foreseeable advantages and disadvantages. Finally, the report contains a financial estimate as well as a proposed strategy and plan for technical and organizational realization of the vision(s) with the highest priority.

```
0. Summary

1. Objective
    1.1 Objective and premise of the design project
    1.2 Main points of the in-line analysis phase
    1.3 Main points of the in-depth analysis phase

2. Visions for overall change
    2.1 Technology
        2.1.1 IT systems and IT platform
        2.1.2 Functions
        2.1.3 User interfaces
    2.2 Work organization
    2.3 Qualification needs

3. Advantages and disadvantages
    3.1 The company's business and IT strategies
    3.2 Groups of staff and interdepartmental relations
    3.3 Customers and suppliers

4. Finances

5. Implementation strategy and plan
    5.1 Technical
    5.2 Organizational

6. Recommendations and priorities
```

Figure 7.3 Suggested outline of a design project report

7.6 Possible Results of the Phase

The results of the innovation phase provide the basis for the design project's final end product. Requirement specifications and tender materials for IT systems often focus on what the systems should offer in terms of functionality. The objective of the MUST method—cohesive visions anchored with the organization—requires that the design visions should also include answers to questions of why the IT systems are relevant and how they will be integrated and used in the company's work practices. The overall result of the innovation phase thus touches upon a large number of conditions, as summarized in figure 7.4. The main result of the phase is a design project report, which may be supplemented by mock-ups and prototypes illustrating ideas central to the proposed IT systems.

As in the three previous phases, described in chapters 4 through 6, all the potential results of the innovation phase are indicated in terms of the six aspects mentioned in

Visions for the overall change
- Function and interface of the system
- IT platform
- Work organization
- Employee qualifications
- New services and products

Costs, advantages, and disadvantages
- The IT systems
- Work organization and qualification needs
- The company's business and IT strategies

Implementation strategy and plan
- Technical
- Organizational

Mock-ups or prototypes, if applicable

Figure 7.4 The result of the innovation phase

	Aspect	Innovation phase
Project context	Design project	-
	Implementation project	●
Usage context	Business strategy	○
	Work practices	●
Technical context	IT systems	●
	IT platform	○

Figure 7.5 The relevance of the results of the innovation phase in terms of six different aspects: (●) indicates primary relevance; (○) indicates secondary relevance; (-) indicates that this aspect is relevant to the phase only in certain situations

chapter 3 (see figure 7.5). Thus, sections 7.6.1–7.6.6 constitute a total list of conditions that may be relevant to document in the innovation phase.

7.6.1 Results in Terms of the Design Project

The innovation phase concludes the design project, and the results of the phase are usually limited to a summary of previous decisions and an anchoring of the results of the phase. These goals may involve two steps:
- Providing summary of, or references to, the backdrop of the project and a baseline plan
- Informing stakeholders, plus incorporating or documenting their comments

7.6.2 Results in Terms of the Implementation Project

Decisions regarding the proposed IT applications require a certain grasp of the subsequent implementation project. The most important results of the design project in terms of the implementation project are proposals for a strategy and plan for implementing the project. This strategy may include several components:
- An overall plan for the technical implementation of the visions, including a specification of the order in which individual vision elements should be implemented, plus an overall procedure for a tender and outsourcing of supplies

- Identifying subprojects, their interdependency, and their interaction
- A plan for organizational change and training, based in part on the company's readiness for change, its traditions, and its culture
- A strategy for overall risk management of the implementation project
- Estimate of the financial parameters and time frame of the project
- Preliminary estimates of the scope of main activities
- Identifying and characterizing links to other initiatives and projects at the company upon which the implementation project depends

7.6.3 Results in Terms of Business Strategy

The design visions must be evaluated in terms of their relationship to the company's business strategy, which was analyzed in the in-line analysis phase. In the report, the results of such evaluation may include three elements:

- Reference to, or summary of, the main points of the strategic analysis report
- Description and characterization of new or improved services and products resulting from the design visions
- Effects and consequences of the design visions with regard to the business strategy, including an evaluation of the visions' alignment with the organization's short-term and long-term objectives

7.6.4 Results in Terms of Work Practices

The main result of the in-depth analysis phase as concerns work practices is an accounting of the reasons why the proposed solutions are necessary—in light of business-related goals and conditions of the existing work practices. In the innovation phase, the main result consists of describing what these solutions will look like—that is, how the new work organization may function and how the IT systems are envisioned to be used in specific, real-life work contexts. The project team must also consider the advantages and disadvantages of the proposed solutions, plus the cost of establishing the new work practices. In the design project report, results may include some of the following aspects:

- Reference to, or summary of, the main points of the analysis report (answers to the questions "why?")
- A description of the new work organization in the design visions, that is, a review of how tasks are performed using the proposed IT systems (typically supported by scenarios)
- A list of all advantages and disadvantages that a new work organization may conceivably entail—for instance, the performance of new tasks, working conditions, competencies, cooperation between different groups of employees, and so forth
- A review of required qualification, including estimates of the scope and content of training programs for various groups of staff
- Estimates of the costs of changing the work organization and of the overall training needs
- Overall evaluation of advantages, disadvantages and costs, that is, a cost-benefit assessment of changing the work practices—excluding the cost of procuring and developing the IT systems

A major challenge in developing the visions of a design project is to provide the organization with a visualization of what future work practices may look like—to make each manager and staff member "see" the nature of his or her future work in the vision. The most important technique for describing future work practices is scenario development. We recommend writing several scenarios describing the future work processes as viewed from the perspective of various categories of users, since there may be significant variation in how management and different groups of staff will be experiencing the use of the new IT systems. Further visualization of IT usage may be supported by mock-ups and prototypes (section 7.6.5).

7.6.5 Results in Terms of IT Systems

The results in terms of the IT systems envisioned involves the question of what these systems should offer by way of functionality, an aspect which often has a high priority in requirement specifications and tender materials. The results are described in the design project report and may favorably be supported by the following types of sketches, mock-ups, and prototypes:

- Drawings providing an overview of the overall portfolio of IT systems in the design—vision for instance, in the form of a design sketch
- Clarification of which parts of the systems are to be realized through (adapted) standard systems and which need to be developed. Consideration of whether system adaptation and development should be put out to tender or be implemented internally by the organization
- Lists of the functions of individual IT systems and an evaluation of their complexity
- Requirements for user interfaces and ways of interaction
- Description of the relations between the proposed IT systems and other existing and planned systems
- Survey of the data basis of the IT systems—for instance, in the form of ER diagrams
- Mock-ups and prototypes illustrating and simulating selected aspects of the systems

7.6.6 Results in Terms of the IT Platform

The IT systems in the visions should be viewed in terms of the organization's IT platform and related plans and strategies. The proposed IT systems' IT platform requirements should be identified and an evaluation should be made of whether the proposed systems set new IT platform requirements and the extent to which this harmonizes with the organization's technical strategy.

7.7 Summary and Literature

In this chapter, we initially clarified the objective of the innovation phase. Accordingly, we described the possible activities and results of the phase. Moreover, we described four prototypical situations to aid a project group in planning an innovation phase according to the specific situation of their project.

Regarding opportunities for developing and testing design ideas in the project group, our main inspiration has been work on "reflection-in-action" (Schön 1983) and "reflection-on-action" (Schön 1987). The use of scenarios is inspired by

Carroll (1995). The use of mock-ups in experiments with prototypes is described by Ehn and Kyng (1991). Hasse Clausen's notion of using narratives in systems development (Clausen 1993) has several points of resemblance with our use of scenarios. We have systematically worked with these ideas in many of the design projects we have conducted (Bødker and Kensing 1994) and (Kensing, Simonsen, and Bødker 1998). Furthermore, Bødker and Kensing (1994) demonstrates how the project group may include evaluations of the readiness for change when developing visions in the innovation phase.

III
Method, Tools, and Techniques

8
An Overview of Techniques

Part II presented the four phases and activities for developing a design project's intermediate and end products. Part III presents a series of techniques for supporting the different activities in the four phases.

In this chapter, we provide an overview of all the techniques and related representation tools that have proven effective when used in IT design projects. The emphasis of this overview is on providing a comprehensive presentation of individual techniques and their application area. Chapter 9 offers a more detailed description of all techniques and related representation tools. A technique describes how an activity can be carried out. The term *representation tools* refers to the notation forms supporting a technique and capturing the results of the work.

An overview is presented in the form of figure 8.1, after which we briefly describe all the techniques in the order in which they are listed in the table. The descriptions refer to further reading on individual techniques, including references to a section of chapter 9 and to other literature.

8.1 Overview

Figure 8.1 provides an overview of the MUST method's techniques. Project management is regarded as an integrated part of the method. For instance, the project group is in charge of planning the individual phases, including the choice of approaches and techniques. Accordingly, the MUST method includes management-oriented techniques focusing on IT design as a process as well as performance-oriented techniques supporting analysis and design activities. The table first lists three project management techniques, followed by thirteen performance-oriented techniques:

Technique	Phases	Principles	Knowledge areas	Representation tools
Management-oriented				
1. Baseline planning	**1**,2,3,4			Baseline plan
2. Review	1,2,3,4	2,4		Summary
3. Hearing	1,2,3,4	**2,4**		Summary
Performance-oriented				
4. Interview In situ interview	**1**,**2**,3,4 3,4	2 3	A,B,C D,E,F	Summary
5. Document analysis	**1**,2,3		A,C	Notes
6. Functional analysis	**2**	1,4	A	Functional model
7. SWOT analysis	1,**2**	1,2,4	A,C	SWOT model Risk matrix
8. Observation	1,**3**	1,**3**	D,E,F	Summary
9. Thinking aloud	3,4	1,2,**3**	D,E,F	Notes
10. Workshops	**3,4**	**1,2,3,4**	A,B	Freehand drawings Collages Dead Sea scrolls Affinity diagrams Role lists Communication models Timelines Design sketches Data models
11. Future workshop	3,4	1,2	A,B	Open notes on big sheets of paper
12. Mapping	**3**,4	2,4	A,B,C	Virtual maps and diagnostic maps
13. Prompted reflection	3	2	A	Freehand drawings Notes
14. Company visit	**4**	2,3	C,F	Summary
15. Experimenting with prototypes	4	**1,2,4**	B,E	Mock-ups Prototypes
16. Developing scenarios	**4**	**1,4**	B	Scenarios

Figure 8.1 Overview of MUST method techniques: The three most important techniques for each phase and principle are in boldface

There are a number of approaches to selecting techniques. We have decided to support a selection by providing a number of characteristics for individual techniques that correspond to the table's division into columns.

First, the approach may be a specific phase. The phase column of figure 8.1 indicates phases of the MUST method in which each technique can be applied, highlighting the three most significant techniques for each of the four phases. The phases are described in part II and here are simply referred to by their number:

1. Initiation phase
2. In-line analysis phase
3. In-depth analysis phase
4. Innovation phase

Second, one may wish to locate techniques supporting the realization of a specific principle. The principle column of figure 8.1 indicates which principles are supported by the technique, highlighting the three most significant techniques for each principle. The principles are described in chapter 2 and here are simply referred to by their number:

1. The principle of a coherent vision
2. The principle of genuine user participation
3. The principle of firsthand experience with work practices
4. The principle of anchoring visions

Third, the approach may involve a specific knowledge area to be studied. The knowledge area column of figure 8.1 indicates areas in which each technique can support the generation of knowledge. The knowledge areas are described in chapter 2. For categorization purposes, figure 8.2 assigns a letter (A–F) to each of the six knowledge areas.

	Users' present work practices	New IT usage	Technological options
Abstract knowledge	A. Relevant descriptions of users' present work practices	B. Design visions and proposals	C. Overview of technological options
Concrete experience	D. Concrete experience with users' present work practices	E. Concrete experience with new IT usage	F. Concrete experience with technological options

Figure 8.2 Six knowledge areas in IT design

Fourth, figure 8.1 indicates the most frequently used representation tools for supporting each technique and capturing its results. The representation tools column of figure 8.1 may also be referred to when exploring the use of a specific representation tool. All the techniques and their related tools are described further in chapter 9.

Management-oriented techniques—baseline planning, reviews, and hearings—support central project management activities in a design project. In the previous chapters, we have characterized a design project as marked by a high level of uncertainty. Accordingly, risk management is a central element of design projects. We regard risk management as a collection of techniques for managing the inherent risks of all IT projects. The principle behind the techniques is to identify problems before they occur and become critical in order to safeguard against crises.

Boehm's model of risk management, which we rely on in implementing the MUST method, comprises three overall activities: risk evaluation, risk control, and crisis management (see Boehm (1991) and Fairley (1994)). Risk evaluation identifies risk factors potentially threatening the successful completion of a project. A project's risk factors need to be analyzed and prioritized in order to focus on the most critical elements of each one. The size of each risk is a product of the probability of the risk becoming real and the size of the potential loss.

Risk management starts by determining a strategy for the critical risk factors. Boehm's model of risk management also includes the most effective risk-management techniques. Next, action plans are devised for realizing the risk-management strategy. These risks, against which management decides to seek measures, are managed by the respective action plans.

If an action plan fails, or a different risk factor exceeds a set threshold, the project is designated as critical. This is where crisis management comes in. The most important principle when a project becomes critical is to focus attention on the crisis situation in order to get the project under control with swift, concentrated measures. Once the crisis has been weathered, it is important to actively determine how to proceed with the project.

Day-to-day responsibilities for assigned tasks of risk management rest with the project manager. Likewise, it is the project manager's responsibility to include the company's management in important decisions. Risk management is an integrated part of the MUST method. The overall risk-management strategy is intrinsic to the method's suggestions for intermediate and end products of each phase. The mapping technique, which we describe as a technique for supporting analysis and design activities, may also be used to establish an understanding of problematic project management situations in a design project, as well as of possible solutions and their consequences. For an in-depth description of risk management as a separate technique, see Boehm (1991) and Fairley (1994).

Performance-oriented techniques support the method's analysis and design activities. Analysis involves understanding something that exists, while design targets the creation of something new—change. This may seem like a simple and clear cut distinction, but in practice the two types of activities are closely intertwined. Understanding provides the basis for potential change, and, while working to develop visions of change, one often encounters a need for greater understanding. Accordingly, many activities in IT design will be in the form of continual iteration between analytical understanding and design-oriented change. Both types of activities, however, involve gathering and analyzing information, as well as presenting the results to a broader audience. A number of common features of the techniques supporting analysis and design activities are described in sections 8.2 and 8.3.

8.2 Data Gathering

When it comes to data gathering, a characteristic of the MUST method is its focus on gaining insight into concrete experiences. This may involve concrete experience of users' present work practices, of technological options, or of newly proposed systems (knowledge areas D, E and F in figure 8.2). Chapter 9 describes three techniques, designed for use in knowledge gathering within the areas mentioned. These are in situ interviews, observation, and experiments with prototypes. Moreover, chapter 9 describes three techniques—mapping, future workshops, and prompted reflection—that help in analyzing concrete experiences, but represent them on a more abstract level.

As the techniques bring the IT designers close to the clients' staff, the designers become personally involved in problems encountered by these people in their work and gain insight into these problems via the MUST method techniques. The designers must fundamentally accept that the design project cannot be controlled in the same way as when modeling workflows together with users by way of formalized representation tools. In situations that rely on formalized representation tools, the IT designers are on their home turf, since they are the experts on modeling. However, when using the techniques mentioned here, a client's staff members are on their home turf. The IT designer should strive to get to know the key concepts at the client company and understand why tasks are performed the way they are, as well as what work practices the staff experiences as either good or problematic.

Application of the techniques should be regarded as a process of iteration. For instance, insight into a specific issue gained from observation can be used in a subsequent interview to elaborate the issue or confront it with different information. Thus, data gathering cannot be planned in detail. Rather, one should be prepared to pursue interesting aspects that surface during the course of events. After each activity, it is necessary to take what has just been learned and compare it with previously gathered material. For instance, when an interview produces apparent contradictions with previously gathered information, the experienced IT designer will take up the issue in order to clarify any ambiguities. The act of comparing insight gained by the application of different techniques is known as *triangulation*.

Crucial to applying the techniques is that the *informant*—a neutral term for the person supplying the information—feels secure and, thus, may speak candidly. As a precondition to facilitating this process, the informant should know why his or her opinions and experiences are important, how the information is analyzed, and to what ends the results are put. All informants should receive advance information that will help them understand the design project's objective and data gathering's importance in achieving the design project's goals. The informant should be aware of, and approve, how any potentially confidential information will be handled, possible usage of any recordings, agreements with management regarding feedback from the interview, the approval procedures if direct quotes are used, and so forth. The IT designers must be prepared to gain insight into conditions about which the informant does not want to be quoted on the record. If the informant seems uncertain about a situation, this insecurity should be addressed by the IT designer and discussed before an activity begins or continues.

8.3 Analysis and Presentation

What to include in data gathering, and in subsequent analysis and presentation, naturally depends on the content of the individual design project. In this section, a number of focal points for analysis and design activities are described. These points may also be of use in planning interviews, observations, or other data-gathering techniques:

- Work functions (why are the business processes and tasks performed?)
- Tasks (what do the tasks involve?)

- Work process (how is the work process carried out?)
- Flow of information (what information is used, created, and transmitted, and by what means?)
- Time sequence (who does what when and what are the preliminary and end results?)
- Communication structure (who communicates what with whom and by what means?)
- Coordination of tasks (who handles the coordination of tasks and by what means?)
- Breakdowns in the work process (what are the possible causes of problems or stoppages?)
- Preservable traditions (what works well within the present work organization and with the present technology?)

In the initial part of a design project, these focal points serve to support information gathering for use in analytical activities. Later on in the design project, when more design-oriented activities are at the forefront, the same focal points can be used as starting points for efforts in creating a design vision. Based on this vision, efforts in specifying flow and coordination of information may be undertaken.

Analysis and design activities can seem chaotic. Many factors may be involved which do not seem to fit together and there may be many details that are hard to track. The MUST method's techniques and tools support different ways of arriving at an understanding of a phenomenon in the design process. We may speak of three different types of movement taking place in our thought processes when striving to understand and describe a phenomenon:

1. We explicitly move between concrete and abstract. For instance, we need concrete knowledge of users' present work practices to be able to develop relevant representations of the practices (see figure 8.2). Such representations involve abstraction by emphasizing the most significant qualities and omitting less significant ones. Conversely, we also need to gain concrete experience with an abstract representation of a new IT usage in order to evaluate its functional qualities.

2. We operate with a movement between the whole and its parts. We construct a holistic understanding on the basis of data gathering—for instance, via observation and in-

terviews, which typically provide a wealth of detailed knowledge. As this process consumes many resources, points of potential impact for detailed data gathering are selected according to an overview or a holistic understanding.

3. We may move between a phenomenon and the terms describing it. For instance, when utilizing a scenario to describe IT usage, we use terms emphasizing central qualities of a future phenomenon: IT usage within a specific organizational context. Conversely, in attempting to establish an overview of data gathered about users' current work, we pick or coin terms capturing those qualities of the phenomenon that are relevant to the current design project.

8.4 Brief Description of MUST Method Techniques

This section contains brief descriptions of each of the sixteen techniques in the MUST method. Each description starts by characterizing the technique according to figure 8.1, and each technique is further described in chapter 9.

Technique	Phases	Principles	Knowledge areas	Representation tools
1. Baseline planning	1,2,3,4			Baseline plan

Sources: Section 9.1; Andersen et al. (1990), chaps. 5, 7.

Baseline planning centers on dividing a design project, in terms of time and content, into a number of baselines, which indicate when selected intermediate products must have arrived at a specific, well-defined state. Furthermore, we describe ways of assessing whether this has been achieved. The period between two baselines is called a phase. A phase thus consists of a number of activities collectively contributing to the movement of the project from one baseline to the next.

The course of the entire design project will usually be planned in the initiation phase, taking into account the desired completion date and the available resources. At each baseline, the plan is critically assessed, possible changes are implemented, and the subsequent phase is planned in greater detail. Results of the baseline planning are documented in the form of a baseline plan which, along with the project charter, constitutes the scope of the design project.

Technique	Phases	Principles	Knowledge areas	Representation tools
2. Review	1,2,3,4	2,4		Summary

Sources: Section 9.2; Andersen et al. (1990), section 6.3; Freedman and Weinberg (1982).

A review is an effective technique for systematically assessing the quality of a product. During the course of a design project, the project group may decide to subject a draft of an intermediate product, a report, or a project plan to a review. The creator of a product decides when the product is ready for a review. As a condition for a review, a separate description should be made of the requirements that the product needs to meet. The requirements may be described by a list of contents (if the product is a report) or by a set of criteria that the product must meet.

The actual review consists of a meeting that last for a few hours. The reviewers' task is to point out what is good about the product, as well as its possible errors or shortcomings. As a general rule, the creator of a product should listen to the reviewers' comments and refrain from starting a discussion or an explanation of errors and shortcomings. Responsibility for making the necessary improvements and corrections lies with the product creator. The results of the review are set down in a summary.

Technique	Phases	Principles	Knowledge areas	Represen-tation tools
3. Hearing	1,2,3,4	**2,4**		Summary

Source: Section 9.3.

A hearing is a technique specifically aimed at promoting the principles of anchoring visions and genuine user participation. The idea behind hearings is to provide employees in the company opportunities to review and comment on significant products of the design project before final decisions on them are made.

A hearing may take place by exchanging information in writing, by oral communication at a meeting, or by a combination of the two. The steering committee decides whether a hearing is warranted, while the project group prepares and analyzes the submitted comments in order to inform the steering committee's decision. If the hearing takes the form of a meeting, it will typically feature presentations by the steering committee chairman and the project manager before the discussion is opened to the invited participants.

Technique	Phases	Principles	Knowledge areas	Represen-tation tools
4. Interview **In situ inter-view**	1,**2**,3,4 3,4	2 3	A,B,C D,E,F	Summary

Sources: Section 9.4; Kvale (1983, 1996).

Interviews are one of the most frequently used techniques in IT design. Interviews are used to effectively and systematically gather information from staff, management, customers, and other stakeholders.

IT design chiefly operates with so-called qualitative interviews. Qualitative interviews may focus on a variety of issues and themes, or may center on discussion of a single, general theme. Practices range from interviewing subjects in a room away from their workplace to interviews in situ at the subject's work station, where the informant refers to and demonstrates specific tools, such as files papers, IT systems, and so forth.

Interviews mainly aim at understanding how the informant performs his or her work, what the work involves, and why it is performed the way it is—that is, understanding the informant's current work practice as work process, task, and work function. The results of an interview are set down in a summary—which may be forwarded to the informant for comment and which affords the other participants in the project group insight into the interview's issues.

Technique	Phases	Principles	Knowledge areas	Representa -tion tools
5. Document analysis	1,2,3		A,C	Notes

Source: Section 9.5.

Document analysis involves reading pertinent documents, while noting interesting and relevant information. Document analysis is used in most of a design project's phases. In the initiation phase, it is used to gain an initial overview of the company by studying annual reports and organizational diagrams. In the in-line analysis phase, it is used to analyze strategies and related projects or initiatives that are relevant to the design project. In the in-depth analysis phase, it is used to study documents used in selected work processes more closely, including forms, plans, and so forth. The results of document analysis may be set down in note format, allowing the project group to share the knowledge.

Technique	Phases	Principles	Knowledge areas	Represen- tation tools
6. Functional analysis	2	1,4	A	Functional model

Sources: Section 9.6; Schmidt (1986, 1988).

Functional analysis is a technique for analyzing work functions. It is especially useful in the in-line analysis phase. Functional analysis starts off from the company's overall business strategies, and the aim of the analysis is to identify the work functions (including business strategies and work domains) upon which the design project should focus.

The most important elements of functional analysis are its terminology and its representation tool—functional models. Its terminology is useful for presenting and discussing strategy-oriented representations and considerations with management representatives, as many managers think in terms of work functions. Functional analysis is useful for developing the content of, and the relations between, such terms as environment, business strategy, business processes, work domains, and IT systems.

Technique	Phases	Principles	Knowledge areas	Representation tools
7. SWOT analysis	1,2	1,2,4	A,C	SWOT model Risk matrix

Sources: Section 9.7; Porter (1985).

SWOT analysis charts the company's overall strategic and competitive situation, while providing an overview of the design project's risk factors. The technique can be used in the initiation and in-line analysis phases to establish an overview of the company's market situation or of a department's situation within the company. Moreover, the technique can be used to assess the project's risk factors via a risk matrix categorizing its weaknesses and threats identified in the SWOT model.

SWOT analysis starts from an evaluation of the competitive state of the industry. The company's strengths and weaknesses, as well as opportunities and threats in the industry, are assessed accordingly. Strengths and weaknesses may tie into structural conditions or to the company's ability to carry out change processes. Opportunities involve the company's ability to realize new strategies (product development and the like), while threats involve the risk of other companies doing likewise. Weaknesses and threats in the SWOT model can be entered into a risk matrix and categorized as risk factors according to their probability and consequences.

Technique	Phases	Principles	Knowledge areas	Representation tools
8. Observation	1,3	1,3	D,E,F	Summary

Sources: Section 9.8; Blomberg et al. (1993).

Observation may provide firsthand experience of work practices that cannot be gained by techniques such as interviews and thinking- aloud experiments. Observation of a company's existing work processes contributes to knowledge area D, while observation of the use of prototypes or elements of an implemented system contributes to knowledge area E. Finally, observation of IT systems—for instance, at a company visit—may contribute to knowledge area F.

We distinguish between participatory and passive observation. In passive observation, the observer does not interfere, but acts as a "fly on the wall." In participatory observation, the observer is drawn into the performance of the observed work. Observation is time-consuming and usually requires advance identification of relevant work domains for observation. It may be supported by video or audio recordings, but a project team should keep in mind the time-consuming task of reviewing such recordings. We suggest that project group members set down insight from their observations in summaries, which are divided among the project group as starting points for further analysis.

Technique	Phases	Principles	Knowledge areas	Representation tools
9. Thinking-aloud	3,4	1,2,3	D,E,F	Notes

Sources: Section 9.9; Carroll (1995).

The thinking-aloud technique involves having someone perform an activity while they talk through what they are doing or thinking. The technique may be used in the in-depth analysis phase, as the informant goes about his or her daily work, or in the innovation phase while testing mock-ups or prototypes. The point of this exercise is to provide an outsider, the IT designer, firsthand experience with the users' current work practice (knowledge area D) or with new IT usage (knowledge area E). Finally, thinking-aloud experiments may contribute to knowledge area F, if used in relation to company visits.

The remarks given for supporting observation by video or audio recordings apply equally well for thinking-aloud.

Technique	Pha-ses	Principles	Knowedge areas	Representation tools
10. Workshops	**3,4**	**1,2,3,4**	A,B	Freehand drawings Collages Dead Sea scrolls Affinity diagrams Role lists Communication models Timelines Design sketches Data models

Sources: Section 9.10; Bowman (1997).

To allow for genuine user participation workshops involve users and IT designers working together to produce a joint result according to a relatively focused theme. A workshop can be organized in a variety of ways. They all use simple diagrams or drawings to gather and analyze the participants' knowledge about the theme. A workshop may be mainly analysis-oriented—for instance, aimed at a common understanding of a specific aspect of the users' present work practices. It may also be mainly design-oriented—for instance, aimed at creating relations between the functionality of a series of new IT systems or between the systems and a proposal for a new work organization (coherent visions). Simple diagrams or drawings made in the process may later be refined for purposes of presentation beyond the project group.

Technique	Phases	Principles	Knowledge areas	Representation tools
11. Future workshop	3,4	1,2	A,B	Open notes on big sheets of paper

Sources: Section 9.11; Kensing (1986); Kensing and Madsen (1991); and Jungk and Müllert (1987).

A future workshop is an especially useful technique when large groups of staff in a company participate in a design project. The aim of a future workshop is to create a first joint proposal for changing a situation that a group of people find unsatisfactory. In the course of half a day or up to two days, the group will establish a joint overview of what is wrong with the existing situation and develop ideas for improvement. The workshop concludes by developing a plan for implementing the ideas that are assessed as realistic. When used in a design project, the technique may enable the project group to quickly gather and perform an initial analysis of opinions for possible inclusion in continuing project efforts.

Technique	Phases	Principles	Knowledge areas	Representation tools
12. Mapping	3,4	2,4	A,B,C	Virtual maps Diagnostic maps

Sources: Section 9.12; Andersen et al. (1990), Section 6.4; and Lanzara and Mathiassen (1985).

Mapping is a technique for analyzing and structuring argumentation regarding problem causes, content, consequences, and solutions. We distinguish between diagnostic mapping—focusing on problems, causes, consequences, and solution proposals—and virtual mapping—focusing on solution proposals, actions, consequences, and evaluation.

Diagnostic mapping can be used in the in-depth analysis phase—for instance, to create relations between problems and ideas for solutions (i.e., between knowledge areas A and B). Virtual mapping can also be used in the innovation phase—for instance, to create relations between potential solutions and ways of realizing them (i.e., between knowledge areas C and B).

Mapping can contribute to anchoring visions by creating argumentation for the relevance of the proposed solutions (diagnostic mapping) and for efforts required to realize the solution proposals (virtual mapping). The technique can also be used to analyze other problematic situations, such as cooperation problems within the project group.

Mapping activities are documented in the form of a diagnostic or virtual map. For easy corrections and additions, a whiteboard or something like it may come in handy. The results of the mapping can be set down in a table for inclusion in the design project's intermediate and end products.

Technique	Phases	Principles	Knowledge areas	Representation tools
13. Prompted reflection	3	2	A	Freehand drawings Notes

Sources: Section 9.13; Kensing (1998).

Prompted reflection is a useful technique for IT designers facing a complex work practice that they are having a hard time grasping. This complexity may be due to the IT designers' unfamiliarity with materials, tools, work processes, and products involved in the work, or because the work requires years of schooling and experience. In the in-depth analysis phase, prompted reflection can be used as a technique for producing relevant representations of the users' current work (knowledge area A). It may also provide the first ideas for new IT usage.

The technique can be divided into four overall activities: initiation, workshops, analysis, and discussion of results. Having selecting a theme, the IT designer organizes a workshop with two or more staff members, who each make a drawing of his or her work on a big sheet of paper and explain it to the others. A drawing may illustrate a work process or a product, listing terms, or tools that the staff use in their work. The IT designer subsequently uses the drawings, notes, and possible recordings from the workshop to support his or her own reflections on, and structuring of, the work practice. In conclusion, the IT designer presents his or her representations to the workshop participants and the rest of the project group for evaluation and correction of errors and shortcomings.

Technique	Phases	Principles	Knowledge areas	Representation tools
14. Company visit	4	2,3	C,F	Summary

Source: Section 9.14.

Company visits are a technique for gaining ideas and experiences regarding the types of IT usage that are being considered in the design project. A visit to another company using the relevant new IT usage may generate a wealth of ideas for the design project (knowledge area C). It enables the IT usage's functionality, required infrastructure, or work organization to be studied. A highly valuable aspect of a company visit is the opportunity it affords for listening to and discussing experiences with implementing and using the IT systems in question. Whenever possible, observation of the system in use or hands-on testing of the system will provide more concrete experience (knowledge area F). Company visits may be set up via personal contacts, by cold calls to other companies, or via the supplier of the system that is being considered. The supplier is often more than willing to set up the contact or directly organize a visit with a reference customer. Company visits can provide the project group with useful firsthand experience for their further efforts, which would otherwise be difficult or impossible to gain before the company implements the system itself.

Technique	Phases	Principles	Knowledge areas	Representation tools
15. Experimenting with prototypes	4	**1,2,4**	B,E	Mock-ups Prototypes

Sources: Section 9.15; Ehn and Kyng (1991); Floyd (1984); Budde et al. (1992); Blomberg et al. (1996); Grønbæk et al. (1997).

Experimenting with prototypes supports genuine user participation and it helps anchoring visions. It is a technique for generating ideas for IT usage and making simple prototypes for testing and producing concrete experience relevant to the further design efforts. Even a simple prototype or mock-up, quickly and inexpensively put together, will have specific and tangible qualities resembling the envisioned IT usage. Hence, knowledge from testing and assessing prototypes can be put to constructive use in the further design efforts. We distinguish between experimenting with horizontal and vertical prototypes. A horizontal prototype has no functionality and can only be tested in an artificial setting. A vertical prototype is more complete (within a defined area of the design) and can be tested in real work situations to yield valuable experience about the expediency of its construction, content, and usage contexts. The various prototypes allow the coherent vision to be specified to a level enabling realistic evaluation of what we call the client's readiness for change. That is, assessing whether the company is ready for the change expressed in the coherent vision and concretized in selected areas by the prototypes.

Technique	Phases	Principles	Knowledge areas	Representation tools
16. Develop-ing Scenarios	4	1,4	B	Scenarios

Sources: Section 9.16; Carroll (1995); Clausen (1993).

Developing scenarios is a technique that supports building coherent visions and thus helps ancoring these visions. Scenarios visualize the practical application of a proposed IT system—that is, the potential effects of implementing it. Scenarios are prose-style representations exemplifying a work practice under future use of the system. Scenarios may illustrate application of the system as viewed from the different users' perspectives. Thus, they may also refer to a design sketch or prototype of a proposed system. Scenarios are based on the users' conceptualization of their work context. A scenario typically involves a specific business process. Drawings and design sketches can often be used as points of departure for writing the scenario.

9
Tools and Techniques

This chapter describes all of the MUST method's tools and techniques. The techniques are described in separate sections, in the order in which they appear in chapter 8. The tools are presented as a section under the technique that first introduced them in chapter 8. A number of the examples are drawn from the same design project (at a radio station) to illustrate what contributions the different techniques make.

The chapter is intended to serve as a reference. It does not need to be read all at once or in sequence.

9.1 Baseline Planning

Technique	Phases	Principles	Knowledge areas	Representation tools
Baseline planning	1,2,3,4			Baseline plan

Sources: Andersen et al. (1990), chaps. 5 and 7.

Baseline planning is a technique that supports planning a design project as a work process. Moreover, this technique makes it possible to evaluate the progress of the project. Baseline planning does not, of course, guard against all possible errors, but the technique helps the project group and steering committee to step in and regulate the process when inconsistencies between the plan and the actual situation are noted.

We define a baseline as a project state that has been set down in the project plan, enabling everyone involved in the project to refer to it. Moreover, baselines make it possible to determine whether planned intermediate products and other significant requirements have been achieved when the project group expects to have reached a baseline. The technique thus aids internal coordination in the project group.

The reports and other intermediate products proposed in part II of this volume also help the steering committee and other relevant actors to evaluate whether the project is moving in the right direction.

The technique builds on a graphic representation of the project as a work process (see figures 9.1–9.4). The resulting baseline plan shows what products the project group will be supplying, as well as what intermediate products will be involved. Baseline planning also outlines activities designed to lead to the intermediate products. Finally, criteria are provided for evaluating intermediate products, along with procedures for performing such evaluations.

The actual technique of developing a baseline plan for a design project can be divided into four steps:

1. Draw a baseline for each respective starting situation and desired end situation. Specify criteria for each desired end product, along with procedures for evaluating whether the criteria have been met (see figure 9.1).

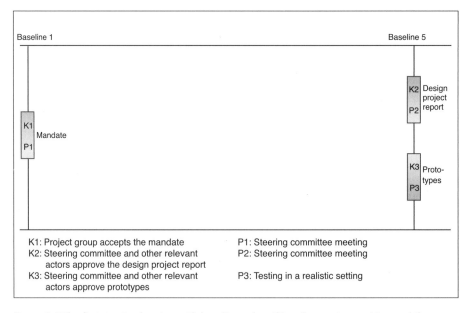

Baseline 1   Baseline 5

K1
    Mandate
P1

                                                                              K2 Design
                                                                                  project
                                                                              P2 report

                                                                              K3 Proto-
                                                                                  types
                                                                              P3

K1: Project group accepts the mandate   P1: Steering committee meeting
K2: Steering committee and other relevant   P2: Steering committee meeting
    actors approve the design project report
K3: Steering committee and other relevant   P3: Testing in a realistic setting
    actors approve prototypes

Figure 9.1 The first step in planning with baselines: describing the starting position and the desired end position

2. Plot three baselines in between the first two baselines representing the beginning and end of the project. These lines indicate the conclusion to the initiation, in-line analysis, and in-depth analysis phases, respectively. Next, add the intermediate products to be contributed by each phase. Again, specify procedures for assessing whether the intermediate products meet the criteria at each baseline (see figure 9.2).

3. For each phase, activities for taking the project from one baseline to the next are now designated, along with techniques and tools for performing these activities. Names of activities are added to the figure, while tools and techniques can be listed in a separate document for ease of comprehension (see figure 9.3).

4. The amount of time for activities planned between each baseline is estimated and corresponding dates are added to the baselines. Finally, the completion date is checked against any possible specification in the project

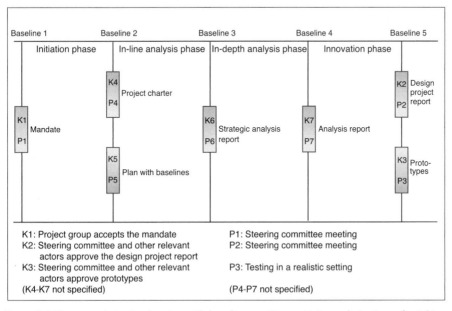

Figure 9.2 The second step in planning with baselines: setting out intermediate stages for taking the project from start to finish

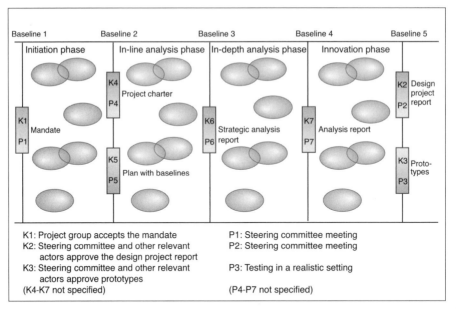

Figure 9.3 The third step in planning with baselines: indicating activities to perform in order to take the project from one baseline to the next

group's mandate. If the estimated completion date falls after what the mandate specifies, the project group must either ask for more time or the ambition level must be lowered. The latter is done by adjusting the expectations for intermediate and end products, as well as the number and scope of activities for producing them (see figure 9.4).

Baseline planning helps clarify the choice of approach for the project. It results in a plan and a specification of conditions under which the plan can be realized. When the project group reaches a baseline, the designated procedures are performed to evaluate whether each intermediate product meets the specified criteria. If an intermediate product fails such an evaluation, it is up to the steering committee to determine whether the project group should simply integrate repair activities into the subsequent phase or whether the intermediate product should be reevaluated before other activities are undertaken. Of course, the steering committee may also decide to lower the ambition level, which is then its responsibility, not the project group's. In any case,

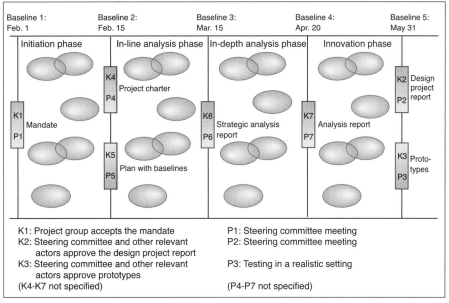

Figure 9.4 Finished plan with estimated dates for each baseline

when developing a baseline plan, it is important to set aside time for possible repair work.

The conventional phase division found in many other planning techniques makes for an unfortunate blend of divisions by time and by content in the project efforts. Planning with baselines, on the other hand, makes it possible to clarify the conceptual distinction between these two division criteria. While a conventional phase plan calls for activities of only one sort in each phase (either analysis, design, specification, and so forth), a baseline plan typically features different sorts of activities in every phase. This is because the phase division in baseline planning is temporally based. The criteria for the baselines are determined by who typically needs what type of knowledge about the project, and when (the "who" will typically be the steering committee). Answering such questions helps to specify the required intermediate products and how to group them into baselines. The division by content—that is, what activities are grouped into each phase—is determined by resolving what activities will take the project from one assessible project state to the next.

As for the number of baselines, the MUST method recommends starting with five—equal to the starting situation and the conclusions to the four phases. However, as we have pointed out in chapters 4–7, the scope of the phases will depend on the inherent uncertainty of the project. At one extreme, some design projects may be limited to three baselines, by merging initiation with in-line analysis or in-depth analysis with innovation. At the other extreme, there may be situations—when the uncertainty level is high and the steering committee needs to closely monitor the project—that warrant additional baselines for several of the phases.

9.2 Review

Technique	Phases	Principles	Knowledge areas	Representation tools
Review	1,2,3,4	2,4		Summary

Sources: Andersen et al. (1990), section 6.3; Freedman and Weinberg (1982).

A review is an effective technique for systematically assessing the quality of a product. During the course of a design project, the project group may decide to subject a draft of an intermediate product, a report or a project plan to a review. The creator of a product decides when the product has achieved a quality qualifying it for a review.

As a condition for a review, a separate description should be made of the requirements that the product needs to meet. If the product is a report, its requirements may be described by a list of contents (see chapters 4–7 for suggested lists of contents for the four reports of a design project). Or they may be described by a set of criteria that the product must meet (see section 9.1 for suggested criteria to specify as a step in baseline planning). A review involves four steps:

1. The creator (the project group) is responsible for distributing the product and setting the requirements by which it will be evaluated.
2. The reviewers cannot be project participants, as the whole point of a review is obtaining an impartial critique. However, they should be knowledgeable about

what they are asked to evaluate. Three to four reviewers should be suitable.

3. The reporter is a member of project group or, at the very least, someone who knows the project well enough to produce a relevant record.

4. The moderator must also be impartial and should, at a minimum, be familiar with the technique to ensure an effective reviewing process.

The actual review takes place at a meeting that lasts a few hours. The task of the reviewers is to point out what is good about the product, as well as any possible errors and short-comings. Responsibility for making the necessary improvements and corrections lies with the project creator. The creator should listen to the reviewers' comments and refrain from defending his or her results or starting a discussion. The most important result of the review is for the creator to absorb the reviewer's comments. Since having one's work critiqued is a sensitive matter, it will often be a good idea for the moderator to remind the reviewers that the product, not its creators, are being critiqued. At some companies the reviewers are responsible for approving or rejecting a product or can demand a new review after the creator has had a chance to correct the indicated errors and shortcomings. Thus, some companies make the reviewers share responsibility for products they have reviewed.

The moderator may choose to have each reviewer make his or her comments in their entirety or to have them take turns as they make comments about particular themes. The project group may have specified in advance a number of conditions about which it is particularly interested in gathering comments, or the meeting can be structured according to the specified requirements. In any case, it is important that the moderator makes sure that every reviewer gets a chance to comment and that the comments are reported for use in the project group's continuing efforts. Moreover, when reviewers share responsibility for a product, they should have a chance to review the report for approval. Although reviewers are not specifically required to suggest solutions to the problems they identify, the project team can set aside time in order to allow this to happen.

A banal yet critical requirement for a meaningful review is allowing the reviewers time to prepare, just as the project group should be afforded time to correct any errors and shortcomings. Accordingly, such activities should be set down in the respective project plans. Figure 9.5 breaks down the requirements for the four roles that take place before, during, and after a review.

Apart from helping ensure the quality of a reviewed product, the technique may also make for uniformity in products supplied by the IT development organization. Finally, some companies also emphasize the technique's potential in terms of personnel training, as it may increase awareness of how co-workers approach a task. The emphasis on the quality of the product and on learning for the participants may present an argument for not letting the creator's managers participate in a review. Likewise, the practice some companies have of publishing review reports can be called into question.

	Before the review	**During the review**	**After the review**
Creator	• makes the product • species requirements for the product	• listens • answers questions	• fixes errors and shortcomings • has main responsibility for the product
Reviewers	• have competency regarding the product	• point out positive and negative aspects of the product • do not propose solutions • critique the product, not its creator • approve or demand a new review or reject the product	• may share responsibility for the product
Reporter	—	• reports the reviewer's evaluations with keywords • provides a clear conclusion	—
Moderator	—	• directs the meeting • makes sure that all reviewers have their say—for example, interrupts the producer if he or she starts arguing or gets defensive • ensures that the review/product requirements are in order or, if not, calls off the meeting	—

Figure 9.5 Requirements for roles in a review

9.3 Hearing

Technique	Phases	Principles	Knowledge areas	Representation tools
Hearing	1,2,3,4	**2,4**		Summary

A *hearing* is a technique for decision makers to use when they wish—or are required—to inform other people about a design project's status and plans. Moreover, the idea behind hearings is to incorporate such responses as the information may elicit into the foundation for subsequent decision making. This technique also promotes the principle of anchoring visions.

Hearings can be employed when the situation calls for communicating with actors who do not directly participate in a design project thus contributing to genuine user participation. As a conclusion to the initiation phase, a hearing may involve broadly informing about the objective and planned course of the project. During the in-line analysis phase, a hearing can be used to consult with managers, both from the candidate work domains and related domains. In the in-depth analysis phase, a hearing with the affected staff can be held to ensure that the project group has a sufficient understanding of the problems and needs. Finally, in the innovation phase, before a decision is made on what design visions to implement, it may be pertinent to inform, and gather responses from, affected staff and managers, as well as from IT or personnel-training departments that may have parts to play in the implementation of the project.

A hearing may take place by exchanging information material and responses in writing, by oral communication at a meeting, or by a combination of the two. The steering committee decides whether a hearing is warranted, while the project group prepares and analyzes the submitted responses in order to inform the steering committee's decision. The hearing will take the form of a meeting that typically features presentations by the steering group chairman and the project manager before the discussion is opened up to the invited participants.

The following example from a design project at a publishing house illustrates the hearing technique. As a step in the in-depth analysis phase, the group has conducted a series of interviews with selected staff and managers. It now wants to ensure that it has sufficient understanding of the involved problems, needs, and solutions before proceeding to design vision development. The project manager has obtained approval at a steering committee meeting to distribute the preliminary analysis report to the entire staff and put the design project on the agenda of the next staff meeting, where the point is organized as a hearing.

The project manager prepared a fifteen-minute presentation that sketched out the project group's understanding of problems, needs, and ideas. A few of the drawings that the project group has used in its work were redrawn and enlarged to serve as illustrations at the personnel meeting. A draft of the analysis report was posted on the publisher's intranet a week before the meeting, along with relations to the previously posted project charter and strategic alignment analysis report.

At the meeting, the steering group chairman set out by restating the objective of the design project and defining the the work domains that the project group had been assigned to analyze in-depth in the current phase. After a couple of questions, the project manager made his presentation which, in turn, generated a few questions. The chairman of the meeting then opened a discussion, allowing the publisher's staff and managers to make their hearing responses in the form of comments on the project group's work. Two project group members took notes.

The comments can roughly be divided into three categories. The first of these type of comments prompted the steering group chairman to clarify what the project group's task has not involved. The second category of comments constituted valuable immediate corrections to the project group's hypotheses and evaluations, while the comments in the third category were set aside for further study in the next phase. The steering group chairman agreed with this breakdown, except for one comment that he believed was so critical to the steering committee's final decision on the analysis report that he requested the project group carry out further analyses and revise the report in preparation for a new steering committee meeting in two weeks.

9.4 Interview

Technique	Phases	Principles	Knowledge areas	Representation tools
Interview	**1,2**,3,4	2	A,B,C	Summary
In situ interview	3,4	3	D,E,F	

Sources: Kvale (1983, 1996).

Interviews are one of the most commonly used techniques in IT design. Interviews are used to effectively and systematically gather information from staff, management, customers, and other stakeholders.

Interview forms range from highly structured to unstructured.

In structured interviews, a series of precisely worded questions are asked. This form is used when the situation calls for asking a large group of people identical questions that have certain pre-fixed response options, allowing for quantitative and statistical analysis of interview responses.

In unstructured interviews, the project team asks broad questions that do not necessarily require specific answers, but answers that may be elaborated upon and lead to a dialogue. This form, centering on subjective answers, is also known as qualitative interviews. Questions in such interviews may often build on knowledge gained from, and discussed in, previous interviews or from applying other techniques.

At an absolute extreme, the structured interview will closely resemble (and could in fact be replaced by) a questionnaire survey, and the qualitative interview can be likened to a chat about one or a few general themes. The following paragraphs describe the qualitative interview, which is the MUST method's main recommended form of interview for design projects.

A qualitative interview may work from a relatively detailed interview guide (i.e., a series of questions and themes) or may center on a discussion of a single overall theme. Subjects can be interviewed in a room apart from their workplace or in situ—that is, the interview takes place at the subject's workplace. During an in situ interview, the informant refers to and demonstrates specific tools, such as files, documents, computer systems, and so forth.

The interview mainly aims at understanding how the informant performs his or her work, what the work involves, and why it is performed—that is, understanding the informant's current work practice as work process, task, and work function:

1. Examining how the informant performs his or her work is aimed at understanding what functions well and what does not function well in the existing work processes.
2. Examining what the work involves is aimed at clarifying a division of the work into tasks and groups of tasks. Groups of tasks often correspond to work functions.
3. Examining why the informant does the things involved in the work process targets current work functions being performed, as well as what future functions could conceivably be performed and supported by IT systems.

The interviews are "open"—that is, the interviewer is free to question anything he or she does not understand during the interview. If an answer includes unfamiliar terms or refers to unfamiliar procedures, the interviewer may ask the informant to clarify the point. A successful open interview is conducted not only in question-and-answer format, but more as a conversation, by which the interviewer, and often the informant as well, learns something new. The conversation may revolve around how the work is organized and performed, why it is done that way, what problems the informant frequently experiences, as well as any ideas the informant may have for changes, improvements, or IT support.

Interviews aim at gathering knowledge about areas A, B, and C in figure 8.2. In situ interviews may provide further access to the informant's concrete experiences (knowledge areas D, E, and F), which can be expanded by applying the thinking-aloud experiments and observation techniques.

The following section divides interview technique into four subactivities: preparation, execution, processing, and summary writing techniques.

9.4.1 Preparation

Preparation for a series of interviews should include decisions about whom to interview, topics for the interview, and how the project group should organize and conduct the interviews.

Choosing people to interview is entirely dependent on how far the design project has advanced. The initiation phase may involve initial interviews—for instance, with management representatives on the objective and content of the design project. In the in-line analysis phase, which aims to identify work domains for further study in the design project, it may be relevant to interview external and internal customers plus suppliers, as well as a broad selection of people handling different functions. In the in-depth analysis phase, when candidate work domains have been designated, it may be relevant to conduct fewer, more in-depth in situ interviews with the people working in these domains. Finally, in the innovation phase, interviewees may include staff at another company who have experience with an IT system like the one that is being considered by the current client. In addition, staff at the project company may be interviewed in order to test and further develop ideas for the IT system that the project group is designing.

Determining what topics to include in the interview involves writing an interview guide that indicates questions and themes for the interviews. The project group may write the interview guide based on joint brainstorming and subsequent discussion on the focal points mentioned in section 8.3. The interview guide is referred to during the interview and may be forwarded to the interviewees beforehand. The interview guide should continually be revised as the project group gains both information and experience from using it.

The project group should make a plan for who interviews whom, a plan for analyzing and reporting back on the interviews, and an overall timetable for conducting the interviews. The group should not plan several interviews one right after the other, but should allow for enough time to review each interview before conducting the next one. An interview will often yield a wealth of relevant information that can be used in the next interview. This consideration is especially critical when expecting to interview a series of subjects only once.

9.4.2 Execution

We recommend making every effort to have two people conduct each interview. First, each can support the other in asking questions; second, both can subsequently discuss and interpret the interview; and, finally, one can concentrate on the interview while the other takes notes.

Recording an interview is always recommended. The course of a qualitative interview is highly unpredictable and an interview may take unexpected turns, which one will later appreciate having "saved." The most important function of a recording is to serve as a memory aid, enabling the interviewer to concentrate on the informant and the issues in the interview guide. An audio recording is an ideal "back-up" of the interview that can always be consulted and used to expand notes from the interview. Before starting the recording, briefly but clearly explain why you would like to ask permission to use the recording as a memory aid—to be able to concentrate on the interview instead of worrying about taking detailed notes.

If no recording is made, the interviewers should take notes in keyword form. If several interviewers are present, we recommend that one take notes while the other concentrate on conducting the interview. When one person conducts the interview, he or she should plan for half an hour after the interview to write a more thorough summary. If hours or days are allowed to pass before a summary is written, many details will be lost. When the informant mentions specific documents or forms during an interview, the interviewer should ask for a copy right away or make a note and ask for copies of all documents mentioned later.

9.4.3 Processing

An interview should always be documented by writing an interview summary. Often, it is during the process of the interviewer writing down the results of the interview—while alone and undisturbed—that ideas for further questions or design ideas occur and valuable insight is gained. Moreover, a written summary is an important source of information for other members of the project group and the informant.

If no recording of an interview was made, a summary is written based on the notes from the interview, in addition to the initial summary that one hopes was written immediately after the interview (this is especially important when there is only one interviewer). If the interview was recorded, the recording can be processed in two ways:

- By transcribing the entire recording. However, producing, reading, and processing a transcript is a labor-intensive task.
- By carefully reviewing the recording while writing a summary of the most significant elements. Experience has proven this to be an efficient way of processing an interview. The next section describes one way of writing this kind of summary.

The interviewer should listen to the recording and pause to take notes each time something relevant is mentioned. In the process, the interviewer may structure the summary under suitable headings (e.g., based on the interview guide). He or she should write down good potential quotes verbatim. The interviewer should also note especially interesting passages of the recording so they are easy to locate again if necessary. Ideas (including design ideas), follow-up questions, and personal hypotheses (which may be tested in future interviews) occurring during the process may be noted in separate documents.

In our experience, it takes about two to three times the duration of the recording to write a summary this way. A summary of a one-hour interview may very well extend to five to ten pages. Summaries will benefit from the inclusion of drawings and diagrams made or presented during the interview, or sketched out during the review of the recording. A summary of an interview should only represent the things the interviewer personally regards as relevant. It may, however, be a good idea for the interviewer to make a list, in keyword form, of subjects one has initially chosen to leave out. This makes it easier to locate them if they later turn out to be relevant. A recorded interview should always be saved until the design project has concluded, unless the informant makes it a precondition that it be erased immediately.

The interview summary is included in the project group's collective, current documentation. It may profitably be forwarded to the informant for comment. If the informant agrees, it may also serve as an appendix to intermediate reports or the final design project report.

As a rule, many direct quotes from the interviews will not be used. However, it is a good idea to gather pertinent quotes when processing the recordings, as a good quote sometimes strikes to the heart of a problem much better than a laborious explanation. This may be the case when it is important to describe a conflict within the organization or when faced with different descriptions of an apparently identical phenomenon.

9.5 Document Analysis

Technique	Phases	Principles	Knowledge areas	Representation tools
Document analysis	**1,2,3**		A,C	Notes

Document analysis involves reading through one or more relevant documents, while taking note of interesting and relevant information. This knowledge can be shared by the project group via a note. Document analysis can be used in most phases of a design project. Typically, it will be used for preparation and follow-up of interviews by studying documents supplied before or during the interview.

In the initiation phase, the design team will benefit greatly from studying organizational diagrams and descriptions of the company in order to gain an overall understanding of the company, its products, and market position.

In the in-line analysis phase, when the focus is on establishing relations between the design project and the company's business and IT strategies, analyzing documents describing these strategies will yield a wealth of important information. Moreover, analyzing descriptions of related projects contributes to an understanding of the relations between design projects and other projects.

The in-depth analysis phase will typically involve analysis of work descriptions, manuals, work documents, and other forms used in the selected work domains, in order to supplement insight established during this phase. The primary value of such documents will often be to serve as a reference for specific experiences or knowledge gained by the project group. Second, copies of documents and forms may be valuable as sources of information about detours in work practices or by providing vital, supplementary information added to the document outside any possible preprinted boxes.

Figure 9.6 shows an overview of types of documents and the phases where they typically will be incorporated into design project activities. It is important to bear in mind that documents may exist in both paper and electronic form.

Phase	Documents
Initiation	Annual report Company presentations on the Internet Commemorative publications Organizational diagrams
In-line analysis	Business strategy IT strategy Project descriptions
In-depth analysis	Work descriptions Meeting records Manuals Work documents Forms Rules and procedures

Figure 9.6 Typical documents and the phases when they are incorporated into a design project

9.6 Functional Analysis

Technique	Phases	Principles	Knowledge areas	Representation tools
Functional analysis	2	1,4	A	Functional model

Sources: Schmidt (1986, 1988).

Functional analysis is an analysis of work functions. It has nothing directly to do with the functions of an IT system. Functional analysis can be used in the in-line analysis phase to clarify the potential of investing in information technology, as well as to identify the goals, needs, requirements, and conditions involved. The technique is especially useful for supporting the in-line analysis phase activities of "analyzing the business strategy" and "analyzing the environment." Functional analysis was developed in Denmark over a number of years. It is a systemic analysis—that is, the starting point for the technique is a decision to view a designated part of a company as a system and then to explore that system's relationship to its environment.

The most important elements of functional analysis are its terminology and its representation tool, functional models. Its terminology is useful for presenting and discussing strategy-oriented representations and considerations with management representatives, since many managers think in terms of work functions. This technique is useful for developing the content of, and the relations between, such terms as environment, business strategy, business processes, work domains, and IT systems (see figure 5.3). Moreover, the technique can be characterized as adaptive, rational, and expert-oriented:

- It is adaptive because it requires relatively stable environmental factors setting requirements on the system that the system tries to meet. Thus, the technique assumes that the company tries to change and adapt as its environment sets new and changed requirements.

- It is rational because it requires viewing the company as expedient work systems that have an overall function in relation to the company's environment.
- It is expert-oriented because it generally requires the IT designer (alone or with a project group) to perform the analysis based on interviews and document analysis, while deriving and representing the results in terms of environments, requirements, needs, conditions, and functions.

The following section describes the terms of functional analysis, the general approach to performing the analysis, and the technique's functional models. Examples are drawn from projects at the Nordic Film Institutes to illustrate aspects of functional analysis. These cinema culture institutes support national film production, while also lending and selling films to private companies, public institutions, and individuals.

9.6.1 Concepts

Functional analysis fundamentally involves analyzing the requirements, needs, and conditions to which so-called work systems are subjected, as well as the functions they accordingly perform (see figure 9.7).

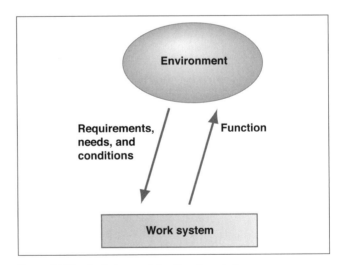

Figure 9.7 The basic terms of functional analysis

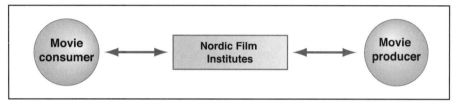

Figure 9.8 Environment of the Nordic Film Institutes

The work system is the part of the company selected for a focused study. The focus of a design project may be on the entire company or on one of its departments. However, functional analysis does not necessarily have to be applied to a specific organizational unit: IT designers may choose to consider as a work system any group of staff who, in one way or another, cooperate to perform a specific overall business function.

In figure 9.8, the work system represents an entire organization—in this case, the Nordic Film Institutes. Figure 9.9 shows the work systems within this organization, some of which correspond to actual departments, such as marketing, order receiving, shipping, and receiving.

The environment represents the work system's setting and, hence, the requirements, needs, and special conditions of the work system's surroundings. If the work system is the entire company, the environment typically involves the requirements and needs of the company's customers and suppliers, as well as conditions of legislation or competition. The needs of the cinema culture institute's customers (the movie consumers) may concern specialized educational and documentary films, that are not widely commercially produced. The requirements of the supplier (the movie producer) may concern financing or production support. Legislative conditions may, for instance, require movie support to promote public service information and education.

If a department of a company is designated as the system, the environment includes the other departments of the company. In figure 9.8, the shipping and receiving department's environment includes the order receiving department, which provides orders for the shipping and receiving department to process.

The work system attempts to answer the requirements and needs of its environment via the function it maintains. Function, in other words, expresses the work system's objective. If the work system is represented by the entire company, its function is expressed by the company's overall business strategy, among other things. The law that created the Danish cinema culture institute outlined the institute's function as a "liaison function." More explicitly, its overall objective is "to promote information, education as well as artistic and cultural activity, by producing Danish short films and otherwise buying short films" and "to promote information, education as well as artistic and cultural activity, by . . . distributing such [short movies] to institutions of learning, associations and individuals."

9.6.2 Procedure

As a starting point for functional analysis, a work system must be identified and defined. The work system is the part of the company included under a design project and should be apparent in the initiation phase of the project's charter. The technique is performed by gathering data via interviews and document analysis and then relating this data to the terms of functional analysis. It may also involve modeling the data in comprehensive functional models.

Interviews are mainly with management representatives of the affected departments of the company (i.e., the departments in the work system). Furthermore, representatives of the environment are interviewed (these representatives are typically selected customers and management representatives from other departments of the company that constitute the work system's environment).

Functional analysis also requires document analysis to be performed on all forms of business strategy proposals and plans, brochures, sales materials for customers, annual reports, legislative texts (for public corporations), and so forth.

Interviews and document analysis should generally aim to seek answers to "why" questions. When asking "why" a certain procedure, workflow, or routine is performed, the answer usually translates into a description of a function. Seeking to answer "why" questions means seeking the reason and objective of what is being performed—hence, indicating a function.

Functional analysis is performed by alternating among interviews, document analysis, and functional modeling. We recommend beginning with an examination of the work system itself before studying its environment. Because the staff in a given work system are all involved in performing the system's functions, members of a project team can gain a relatively quick overview of the system's self-understanding. Next, using this background knowledge, members of a project team can search the environment for related requirements, needs, and conditions. A given work system usually constitutes only a small part of the environment's "consciousness." For instance, library lending of the cinema culture institute's films may only constitute a very small part of a library's total lending.

Functional analysis should be performed on three levels:

1. On an overall organizational level, in order to "take in the scenery." On this level, the organization's environment and overall function are analyzed (as shown by the example in figure 9.8) and function corresponds to the organization's business strategy. This analysis helps describe the terms of "environment" and "business strategy," as indicated in figure 5.3.

2. On a middle level, breaking down the organization into internal functions, as indicated by the example in figure 9.9. On this level of functional analysis, functions correspond to business processes (see figure 5.3).

3. On a base level, breaking down those functions of the organization that are the subject of the design project into subfunctions/work domains, as shown in figure 9.10. The most detailed level of subfunctions is an individual employee's work function. This aspect of func-

tional analysis corresponds to analyzing work domains and identifying existing and potential opportunities for IT support (as shown in figure 5.3).

9.6.3 Functional Models

Functional models are a tool for establishing an overview of functions, as well as their relations to other functions in the company and the company's external environment. The models serve mainly as an internal tool for the IT designer and the project group, but in some cases can also be used as diagrams to present the results of functional analysis to outsiders.

Figure 9.8 and figure 9.9 show two examples of functional models. Each box in the figure corresponds to a function, while the circles (ovals in figure 9.9) indicate a company's environment. The arrows illustrate logical relations (typically information flows) between functions, as well as between functions and environment.

In figure 9.8, the company is viewed in toto, as an overall function. The environment has here been divided into two components: customers (those buying, renting, borrowing, and watching films) and suppliers of film (movie producers). The arrows illustrate the institute's relations (e.g., as dictated by legislation) to both types of environments, as the institute sells and rents film to consumers, while also buying films and subsidizing movie production.

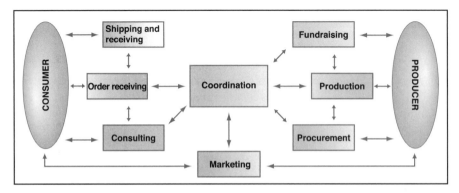

Figure 9.9 Individual functions of the Nordic Film Institutes

Figure 9.9 "opens up" the organization to show the functions into which the organization can be divided. A central function, called *coordination*, seeks to engage the two environments—that is, coordinating and deciding what films to buy and support—partly based on identified consumer needs. Coordination is typically managed by regular executive meetings. Consumer needs may derive from status reports and order-receiving statistics. Some functions may correspond to departments (such as order receiving), but that is not necessarily the case (e.g., customers may receive consultation in connection with order receiving). A function corresponds more to making a certain type of decision than to an organizational unit. Thus, a function indicates the overall objective of a business process more than focusing on how this process is performed in practice. Accordingly, a function's name should reflect what the process is continually trying to achieve.

The lowest level that can be included in functional analysis is individual functions, as shown in figure 9.9. Analysis at this level results in a further division, which usually comes to reflect the practical organization of the functions as aspects of business processes and work domains. Thus, it is generally not expedient to make additional functional models at the individual level—since it then becomes hard to distinguish between the abstract objective of the function and its practical and work-organizational implementation. However, functions may profitably be represented in images or text structured according to the division (as shown in figure 9.10).

Functional models are used as a tool in iteration with interviews and document analysis. When reviewing a recorded interview, an IT designer may make a separate note each time the interviewee expands on why a certain work process is performed. Potential functions are often identified and described this way. In the document analysis, an IT designer should make particular note of sections describing goals, objectives, and strategies. This frequently helps to produce a list of potential functions. Functional models are developed individually or at a workshop for the project group: Functions are set down in separate boxes with arrows indicating their relations to each other and the over-

Order receiving
- By electronic inquiry
- By phone inquiry
- By written inquiry
- By direct counter service
- Long-term loans to libraries
- Domestic and foreign sales
- Remainders and claims

Marketing
- Subscriber maintenance
- Distributing selections of films to new customers
- Sales/marketing follow-up
- Premieres
- Film festivals

Figure 9.10 Practical organization of two functions of the Nordic Film Institutes

all environment. This exercise usually results in a series of new questions to be pursued in new interviews and document analysis.

9.7 SWOT Analysis

Technique	Phases	Principles	Knowledge areas	Representation tools
SWOT analysis	1,2	1,2,4	A+C	SWOT model Risk matrix

Source: Porter (1985).

SWOT is an acronym for Strengths, Weaknesses, Opportunities, and Threats. SWOT analysis charts the company's overall strategic and competitive situation, while providing an overview of the design project's risk factors. This technique is especially useful in the initiation phase to support the activity of "identifying critical factors" and in the in-line analysis phase to support the activities of "analyzing the environment," "analyzing business strategy," and "innovative technology analysis." Analyzing strengths, weaknesses, and threats contributes to knowledge area A, while analyzing opportunities may also contribute to knowledge area C in figure 8.2.

SWOT analysis is used as a technique at workshops with the participation of the project group and invited stakeholders. Necessary tools for this workshop include a whiteboard (or flip chart) and a pad of colored adhesive notes. The workshop starts by introducing the SWOT technique to participants who have not worked with it before.

SWOT analysis is essentially a brainstorming technique. First, a SWOT model is made in the form of a large cross on a flip chart or board (see figure 9.11). Then, a brainstorming session is conducted to name every strength, weakness, opportunity, and threat the participants can identify. All suggestions are written down on colored adhesive notes (by the participants themselves or by a reporter), which are then placed in the appropriate quadrant. As in other brainstorming techniques, the rule is that there will be no discussion during the brainstorming activity and that all suggestions and formulations are permitted.

Strengths and weaknesses may tie into a company's structural conditions or its ability to carry out change. They often describe internal conditions concerning project participants and stakeholders directly involved in the design project.

Opportunities and threats usually involve conditions in the environment of the department, company, or industry. Opportunities may relate to new potential products or services, or be opportunities offered by new information technology. Threats may involve the risk of other companies taking advantage of these same opportunities, thus threatening the company.

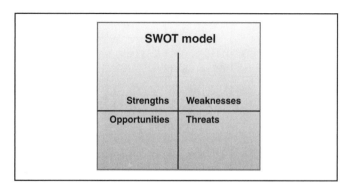

Figure 9.11 SWOT model

Once the participants have written down all their suggestions and situated them in the SWOT model diagram, it may be a good idea to review the suggestions one by one in order to evaluate whether each threat and weakness has a corresponding opportunity and strength that can counteract it. The SWOT model can then be followed up by a risk matrix (see figure 9.12).

This risk matrix, like the SWOT model, should be drawn on a flip chart or board. The risk matrix categorizes risk factors according to their consequences and probability. If a risk factor has a high probability of occurring, it is placed at the right side of the matrix. Correspondingly, if a risk factor is placed at the top of the matrix, it indicates that it may have serious, negative consequences.

The candidates for risk factors are all the suggestions on the right-hand side of the SWOT model—that is, all suggestions placed under weaknesses and threats. These suggestions are discussed and evaluated by the participants and then placed in the risk matrix.

Once all relevant suggestions from the SWOT model have been moved to the risk matrix, a final, in-depth evaluation is made of all risk factors that have high- or medium-level probability and high- or medium-level consequences—that

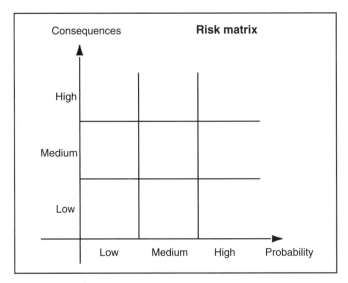

Figure 9.12 Risk matrix

is, all suggestions on the top right-hand side of the matrix, above the dotted line in figure 9.13. For each of these critical risk factors, the participants should discuss what measures can be taken to avoid them or reduce their probability and consequences.

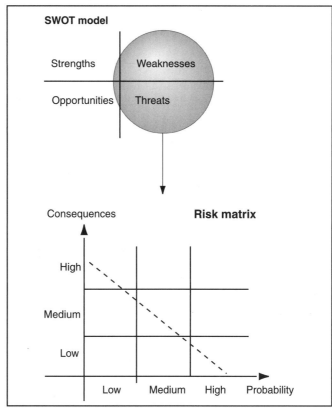

Figure 9.13 Placing weaknesses and threats from the SWOT model in a risk matrix

9.8 Observation

Technique	Phases	Principles	Knowledge areas	Representation tools
Observa-tion	1,3	1,3	D,E,F	Summary

Source: Blomberg et al. (1993).

Observation is a useful technique for gaining firsthand experience with present work practices, technological options, or a proposed new system (knowledge areas D, E, and F in figure 8.2). Observation makes it possible to study how specific tasks are performed in practice, how the tasks are actually coordinated, and how patterns of cooperation come into play under actual conditions.

The main reason for using observation is an acknowledge-ment of the possible variation between what the staff say they do (knowledge area A in figure 8.2) and what an out-sider may observe them doing (knowledge area D in figure 8.2). This is sometimes referred to as the "say/do-problem" (see section 2.3). When an IT designer asks staff members about what they do, how they do it, or why they do it a cer-tain way, their answers are likely to contain a good measure of what they are expected to do or should do. However, it can be important to understand why certain things cannot be done as expected or why it may not be a good idea to do as expected. Hence, the IT designer must confront informa-tion about an ideal workflow with what an outsider may observe as what is actually happening. In other cases, obser-vation is called for when staff members are unable to explain what they do or how certain assignments are solved. These shortcomings do not exist because of any ill will, but because staff members are so accustomed to certain work patterns that they are not aware of—or are not used to putting into words—how the tasks are solved or coordinat-ed.

There are several forms or methods of conducting an obser-vation. An extreme method is the proverbial fly-on- the-wall situation, where the observer tries to be as out of the way as possible. To be able to act as a fly on the wall, the IT designer should choose a form or method that seems fair and reasonable for observing activities in a specific work situation. At the other extreme is what is called *participatory observation* where the observer becomes part of the group of staff members whose work is being studied. Participatory observation requires the observer to become able to perform the work he or she is studying and, while performing the work, to take the necessary notes for subsequent analysis. In many design projects, IT designers cannot realistically get to know the users' work well enough to carry out participatory observation, while user representatives in the project group may have an easier time doing so.

For example, spending a day in a secretarial office enables a project group member to note the number and types of inquiries. It may cast a light on how secretarial workers coordinate parts of their work by passing on messages from one person to another. Likewise, following a staff member over the course of a workday will provide a vivid impression of the communication in which the staff member is involved—possibly including negotiations and decisions to be made with co-workers, with people from other departments of the company, or with clients and suppliers. Both examples reveal conditions that are not typically brought forth in interviews.

The following sections describe the observation technique in three steps: preparation, execution, and processing.

9.8.1 Preparation

In section 8.2, we discussed how the IT designer must learn to accept the loss of control inherent in data gathering techniques such as observation. However, this should not imply that there is no need to prepare for observation. In planning observations, as in preparing interviews, it is important for the project group to clearly specify whom and what will be observed, who will be doing the observing and for how long, as well as how to incorporate the results of observations into the continuing design project. Answering such questions depends, of course, on the scope and content of the design project.

In some design projects, a few observations will suffice to provide a good overview of the workflow and an impression of the nature of the work. For example, one or more staff members can be followed over the course of a workday. For reasons of resources, detailed observation will not come into play in a design project until the point when enough information is available that it becomes possible to focus the observations. An observation can be focused according to four focal points:

- Event
- Person
- Place
- Object

In a design project—for instance, one involving potential IT support for task planning—it will be natural to study planning and decision-making processes as they unfold before and during meetings (event focus). Observation of meetings will clarify on what basis decisions are made. It may also be helpful to observe a central actor in a design project (person focus)—for instance, someone in charge of producing a proposal for decision making: how it is done, who consults this person, what information is used, and how the work is coordinated when others are involved.

Another design project may focus on how certain tasks are coordinated. In that case, it may be relevant to observe a secretarial office (site or place focus) to study how secretaries play a part in communication and coordination among various people at a company. At times, some of the coordination occurs via lists or messages, so-called *coordination mechanisms*. In this instance, it may be useful to observe the flow of such lists or messages through one department (object focus).

Thus, the attention in the observation process is on what actually takes place, whether something works well or is inexpedient, who participates, what information is available or lacking, and by what media (paper, telephone, IT system, and so forth) information is supplied, processed, and distributed. The choice of focus, along with related aspects and points, is set down in an observation guide. When planning an observation, one should consider scheduling observations at different times. The work of a secretarial office may vary greatly depending on the time of the day, week, or month.

9.8.2 Execution

We recommend that observation be performed by a single person, mainly out of the concern to cause as little disturbance as possible. As a matter of course, an observation should always be agreed upon with the relevant staff member or members in advance. Likewise, it should be agreed how the results of the observation will be used in further design efforts. It is particularly important for the project team to be aware of any issues of confidentiality. Also, the observer should keep in mind that although staff members have agreed to be observed, it takes a while for them to get used to the observer.

As with interviews, observations can be conducted by following a guide and taking notes. The observation guide only serves to indicate a possible direction; notes should be made of all observations of apparent interest to the focus. Moreover, some situations will allow the observer to ask brief questions or request copies of specific work documents.

Depending on the focus of the observation, it may in some cases be useful to make audio or video recordings to supplement the notes. When this is the case, preparations are in order. Video recording, for instance, involves such considerations as camera placement and focusing. Only in very special cases do we recommend basing an observation entirely on video recording. As a rule, there are many events that cannot be recorded due to the camera angle and conditions of distance, sound, lighting, and so forth. Accordingly, we recommend using video recording only as a supplement to participatory observation.

If video or audio recordings are used, it is important for the project team to be aware of issues that are sensitive on a personal level. Video recordings, in particular, can be very revealing. If video sequences are going to be played back in other forums, the project group should carefully consider any personal issues contained in a sequence, and direct permission to use the material should be obtained in each case.

9.8.3 Processing

Notes, supplemented by examples of work documents, are the most significant and immediate products of an observation. As with interviews, it is important to make at least one preliminary summary of the observation before new observations are undertaken. Details or specific conditions are quickly forgotten.

When reviewing audio or video recordings, it will initially suffice to write a record of the contents, or a log. Interesting passages are noted in the log, with indications of times and keywords describing the observation. When using certain digital media, such marks can be directly entered into the medium, enabling quick retrieval of any given sequence.

At the end of the observation process, a summary is written based on the notes, capturing interesting and relevant observations. Since the summary represents the observer's reflections on his or her own observations, it makes no sense to forward the summary to the persons observed for comment. However, in some cases, confusion may arise in the course of compiling the observations, confusion that can be clarified by the relevant informants.

9.9 Thinking Aloud

Technique	Phases	Principles	Knowledge areas	Representation tools
Thinking aloud	3,4	1,2,3	D+E+F	Notes

Source: Carroll (1995).

Thinking-aloud experiments were originally developed in relation to usability studies of user interfaces and prototypes. In IT design, this technique is especially useful for gaining firsthand experience with work practices. It can be used as an alternative to observation of work processes that are hard to "see"—for instance, when a person works alone, with papers, or at a computer. The technique can also be used in place of an interview if the informant has a hard time describing what he or she does in the work environment. We will not repeat here the recommendations described in sections 9.4 and 9.8 regarding interviews and observation, respectively. However, those recommendations may also be useful in thinking-aloud experiments.

A thinking-aloud experiment involves having someone perform an activity, while he or she talks through what he or she is doing or thinking. This technique may be used during the in-depth analysis phase, as the informant goes about his or her daily work, or during the innovation phase, while testing mock-ups or prototypes. The point is to give an outsider, the IT designer, access to the users' concrete experiences with their current work practice (knowledge area D) or with new IT usage (knowledge area E). Finally, thinking-aloud experiments may contribute to knowledge area F, if combined with a company visit.

During a thinking-aloud experiment, an informant will frequently pause and forget to say what he or she is doing or thinking—either because the experiment may seem a bit contrived, or because the informant has become absorbed in his or her work. In such cases, the IT designer should prod the informant by asking what is happening at that moment. In other instances, the informant may be more concerned with explaining to the IT designer what is going on than with the task he or she is performing. The experiment then develops more in the direction of an in situ interview. At that point, the IT designer must make a choice either to try to get back to the thinking-aloud experiment or to switch techniques. The choice may depend on how many times this happens and on an assessment of whether it is because the informant feels insecure about the format.

Thinking-aloud experiments can be supported by video or audio recordings, but the project team should be mindful of the time-consuming task of reviewing such recordings. We suggest setting down the insight gained from thinking-aloud experiments in notes, which should be distributed among the project group as starting points for further analysis.

9.10 Workshops

Technique	Phases	Principles	Knowledge areas	Representation tools
Work-shops	**3,4**	**1,2**,3,4	A,B	Freehand drawings Collages Dead Sea scrolls Affinity diagrams Role lists Communication models Timelines Design sketches Data models

Source: Bowman (1997).

Workshops are useful when the project group needs to develop an understanding of the users' current work or when developing sketches of future IT usage (coherent visions). Because workshops are product-oriented and typically last only a few hours, they will benefit from taking either a mainly analytical or a mainly design-oriented theme. This section describes some general features of workshops, and sections 9.10.1–9.10.7 present a number of different representation tools for supporting the activities of a workshop and capturing the results. Each representation tool focuses on different aspects of the work at a company, its IT systems, or the relations between them. The tools are simple diagrams or drawings with no special formalisms. Formalisms include diagramming rules and notation forms from dataflow diagramming, class diagrams in object-oriented analysis, or entity-relation diagrams in data modeling. Aiming at genuine user participation we recommend avoiding such formalisms because staff members participating in the workshop, as well as those to whom the results are later presented, typically have no experience with technical descriptions using IT-oriented formalisms. The results of a workshop may later be processed for purposes of presentation beyond the project group.

In a workshop, the project group works together to gather and analyze information concerning a selected theme. Additional participants may be called in if their knowledge and opinions are needed. It may be a good idea to pick one or two project group members to serve as secretaries who are responsible for setting down the results of the work. It may likewise be a good idea to have a facilitator responsible for securing the forward progress of the workshop.

Data gathering—for instance, by interviews or observation of current work practices—will often leave the project group with a chaotic impression involving a lot of specific information. Where is the cohesion? What is general and what is specific to the relevant work practice? A workshop may thus be held to establish an overview of, and create cohesion in, the gathered information. In the case of a work domain characterized by an extended process in terms of time, such overview and cohesion can be established by modeling the workflow in cooperation with representatives of the staff performing the work. With a starting point in the event that sets it off, the workflow is represented, along with the content of the information involved in the tasks. Here, a so-called Dead Sea scroll may be useful (see section 9.10.3).

Another way of establishing an overview is by generalizing—starting from stand-alone situations or observations and proceeding to common features. The starting point may be individual notes or insight gained from observation, interviews, or other data-gathering techniques. The notes—in the form of statements written on colored adhesive notes—are organized hierarchically or in groups to serve as points of departure for formulating terms and broader terms capturing the noted insight. This is a "bottom-up" process and gradually advances toward an overview of the selected theme or problem field. This technique is also called affinity diagramming, and the result of the process is called an affinity diagram.

While the workshop technique described in the previous paragraph aims to establish an overview by generalizing and focusing on understanding the entirety, a workshop may also focus on concrete aspects of the work practice. A more focused cross section can be taken, based on a more or less developed understanding of the entirety of a specific design idea or of a specific aspect of the work practice.

The cross section is taken according both to the focus and situation of the design project. In some design projects, central job functions may be highly complex. For example, certain elements of the work may have a strong individual component, while others are more cooperatively oriented. In such cases, the project group may profit from writing a simple role list to separate the different work situations. Focusing on one role at a time makes it easier to obtain in-depth understanding of the work and develop ideas for appropriate IT usage, which later need to be evaluated in terms of the overall work situation. Such role lists, and how they support design considerations, are described in section 9.10.4.

In other design projects, a central work domain may perhaps be characterized as a sort of command center, where a lot of coordination and communication takes place. As a means of modeling such situations, we recommend communication models—which describe who communicates with whom, about what, by what medium, and what problems are involved. Some of the individual conversations thus modeled are typically part of more overall processes. This type of information can be modeled as a timeline, indicating participants, media, content, and breakdowns in a time sequence. Communication models and timelines, described in more detail in sections 9.10.5 and 9.10.6, illustrate how design considerations can take off from such models and representations. We also describe design sketches, a recommended tool for documenting general ideas about the functionality of IT usage, in section 9.10.7.

Contrary to the general caution against formalisms mentioned in the introduction to this section, it may be expedient to perform formalized modeling of data involved in selected work domains in preparation for experiments with prototypes. One option is entity-relation diagrams. These types of diagrams may be required when developing a prototype for testing in real work situations, which may involve combining the prototype's data with data in existing IT systems. In certain other situations, it may also be necessary, as a step in the design project, to perform thorough data modeling extending to the entire work domain that is the design project's object field. This may happen if it becomes clear that the target calls for a tender involving customized IT systems. In that event, a data model will be a natural part of the design project's end product.

Finally, we should mention a form of workshop that is typically used late in a design project. Often, a project group's work involves detailing the content of a coherent vision by experiments with prototypes, described in section 9.15. One of the most important characteristics of a prototype is that it concretely and tangibly demonstrates its capabilities. Essentially, this is what allows a prototype's qualities to be evaluated. However, it also enables what is known as a mental test of the company's readiness for change as regards the coherent vision concretized in the prototype. Such a mental test assesses the extent to which the rationale behind the prototype harmonizes with the company's readiness for the overall change and, thus, to what extent the design is viable. The test can be made at a workshop by judging the basic idea of the design against hypotheses about the work formulated from insight gained from observations and interviews (e.g., see the example in figure 9.14). If inconsistencies are noted, it becomes necessary to assess whether the design's requirements can realistically be met by changing the work practices or whether the noted inconsistencies are so significant that the design vision must be changed to accommodate the relevant points.

In a design project at a radio station, the IT designers, after experimenting with a vertical prototype, came up with an overall design that was approved by the journalists. On certain points, however, there were premises of the design—i.e., the IT system and its use—that the designers regarded as significantly different from existing practices. To examine the potential consequences of this, the designers carried out a series of follow-up observations. Insight thus obtained was set down in a series of hypotheses about the radio station's work practices, which challenged the design. A workshop was organized, with the prototype available and the hypotheses posted on the walls of the room where the workshop was held. The journalists were asked to identify the links between the hypotheses and the design vision.

The design vision called for making the editorial process involved in composing a daily program more transparent to the journalists and enabling them to see the context in which their feature would be part. However, the observations had prompted hypotheses that, as many types of negotiations took place during the day regarding the composition of the program, increased transparency for the journalists would significantly complicate these negotiations as far as the producer and the presenter were concerned. By putting this contradiction on the agenda, the IT designers set the stage for an explicit design choice to be made. Maintaining the producer and presenter's negotiating position required reducing the IT system's transparency to the journalists. Conversely, maintaining the vision of transparent program planning required major changes to the way decisions about the composition of a daily program were made. The journalists alternately played the roles of producer and performer. As a result, they decided to go with the first alternative, even though it conflicted with what they had originally agreed to based on the prototype test.

Figure 9.14 Example of a mental test of a company's readiness for change

9.10.1 Freehand Drawing

Freehand drawings are representations of the current work practices in the form of "childlike" drawings on large sheets of paper or the like. The idea is to present an overview of the work domain that is being studied in the design project in a single drawing. A freehand drawing will typically be the first product that results as the project group moves from notes of the participants' individual understanding to collaborative representations.

A freehand drawing serves two purposes. First, it gives participants in the project group an opportunity to test their understanding of the work domain. Second, it constitutes a point of reference in the form of a relevant structure that can be called on later in the project.

Producing a freehand drawing typically involves the project group's IT designers presenting their understanding of the work domain in the form of preliminary sketches for a drawing. Workshop participants then set to work, jointly correcting mistakes, refining the drawing, and adding any missing aspects.

Figure 9.15 shows four examples of freehand drawings with varying degrees of "artistic" ambition. The top left drawing focuses on data recorded in the business process of "car rentals." The top right drawing is an overview of the flows of materials and information, plus controls, involved when a main office distributes prices and special offers to a number of stores. The center drawing illustrates the information that a journalist at a radio station needs to be able to access. The top three drawings are all drawn on flip chart sheets. The drawing at the bottom of figure 9.15 is a section of a sheet of paper measuring 3 by 1.5 meters overall. A cross between a freehand drawing and a collage (see section 9.10.2), the drawing illustrates the different steps involved in a company's gathering, evaluation, and distribution of press overviews. Each step is drawn and made into a collage, using clippings from magazines and printouts of computer-generated drawings.

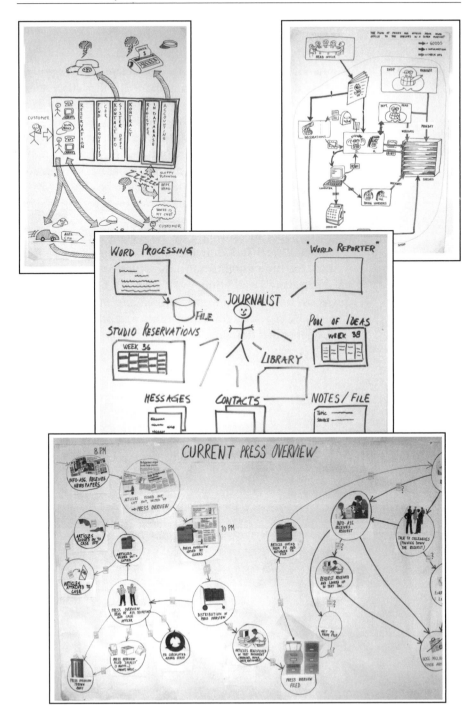

Figure 9.15 Examples of freehand drawings

9.10.2 Collage

Collages are a special kind of freehand drawing. A collage offers a lively, tangible image that includes people by name, represents documents by copies of forms, and illustrates working tools with clippings from magazines, sections of screen shots, and so forth.

The idea behind a collage is to present an overview of the work domain that is being studied in the design project in a single drawing. The collage will typically be the first joint product that is presented to individuals outside the project group. A collage serves two purposes. First, it affords the project group an opportunity to test its understanding of the work domain. Second, it serves as a point of reference in the form of a relevant structure that can be called on later in the project.

Producing a collage typically involves the project group's participants. It expresses their understanding of the work domain and may be based on a freehand drawing. The collage can later be included in the project group's presentations to the steering committee and may also be used in future meetings of the project group. If the project group has an office available, the collage may find a permanent spot on the wall.

Figure 9.16 shows a detail of a collage from a design project at an editorial unit of a radio station. The figure shows only a small section of the total collage (measuring two by three meters). In its entirety, the collage represents the communication and workflows involved in planning, producing, and broadcasting a radio program.

The collage in figure 9.16 illustrates cooperation between the producer and the presenter. At an editorial meeting, ideas for features for the daily program or suggestions for other decisions are submitted to the producer and the presenter. The secretary, Bente, may serve as a connecting link between the editorial meeting and the producer and presenter. Journalists submit features (and other information) in various media (demonstrated by the arrows at the lower left-hand corner). On the basis of this information, the producer and the presenter cooperate closely to develop a plan for the day's program. The central element of the communication involves topics for the program. Thus, the communication revolves around a feature's placement, length, and degree of specificity, along with other suggestions. A program topic may also involve studio guests. In these instances, specific times must be scheduled, technicians need to prepare microphones, and so forth.

A significant part of the communication between the producer and the presenter occurs over the telephone, since they spend most of the day in separate offices seeing to other business. Plans for the day's program are continually discussed with the chief subeditor. Discussions and disagreements may, of course, arise over details of the program's composition, both between the producer and the presenter and between the two of them and the chief subeditor (these disagreements are in figure 9.16 represented by "lightning bolt arrows"). Although the program will not air until late in the afternoon, the producer and performer need to submit a list of contents for the program schedule and,

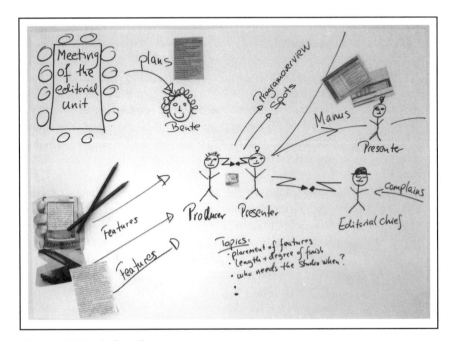

Figure 9.16 Detail of a collage

possibly, a sequence from a finished feature to be used as spots during the day.

When the collage was presented at a meeting, the discussion gave rise to adding a particular aspect of the communication between the presenter and the producer (indicated in figure 9.16 by a star), which was depicted more thoroughly in an available corner of the collage. As the collage also shows, the meeting specified the studio text—co-written by the producer and the presenter, and used by the producer in the studio (located at the center right of figure 9.16)—as a script indicating exact times for individual features.

9.10.3 Dead Sea Scroll

A Dead Sea scroll shows the chronological progress of a business process. Scrolls are especially useful for establishing a joint understanding and overview of complex workflows. Such workflows may involve many actors and an extensive division of labor, resulting in a great need for coordination, or take place over an extended period of time. In consequence, it may be hard for an individual staff member in a department to know what has taken place earlier in the workflow or what will happen next.

Textual in nature, Dead Sea scrolls are written on a roll of paper about a meter wide (wrapping paper or the like), corresponding in length to the extent of the workflow (up to 10 meters)—hence the name. Dead Sea scrolls are made by the project group in cooperation with the people performing roles or functions not represented by the users in the project group. Working with a Dead Sea scroll thus develops a holistic understanding of an overall case flow or workflow. A scroll can be included in the project group's documentation from the in-depth analysis phase. Often, a scroll will serve as a reference point for discussion—for instance, about possible uses of IT.

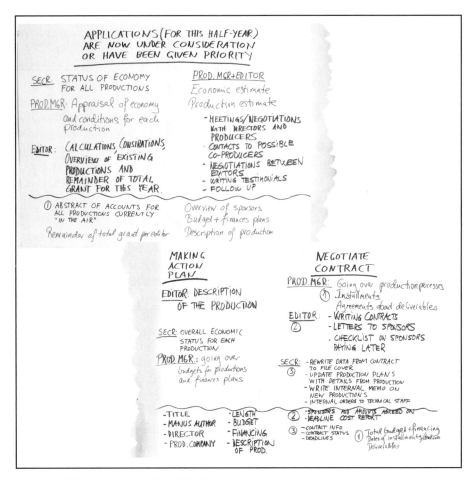

Figure 9.17 Two sections of a Dead Sea Scroll

Figure 9.17 shows an example of a Dead Sea scroll. The left side of this scroll describes the start of the business process. It may be a good idea, as we have done in figure 9.17, to divide a scroll into a top and a bottom part. The top part of the scroll in figure 9.17 describes who does what in the different steps of the process. The bottom part describes the data or information involved. Use of different colors will help clarify contributions made by different people, as well as different roles and functions.

Figure 9.17 shows two sections of a ten-meter Dead Sea scroll from the Danish Film Institute. The scroll describes the overall business process from when an application for production support is received to when the movie premieres. Figure 9.17 shows details of this business process from "a term's proposals under consideration" to "contract negotiations." The bottom third indicates data or information that are central factors in the described process. The scroll was produced at two workshops with the participation of secretaries, script editors, and the head of production. Each person has described his or her part in the process using a different color.

9.10.4 Role List

A role list is an overview of the roles or functions performed by a person in a specific job or by a specific department. The role list is a textual representation that can be used in the in-depth analysis phase to establish an overview of the different functions handled by a specific person or class of employees, in order to clarify problems or challenges with the different roles. A role list can also be used in the innovation phase to clarify ideas for IT support of the different roles and to evaluate whether a design vision answers the needs of the different roles.

The role list in figure 9.18 was used to establish an overview of the different roles played by a central job function. The tasks and conditions of the different roles varied greatly and separating them proved necessary in order to develop ideas for IT support of the different roles. The role list was also used in a design workshop to gather experiences with the use of existing tools and to solidify ideas for IT support of the different roles.

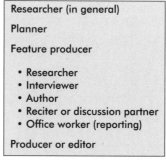

Figure 9.18 Journalist's role list

9.10.5 Communication Model

A communication model describes the communication between a person or a small working group and its context, including:

- Who communicates with whom?
- By what medium do they communicate?
- About what do they communicate?

A communication model will typically be applied to work domains, whose complexity may derive from a high level of communication and coordination of the work.

This model provides an overview of the many conversations taking place between the people in the working group and their context. Accordingly, breakdowns or problems, deriving in communication from one or more of the previous points can be identified for each conversation. Likewise, for a given design idea or a coherent vision, each type of conversation can be reviewed and evaluated to ascertain whether the identified breakdowns and problems have been resolved. The individual conversations modeled may be part of more overall conversations relating to the performance of a larger task taking place over a longer period of time. The flow of such overall conversations can be modeled on a timeline, as described in the next section.

Figure 9.19 shows a communication model of an operations room at an American airport. Four people work in the room: OPS 1, OPS 2, a manager, and a secretary. Some conversations are prompted by operations room tasks (e.g., announcements of departures via "FIDS" to passengers in the departure hall), while other conversations are initiated by the surroundings. This latter scenario is the case, for instance, when a pilot calls the operations room requesting assistance from a mechanic, who is then called by the operations room. Here, the operations room serves as a link between the pilot and the maintenance personnel.

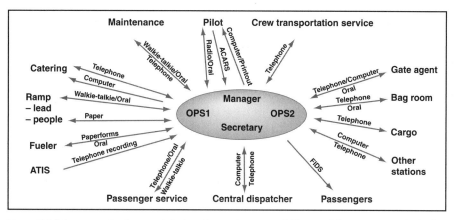

Figure 9.19 A communication model of an "operations room": The model represents only the first two of the three points from the communication model (the "who" and "how"), while the content of the communication (the "what") was described in a separate document for reasons of comprehension

9.10.6 Timelines

A timeline illustrates the flow of conversations involved in tasks performed over a period of time. The time of the individual conversation, as it was concretely observed, is marked on the timeline along with the content of the conversation and the parties to it. In addition, actual breakdowns and problems are noted.

Figure 9.20 shows the flow of conversations involved in determining the number of meals ("the meal count") for the next day's flights. The example is drawn from an operations room at an American airport. The right-hand side of figure 9.20 indicates those parts of the conversations that take place in the operations room, while the left-hand side shows the other actors' parts of the conversation. These include catering (the food supplier), travel agents or the airline's own staff (gate agents and reservation agents), and, finally, the airplane's pilot. Circles on the timeline represent breakdowns and problems, whose content and causes are described separately.

The breakdown situations in figure 9.20 are explicitly indicated in order to mark them as potential candidates for three types of IT support:
• Automation (e.g., automatic data transmission)

- Support (e.g., the system making data available to the operator) A "trigger" function (e.g., a system reminding the operator when to perform a certain action once set conditions have been met)

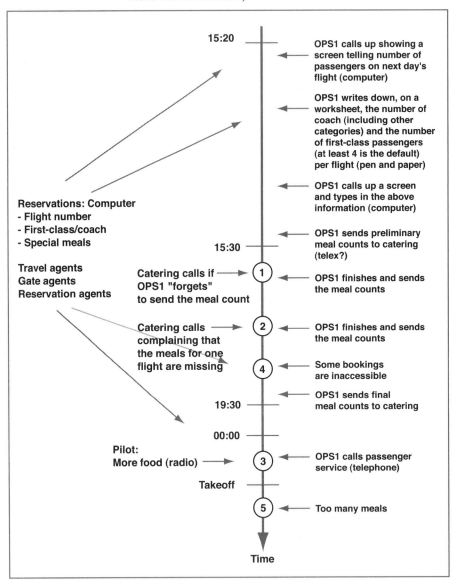

Figure 9.20 Timeline for a meal count in the operations room

9.10.7 Design Sketches

A design sketch provides a comprehensive overview of the elements of a design vision. During the early stages of the in-depth analysis phase, design sketches can offer the first suggestions for elements of a cohesive design proposal and serve as starting points for further design efforts. Later on, during the innovation phase, the design sketches can provide a comprehensive overview of the elements of a coherent design vision.

IT designers may develop a design sketch on the basis of the many ideas for IT usage that typically surface in the course of interviews, observations, thinking-aloud experiments, and so forth. In the in-depth analysis phase, these ideas are listed and possibly compiled into a separate document. These ideas can be presented in collective form as a starting point for an initial discussion at a design-oriented workshop. In the discussion, the project group may relate various elements of the design sketch to specific work situations (represented by collages or communication models) or to specific roles (described in a role list).

The design sketch in figure 9.21 was made following the first project group workshop during the innovation phase. At the workshop, all the design ideas were reviewed and related to the role list. The group clarified how the different ideas for IT usage could aid and improve documents used in planning the editorial unit's programs. The design sketch shows how the various elements contribute to finalization decisions from meetings. Moreover, it shows how data may be transferred to other parts of the design and be reused in other work contexts, with no need to re-enter data and no loss of data. A design sketch—to be read clockwise, starting from the top left corner—also illustrates a daily workflow, as well as how different parts of the design support different work situations.

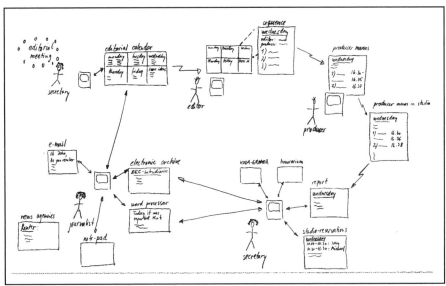

Figure 9.21 Design sketch from a radio station

In finished form, a design sketch can be used as a common framework for representing the uses of IT involved in a design vision, possibly as a supplement to scenarios. Then, the design sketch and supplemental representations can illustrate functional and data relationships or temporal relationships (workflows).

Figure 9.22 shows a design sketch. The sketch provides an overview of all the elements (the systems portfolio) available to each journalist. The circle at the bottom of the figure, linking the five work stations, illustrates how certain parts of the design proposal support cooperation and coordination between individual journalists. The design sketch here serves as an initial overview of the design vision before the project group makes a more detailed review of the individual elements.

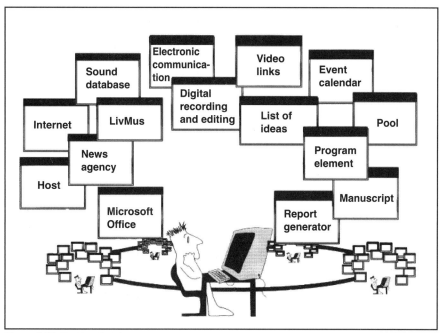

Figure 9.22 Design sketch

Parts of the elements in figure 9.22, and the relations between them, are illustrated by the slightly more detailed design sketch in figure 9.23. This design sketch shows how the various editorial units of the radio station can book an event and indicate their chosen angle for covering it. Data from the event calendar can be dragged into the list of ideas and from there into the program manager. Ideas evolve into program elements, which are linked to the program's manuscript, broadcasted, and finally used by the report generator.

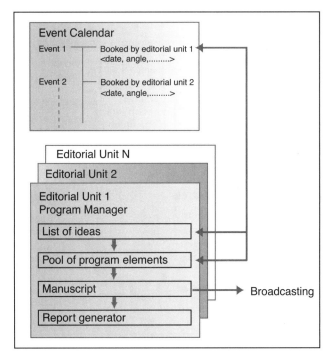

Figure 9.23 Design sketch of six elements from (the right-hand side of) figure 9.22. This figure shows the relationships between the elements

9.11 Future Workshop

Technique	Phases	Principles	Knowledge areas	Representation tools
Future workshop	3,4	1,2	A,B	Open notes on big sheets of paper

Sources: Kensing (1986); Kensing and Madsen (1991); Jungk and Müllert (1987).

The objective of a future workshop is to create an initial joint proposal for changing a situation that a group of people find unsatisfactory. Over the course of half a day to two days, the group establishes a joint overview of what is wrong with the current situation and develops various ideas for improving it. The workshop concludes with the group developing a plan for implementing the ideas that are assessed as realistic. In a design project, the future workshop allows the project group to quickly gather various viewpoints in a company and perform an initial analysis of them, for possible use in the continuing efforts. Future workshops are an especially useful technique when large groups, such as an entire department staff, are collectively contributing to a design project.

A future workshop is divided into five phases: preparation, critique, fantasy, realization and follow-up. A workshop may be organized by the project group and coordinated by one or two so-called foremen (facilitators). The structure of a future workshop alternates between collective brainstorming and work in small groups. If the workshop is short, a lower priority must be put on group work. The aim of brainstorming is to provide all the participants opportunities for expressing their dissatisfaction with the current situation or to freely generate ideas for alternatives. Critiques and ideas are formulated in keywords and written on large sheets of paper on the wall, which serve as an open note and as inspiration for further brainstorming. The aim of this group work is to analyze and expand the critique and ideas for presentation to the other participants.

The aim of a future workshop is for all participants to gain a shared understanding of the problematic situation, to experience how others perceive it, to give structure to the expressed ideas for improvement, and to draft a plan. The first stage of the plan needs to be detailed enough for everyone to know who will be doing what in the time following the workshop. The project group compiles the results into a brief report, containing an overview of the critiques, structured ideas for improvement, and a plan.

If the situation is marked by conflict between various staff groups, between departments, or between the company and its suppliers and buyers, we recommend organizing several future workshops where the participants in each workshop have shared interests. This will allow the participants to clarify their position. Mixing staff and their managers can be a problem. It may not facilitate the open environment that a future workshop requires. If several workshops are held, the coordination of critiques, ideas, and actions to prioritize as a step in the design project becomes a task for the project group and steering committee to handle after all the workshops are done.

By way of its focus on critique and ideas, a future workshop is especially relevant in the in-depth analysis and innovation phases. It may be held to gather more opinions than are represented in the project group. Or a workshop may be held after the initial interviews if, in the project group's evaluation, the true nature of problems in the relevant work domains remains unclear. In both cases, a future workshop will also contribute to anchoring, since a larger group of people is drawn into formulating the problems and their possible solutions.

In our experience, a future workshop also generates considerable enthusiasm among the participants. When using this technique, as with other ways of realizing the principle of genuine user participation, management should be ready to include staff opinions in its priorities. Otherwise, the technique could have an outright negative effect on the project and should not be employed.

Future workshops contribute to two of the six knowledge areas targeted by a design project (see figure 8.2). The critique phase may yield ideas for relevant structuring of the users' current work practices (knowledge area A) and the fantasy phase may inspire design visions and design proposals (knowledge area B).

In the following section, we describe how to approach each of the five phases of the MUST method and their results. Figure 9.24 shows three suggestions for dividing the time between the four phases of the future workshop relative to the various durations of a future workshop.

Phase	2-day schedule	1-day schedule	1/2-day schedule
Preparation phase Designing the room; introducing the theme and working method	1 hour	1/2 hour	1/2hour
Critique phase Creating a richer, common image of the problematic situation	4 hours	2 1/2 hours	1 hour
Fantasy phase Generating visions of an improved situation without restrictions	6 hours	2 hours	1 1/2 hours
Realization phase Bringing the visions down to earth and developing a plan	4 hours	2 hours	1 1/2 hours

Figure 9.24 Three suggestions for structuring future workshops of various durations

9.11.1 Preparation Phase

The project group is responsible for picking the theme of the future workshop. The theme should be as specific as possible and reflect the project group's preliminary understanding of the situation. A possible theme might be "new technology to support communication with clients and suppliers," or "how to organize the work to better use standard system X."

The project group should write an invitation that states the objective, lays out the theme, and describes the structure, time, and place of the future workshop. Experience has shown that approximately twenty participants is an optimum number for creating the necessary dynamics. A suitable room should be obtained, with space enough for everyone to work together and in small groups, as well as for down time, dining, and so forth. The project group should also make sure to provide all workshop materials, including large sheets of paper, markers, tape, and food, if the workshop is of longer duration.

To foster a relaxed atmosphere, the foremen of the future workshop may ask the participants to help design the room, such as setting up chairs in a half-circle facing the wall where the large sheets of paper have been taped up. The foremen start by introducing the technique and their own role. They act as moderators and make sure that the timetable is kept. They see to it that everyone has his or her say and encourage new ways of considering the situation, while remaining neutral in terms of the subjects being discussed and the potential courses of action. The idea is to make it the participants' workshop.

9.11.2 Critique Phase

The critique phase begins by everyone being asked to critique the current situation in keyword form. The critique may be open, or the participants may take turns if it is hard to get everyone to speak up. Issues may revolve around the organization of the work, the available tools, relationships to customers and suppliers, internal relations within the company, qualifications, and so forth. The keywords are written on large sheets of paper to serve as a common, open note and as inspiration for further brainstorming. Long-winded argumentation is "banned" (the limit is roughly thirty seconds for each participant per turn). The point is to get some brainstorming going, enabling the participants to unload their own points of criticism and be inspired by the other participants' points.

The goal is to get the participants to make new connections, give them a shared experience of what needs to be changed, and make them aware of the fact that they are not alone in their criticism. The critique phase ensures the creation of a common foundation for the work in subsequent phases.

Some companies have no tradition for openly voicing criticism. In such cases, it is up to the foremen to get the critique going by asking questions such as "Although you are generally satisfied with your job, could certain things be improved?" Another way of evoking responses from participants is directly referring to criticism stated in interviews—though without referring to specific people who made these points.

When the foremen are unable to elicit any new points of criticism, or when the allotted time is up, the participants will prioritize points of criticism that need to be worked on further. To promote comprehension, some foremen elect to order the points of criticism by theme, since many of the points will be related. At this point, a vote should be taken to determine the most important keywords or themes—for instance, by giving each participant five points to divide among the keywords. The vote can either be open or by secret ballot. Rejected themes are saved for future treatment by the project group. The keywords or themes that receive the most points are assigned for work in small groups (of four to five people) to expand the critique. Here, there are no restrictions on the discussion and the groups generally organize their own work.

After these small group discussions, the participants come back together and present their critiques according to theme, possibly supplemented by the others. If the themes are too numerous, another vote is taken to decide which ones to continue working on in the workshop. The rest are again saved for future treatment.

9.11.3 Fantasy Phase

The objective here is to develop ideas and utopian proposals for the future situation without any kind of restrictions (which will be returned to in the realization phase). How would the participants like to have the results of their work appear to co-workers and customers? How would they like the work to be organized? What forms of technology would they like to be able to access? What qualifications would they like to have? What should the communication with suppliers and customers be like? These are some questions that the foremen can use to introduce the fantasy phase.

The method of this phase is the same as the previous one: brainstorming, with brief periods allotted for speaking and notes written in keyword format on large sheets of paper. The foreman should step in to block such statements that hinder creativity, such as "that's not realistic!" Sometimes it can be hard to get this phase going because the participants are not used to thinking creatively or developing wild ideas together with co-workers, or because they are afraid of "looking stupid" in front of the others. If this happens, the foreman can suggest taking starting points in the critique keywords and turning them around into positive statements, or making a drawing of an ideal work situation and describing it to the others. Games for stimulating imagination can be played, depending on how far the foremen think they can make the participants go. In the fantasy phase, it may be useful for the foremen to encourage participants to change their perspectives (i.e., viewing the situation from another position, incorporating different aspects, or proposing alternative interpretations).

When the foremen are unable to elicit any new ideas, or the allotted time is up, the keywords are grouped into themes, or specific keywords are made to serve as starting points. A vote is taken on which themes to continue working on. The rest are saved for future treatment. If no division into themes has been made yet, one is made at this point, in order to aid subsequent group work. Each group is assigned one or more themes. The task now involves gathering and developing the ideas into one or more utopian proposals for improving the problematic situation. Each group will try to integrate as many of the keywords relating to the group's theme as possible.

9.11.4 Realization Phase

The realization phase starts with the groups presenting their utopian proposals. Some can perhaps be combined. Otherwise, a new vote is taken to determine which proposals to continue debating in the workshop. The project group saves the rest for future treatment.

Next, the selected utopias are evaluated to assess whether they can be realized under the present conditions at the company or whether new conditions should or could be established. At times, it may be necessary to obtain evaluation and consultation from outside the workshop as far as realizing some of the utopias is concerned. This should be noted in the plan that is written toward the end of the phase. In this phase, criticism is once again welcomed, this time in order to point out conditions that are viewed as barriers to realizing the utopias. The most unrealistic proposals are sifted out. The remaining proposals are once again discussed in small groups, which develop plans for activities that need to be initiated to realize the proposals. The groups come together and present their plans, which are then shaped into a common plan. The workshop concludes by detailing the first steps of the plan, so that everyone knows who will be doing what.

9.11.5 Follow-Up Phase

The project group writes a report summarizing the critique, visions, and plan. In addition, the group is responsible for following up on the plan or for handing over aspects of it that lie beyond the project group's field of competency to others in the company.

9.12 Mapping

Technique	Phases	Principles	Knowledge areas	Representation tools
Mapping	3,4	2,4	A,B,C	Diagnostic maps Virtual maps

Sources: Andersen et al. (1990), section 6.4; Lanzara and Mathiassen (1985).

Mapping is a technique for treating a problematic situation, sketching out alternative solution models for the situation, and assessing what it will take to solve the problem.

Mapping can be used to structure and capture opinions expressed in a discussion among several people regarding problems and potential solutions. This, of course, requires the group to be prepared for a fairly open discussion of the problems. Problems, ideas for solutions, and so forth are written on a large board or on big sheets of paper and organized into columns under different headings. These notations constitute a map of the problematic situations.

Mapping is an effective technique for establishing an overview and joint understanding of a problematic situation, while describing possible courses of action for leaving the situation behind. It may be used by an individual or by a group, allowing the participating actors to express and solidify their statements, interpretations, and ideas for solutions regarding a situation that they all want to improve.

There are two common mapping techniques:

- *Diagnostic mapping.* This technique focuses on analyzing (diagnosing) problematic situations. Possible problems, causes, and consequences of each problematic situation are outlined, along with any ideas for solutions. Various statements about causes, consequences, and so forth are examined to reveal connections or contradictions and to test whether they are serious and credible.
- *Virtual mapping.* This technique focuses on testing the ideas for change (such as potential design solutions) before an attempt is made to implement them. In other words, the technique describes potential and desirable (virtual) actions and situations. The project group outlines the actions required for realizing each idea, the consequences of doing so, along with an evaluation of the outcome in terms of the problematic situation that an idea seeks to improve or resolve. Virtual maps can be used in combination with diagnostic maps by further analyzing the ideas in a diagnostic map with a virtual map.

The mapping techniques apply to problematic situations (diagnostic maps) or ideas for change (virtual maps) that need to be understood systematically before they can be put into action. Potential mapping situations include:

- As a follow-up to interviews. On the basis of an interview, a diagnostic map is made for the interviewed staff members, possibly in collaboration with them. Analyzing an interview frequently reveals a number of problematic situations, including some that were not sufficiently covered in the interview. Following up on an interview may involve mapping such situations in collaboration with the interviewees in order to create an overview of inexpediencies in the interviewees' work and generate ideas for improvement.
- When working together with a group of staff members (a department or other group), cooperating on tasks in day-to-day operations, and establishing an overview of problems for possible inclusion in the design project, along with ideas for solutions. In preparation for a mapping session, each participant may profitably make his or her own map, specifying his or her individual take on the problems.

- As a project group tool for outlining and establishing an overview of the total volume of problems, needs, and solution proposals that the design project has revealed so far—in order, for instance, to assist the steering committee in its prioritization.
- Internally in the project group, if the group finds itself in a problematic project management situation. The project group can use diagnostic maps if the group feels it has run into significant problems or is losing its overview. The project group can likewise employ virtual maps to survey possible courses of action for leaving the problematic situation behind.

Mapping is aimed at developing knowledge in knowledge areas A, B, and C from figure 8.2. Diagnostic maps especially target knowledge areas A and B and the relations between them. Virtual maps especially target knowledge areas B and C and the relations between them. Diagnostic maps are particularly effective during the in-depth analysis phase when the focus is on gaining an understanding of present work practices or experienced problems and needs. Virtual maps are especially useful in the innovation phase when the focus is on formulating and evaluating design proposals, plus planning their implementation.

The mapping techniques are usually organized in the form of a one- to two-hour session. Someone may be picked to serve as the recorder. For the session, a board or big sheets of paper, for example, a flip chart should be provided and, preferably, pads of adhesive notes should be supplied as well.

For diagnostic as well as virtual maps, situations are analyzed, discussed, and set down in keyword form in one of four columns under a different heading. The headings for diagnostic maps are: problems, causes, consequences, and ideas for solutions. The headings for virtual maps are: ideas for solutions, actions, consequences, and evaluation.

Mapping can be used as a technique for understanding and presenting aspects of a process, such as "poor cooperative environment in the project group," or "it takes too long to gather the information required for quarterly reports."

Here, the focus is on how to move from the problematic situation to a more expedient one. This may involve testing one or more of the participants' "wild ideas."

Mapping can be used as a technique for understanding and presenting aspects of a product. Points of departure may be taken in ideas for a specific design involving a future system. Here, the technique can help put a focus on, and test, what it will take to implement a design idea. A technological solution may turn out not to be relevant in terms of the problems that are experienced, or perhaps, living with the consequences of a problem may seem preferable to the cost of eliminating it.

In addition to these mapping objectives and applications, the mapping structure itself may serve as a form of documentation. The results of a design project can be presented in comprehensive form using the map column headings. Diagnostic maps may serve as a collective report to the steering committee by briefly presenting the problems and needs in table form using the headings from the diagnostic map. Reports to the steering committee proposing alternative solutions that need to be prioritized may likewise be presented under the headings of the virtual map to present an overview of the actions required for implementing each solution and the costs involved.

9.12.1 Diagnostic Maps

The following is an example of a group of people meeting and mapping a problematic situation using a diagnostic map. In preparation for the session, the group should agree on what problematic situation or situations they will be treating. The definition of a problematic situation serves as the theme and heading of the diagnostic map. If several problematic situations are treated, a map should be made for each. Problematic situations should preferably be described and defined using the terms of the situation that is experienced as problematic.

Ideally, each participant should have prepared for the mapping session by making a map, specifying that individual's take on the problematic situation. In the process, each will prepare the arguments informing his or her own take on the situation.

The mapping is done on a board or on big sheets of paper on the wall with four (empty) columns headed: problems, causes, consequences, and ideas for solutions (see figure 9.25). The problematic situation that is being studied provides the title of the map.

Start by listing the possible interpretations of the problematic situation, that is, problem candidates. Write down all the suggestions in the problems column in sentences. Let the person who suggested the problem propose the wording. Other participants may also help define the problem, but they are not very helpful if they merely reinterpret or rephrase the problem. If that happens, the group should stick with the original formulation of the problem and add the other formulations to the list as separate candidates. If adhesive notes are used, it is easy to move the suggestion to a different spot on the map. Often, something that is perceived as a problem later turns out to really be a cause or a consequence.

Next, take up the problems one by one and outline the causes, consequences, and potential solutions for each. There are some questions that can help frame this task:
- *Cause:* What is causing the problem? What are the reasons we are having this problem? Where do the causes of the problem lie?
- *Consequence:* What are the most negative consequences of the problem? What consequences and additional problems does the original problem entail? What effects of the problem are we unwilling to accept?

Problems	Causes	Consequences	Ideas for solutions

Figure 9.25 Template for a diagnostic map

• *Ideas for solutions:* What potential solutions to the problem can we come up with? What do we imagine would eliminate or remedy the problem?

If the consequences of a problem are few, or there are no suggested unacceptable consequences, the problem may be superficial—that is, the interpretation of the problematic situation is irrelevant and invalid. If, on closer consideration, the consequences of a problem are found to be bearable, the problem does not warrant further study.

It may be hard to distinguish among problems, consequences, and causes. The consequences of a problem are perhaps seen as constituting problems in themselves. If a consequence of a problem is regarded as a significant separate problem, we recommend putting it down on the list as a new problem (for later consideration) and return to the problem being discussed.

Figure 9.26 shows a diagnostic map from a department of a video-rental company. The problem here involves the risk of customers reserving a video that is not in stock when they come to pick it up. The project group did the mapping of this problem in collaboration with staff from the affected department. Figure 9.26 is one result of the mapping session. The mapping was done on a flip chart with colored adhesive notes. The notes were prioritized from the top down and organized into cohesive groups. Notes that have been crossed out are the project group's suggested causes and solutions that the invited staff members considered irrelevant (see figure 9.26).

9.12.2 Virtual Maps

The approach to virtual maps is basically the same as for diagnostic maps. The title for a virtual map may be the same problematic situation as on the diagnostic map, but the focus is now forward-looking rather than analytical and diagnostic. The agenda for a virtual map is how to get out of the problematic situation—what actions must be taken, what their consequences will be, and how to evaluate the resulting future situation. For an example of a virtual map template, see figure 9.27.

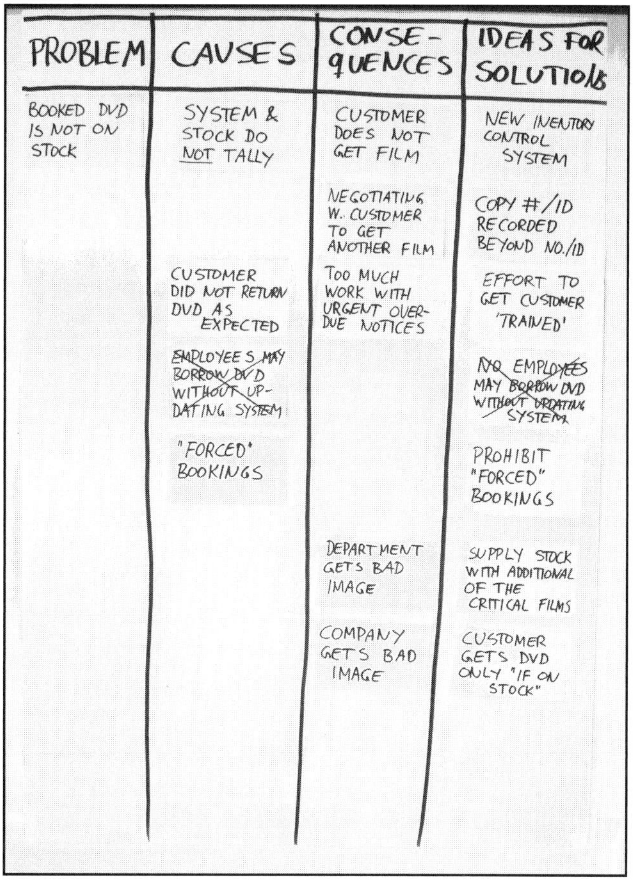

Figure 9.26 Example of a diagnostic map

The ideas for solutions column of a virtual map may describe technical ideas—both design ideas and more broadly formulated future situations that one would like to see realized. Ideas for solutions from the diagnostic map

Ideas for solutions	Actions	Consequences	Evaluation

Figure 9.27 Template for a virtual map

may also serve as starting points when working with a combination of mapping techniques. For each "idea for a solution" the participants discuss and outline which specific actions could, and should, be initiated for implementing it.

The expected consequences of such actions are also calculated and, finally, the situation that would result is evaluated. This should be regarded as a concluding (and, frequently, a very brief) evaluation of whether the end result satisfactorily answers the original problem: How does this situation appear in terms of the starting point (the problematic situation)? In short, did we get what we were looking for?

Virtual maps are a useful tool for presenting a series of alternative design solutions to be prioritized. The maps can also serve to provide an initial overview of a plan for implementing design visions. Then, the ideas for solutions column lists elements of the design visions, the actions column constitutes the plan's overall activities, the consequences column offers ideas for intermediate products, and the evaluation column provides an outline of a cost-benefit evaluation.

9.13 Prompted Reflection

Technique	Phases	Principles	Knowledge areas	Representation tools
Prompted reflection	3	2	A	Freehand drawings Notes

Source: Kensing (1998).

Prompted reflection is a useful technique for IT designers facing a complex work practice that they have a hard time grasping. The complexity may be due to the IT designers' unfamiliarity with materials, tools, work processes, and products involved in the work, or because the work requires many years of schooling and experience. In the in-depth analysis phase, prompted reflection can be used as a technique for producing relevant representations of the users' current work and may also provide the first ideas for new IT usage. Prompted observation may be appropriate when the IT designers have conducted a series of interviews that produced no significant understanding of what is involved in the company's work, how it is organized, or what the potential for IT support is. They have ruled out observation, because the staff members apparently "only" sit at their computers with no significant degree of interaction. The work domain may seem incomprehensible, even disorderly. However, in order to develop sustainable visions of new IT usage, the IT designers need to gain an understanding of the work—which frequently, upon closer examination, turns out to be quite well-organized.

Developing prototypes can be a way of engaging staff members in dialogue. However, if they have only vague notions about their needs, and if the IT designer is not familiar with their work domain, it may be hard to figure out what part of the work to focus on and for what ideas for future IT systems to develop prototypes.

In such situations, the IT designers' first task is to ask broad questions such as "What internal or external goals and needs entail what requirements for changing the work domain? What problems and ideas for solutions do the various actors in the work domain have?" Prompted reflection is a technique for arriving at productive answers to such questions—answers that may be included in the project group's further efforts.

The technique can be divided into four overall activities: preparation, workshops, analysis, and discussion of results. Having selecting a theme, the IT designer organizes a workshop with two or more staff members, who each makes a drawing of his or her work on a big sheet of paper and explains it to the others. A drawing may illustrate a work process or a product, indicating the terms and tools that staff members use in their work. The IT designer acts as moderator, asking questions to make the staff reflect on what works well and what is inexpedient within the existing work organization and current IT systems. The IT designer documents the process in notes or by audio or video recording. The IT designer subsequently uses the drawings, notes, and possible recordings from the workshop to support his or her own reflections on—and structuring of—the work practice. This may require coining new terms, making generalizations, or describing and illustrating work processes in new ways to better enable a discussion of the needs and the potential for change. Follow-up interviews or data gathering by other means may also be required. In conclusion, the IT designer presents his or her representations to the workshop's participants and the rest of the project group for evaluation and correction of errors and shortcomings.

9.13.1 Preparation

Select a theme that is hard to grasp—for instance, the flow or intermingled stages of a certain work process; the communication structure enabling the necessary coordination; project management, if the work is organized by project; or quality assurance.

Select a group of staff members to participate in a series of workshops. Choose participants who can provide knowledge, experience, and interests that have been hard to uncover by such techniques as interviews and document analysis. Ask each participant to prepare for the workshop by making a freehand drawing on a large sheet of paper that illustrates how he or she understands the selected theme. Have the members of the group indicate what tools and materials they use in their work, the products of the work, and what relations with others are required for performing the work. They should use no specific formalisms to represent the theme. Rather, they should use their own terms. On the drawing, they may also mount copies of documents or screen shots to illustrate their work (see the freehand drawings and collages in sections 9.10.1 and 9.10.2). The point is not for them to make an idealized version of their work, but to represent what they perceive is actually taking place. If getting members of the group to draw is a bit like pulling teeth, the IT designer should make a drawing of how he or she understands the theme.

9.13.2 Workshops

The two participants in each workshop take turns—without interruption for anything but clarifying questions—to explain his or her drawing to the other person. Next, the IT designer from the project group moderates a discussion between the two, asking possible clarifying questions. The aim is to use the drawings as a means to make the participants reflect on and put into words what the theme involves. The moderator's job is to encourage the participants to explain and discuss the theme in their own words and terms. Moreover, the moderator or an assistant should document the process by taking notes or by an audio or video recording.

The point here is not to get the participants to agree on the theme. Rather, it is the moderator's job to help them understand the other person's interpretation. At times this can be difficult if the participants are more intent on convincing one another than on depicting the situation. The desired outcome of the workshop is enriching the participants' own understanding of the theme, while increasing their understanding of the other person's point of view. This is a requirement for arriving at a shared understanding of what the situation requires. The aim for the moderator is to understand the terms the participants use, significant aspects of their work practice, the products or services they supply, as well as what works well and what is inexpedient. Finally, ideas for improvement may also arise.

Continue workshops until all the selected participants have explained their drawing to a co-worker. The IT designer may also choose to link a series of workshops by having a participant move on to a new workshop with another co-worker and so on, until the cycle is completed. Or, simply call them in two at a time. The advantage of linking workshops—or even having all participants present at the same time—is exposing them to multiple points of view on the needs for possible changes and what those changes might involve. This procedure promotes the anchoring principle, but, of course, the participants have to be able to set aside the required amount of time.

9.13.3 Analysis

The next step in the prompted reflection process is analyzing the documents—the drawings, notes, and possible recordings from the workshops. This is an intellectually demanding task and may take many different forms, depending on what media were used for documentation and how much time can be spent on the analysis. To gradually build up his or her understanding of the theme and to become a better moderator at the next workshop, the IT designer who served as moderator should always perform an initial analysis immediately after each workshop while events are still fresh in mind.

If audio or video recordings were used, the moderator should start by writing a log of the content of the recordings and the notes. Specially developed IT systems are available for supporting transcription, for inserting notes into the transcript, and for linking events and statements across the transcript.

As an alternative, the moderator can study the drawings, read through the notes, review the recordings several times, and write a summary of what took place and what was said. Every detail does not need to be included. Rather, the moderator should focus on significant subjects, statements that are repeated in various wordings, conflicting interpretations of the same phenomenon, problems with the work, and any ideas for improvement. On the basis of the log, the moderator should pick out elements of the notes and recordings for closer analysis.

In the project team's analysis, the drawings, notes, and recording transcripts serve to support reflection on the work and how to improve it. The point is to discern structures in the work process as well as in the interrelations of staff members and their use of materials and other available resources. One may look for specific issues, or issues may be generated by working with the drawings, notes, and recordings.

Next, the project team should start grouping and linking instances of events or statements in order to make generalizations and hypotheses about the selected theme and the issues in focus. This requires the project team to study the drawings, read the transcripts, and review the recordings several times, while grouping and regrouping issues and statements until a pattern forms or a basis is created for formulating issues for later examination. Hypotheses and generalizations formulated in the analysis should always refer back to something that was heard or observed in a recording or set down in one's own notes.

Hypotheses and generalizations may revolve around certain terms used in different or similar situations, good or problematic practices, causes of repeated breakdowns, ideas for improvement, differences and similarities in perceived relations between identified issues, and so forth. Each of these preliminary conclusions is linked to the observations that prompted it. This makes it easier to assess its validity in the next step.

9.13.4 Discussing the Results

Regardless of whether recordings or simply notes were used for analysis, the next step involves the IT designers evaluating the preliminary conclusions and discussing issues arising from the analysis with the rest of the project group and the participants in the workshop series. In preparation for a joint meeting or separate meetings, a report can be written describing what has been discovered about the selected theme. The aim of such meetings is challenging the preliminary conclusions, while giving the participants new knowledge about the theme. The IT designers should pay attention to any new issues and angles that might arise. They can try stimulating the discussion by comparing their own interpretations with what is said at the meeting with statements from the workshops. If recordings were made, segments of them may be subjected to a joint analysis. Again, the participants should relate what they are saying to what can be observed or heard in the recordings and what the drawings make clear.

The designers should think of challenges to their own interpretations as sources of further insight into the theme. Again, they need to document the procedures in notes or recordings for use in the further work.

The IT designers should return to the notes and recordings. At this point, they look for things that confirm or invalidate what the meeting yielded and adjust the report accordingly. The designers continue to do so until nothing new of significance emerges or until there is no more time to spend on that part of the analysis. In our experience, two or three rounds of this kind of editing will be sufficient.

This process will serve to increase not just the IT designers', but also the staff's, understanding of the selected theme and its relationship to the change that the design project is preparing. Issues that remain unresolved, or on which no agreement is produced, are candidates for follow-up interviews, observation sessions, thinking-aloud experiments, or document analysis.

9.14 Company Visit

Technique	Phases	Principles	Knowledge areas	Representation tools
Company visit	4	2,3	C,F	Summary

Company visits are a vital technique in the innovation phase and when trying to obtain firsthand experience with work practices. This technique is highly effective for gaining insight into experiences with new technological options (see figure 8.2). A company visit involves the project group paying a visit to an organization that uses the specific system that the design project is considering or that uses technology of the type that the design project aims to clarify.

There are a number of different techniques for clarifying new technological options:
- Studying suppliers' sales material describing their systems. This is a good way to gain an initial overview of the different products on the market.
- Witnessing supplier demonstrations of their systems, either with the suppliers or at fairs and expos. Here, the focus will usually be on a system's functionality and interface.
- Studying descriptions and reviews of systems in various trade magazines. Available reviews may offer more critical views of the system. Occasionally, comparisons can be made between the products of different suppliers (benchmarking).
- Organizing tests of vertical prototypes. This offers the advantage of the company's own staff gaining experience

with a technological option. However, such experience will often be limited to a first impression of parts of the envisioned systems.

- Testing parts of an envisioned standard system for a period, if the supplier will lend or lease the system. In such pilot experiments, the system usually will not be fully integrated—for example, it uses a database of test data. However, it allows selected functions of a given generic system to be tested in the context of the company.
- Finally, a company visit can provide information on how a system is used, as well as opportunities to hear about the experiences of management and staff with implementing and running the systems.

Of the techniques described in this section, company visits are among the few that offer opportunities for experiencing a technological option in an entirely realistic context. Observing a system in use, or personally testing a system, contributes to concrete experience (knowledge area F in figure 8.2). Moreover, company visits are the technique that gives the truest impression of the experiences others have with a system, including its organizational and qualificational consequences.

Sometimes organizing a company visit may pose a problem if the only companies that might be relevant to visit are direct competitors. Then, it may be worthwhile to look at a corresponding use of IT in a different industry. However, most public or semipublic corporations have no such competitive issues—on the contrary, many public corporations will agree to a visit without hesitation.

Company visits may be set up via personal contacts, by cold calls to other companies, or via the supplier of the system that is being considered. The supplier is often more than willing to set up the contact or directly organize a visit with a reference customer.

Company visits may provide the project group with valuable and constructive experiences for their further efforts, which would otherwise be difficult or impossible to gain before the company itself implements the system (see the example in figure 9.28). A company visit will, of course, be most effective if the project group is able to carry out various exploratory activities, including

- interviews with management representatives about their aims and experiences with the system;
- interviews with IT managers about operating and maintaining the system and its integration with other systems;
- interviews with various types of users of the system about their experiences with it (functionality, work organization, qualification requirements, etc.);
- observation of the system in use;
- video recordings of selected system-usage situations;
- project group members testing parts of the system.

A company visit may be documented in a summary or by video recordings. Video recordings are often a highly effective way of communicating and anchoring the project group's impressions of the system to and with other stakeholders.

As an activity in the innovation phase of a design project at a radio station, the project group paid a visit to a radio station in Vienna, which at the time was one of the most sophisticated in Europe in terms of applying digital recording, editing, and broadcasting technologies. This one-day visit offered the project group opportunities to observe all the different activities at the radio station, from planning through broadcasting of the daily programs. Although the project group had studied digital technology beforehand, both at a big trade fair and with a supplier, the visit provided a wealth of new impressions.

A member of the project group videotaped how journalists personally edited their interviews using digital technology and how the evening news broadcast was presented in a mix of prerecorded and live features, without requiring technical assistance at any point—the radio station was operated entirely by journalists.

The project group also witnessed how the radio station automated its overnight program. The broadcast was "recorded" over a few hours during the day: a selector system automatically picked all the music titles to play overnight, and a journalist reviewed the segues between the musical numbers, adding the connecting features, including such announcements as "It's three minutes past four in the morning . . ."

Figure 9.28 Example of the results of a company visit

9.15 Experimenting with Prototypes

Technique	Phases	Principles	Knowledge areas	Representation tools
Experiment-ing with prototypes	4	**1, 2, 4**	B,E	Mock-ups Prototypes

Sources: Ehn and Kyng (1991); Floyd (1984); Budde et al. (1992); Blomberg et al. (1996); Grønbæk, Kyng, and Mogensen (1997).

A prototype is a simple version of part of an envisioned IT system. A prototype should not, of course, be confused with a finished system. However, a prototype offers significant advantages over abstract representations of a system by displaying specific and tangible qualities resembling a finished system in selected areas. Accordingly, a prototype can be subjected to a whole other level of qualitative evaluation regarding its planned usage situation thus supporting genuine user participation. Running the prototype in a simulated or real usage context allows users to concretely relate to the design of its functionality, interface, and forms of interaction. Experience has proven the wisdom of conducting such experiments, both very early on and at a later stage of the design process.

The aim of experimenting with prototypes is to produce experiences—and make constructive use of these experiences in the continuing efforts in efforts towards anchoring visions. Experimenting with prototypes consists of three activities—developing the prototype, testing the prototype, and evaluating the experiences—that are repeated several times in sequence (see figure 9.29).

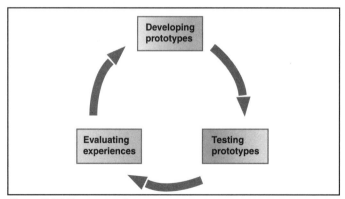

Figure 9.29 The prototyping process

9.15.1 Mock-Ups and Horizontal Prototypes

Very simple prototypes, in the form of *mock-ups* or *horizontal prototypes,* can be used early on in the innovation phase of the MUST process. Simple prototypes have no functionality whatsoever and are quick and inexpensive to make and change. Perhaps they contain only the top level of all aspects of a design. Prototypes may be presented as a mock-up of screen shots on an overhead projector, or as models on paper and board (see figure 9.30). A mock-up may also be in the form of flat screen shots in a presentation or graphics program.

Figure 9.30 shows two mock-ups at the top and a design sketch at the bottom, illustrating the relationship between the mock-ups and an overall systems design for the editorial office of the Nordic Film Institutes. All three of these graphic depiction pictures were made on flip chart sheets. The very top of the mock-up sketches out two windows in a screen shot. The front window presents a spreadsheet-like overview of the productions that a script editor is considering. Each production can be opened in a separate window—as shown by the back window in the screen shot—providing a detailed overview of the production. The center mock-up in figure 9.30 also presents a spreadsheet-like overview, this time showing all the editorial office's current productions. The bottom part of the mock-up indicates who logs in the financial data shown in the overview. The bottom third of the figure shows a detail of a design sketch (see section

9.10.7) for the overall system. A detailed description of the significance of the arrows in figure 9.30 in the design sketch was attached separately. The left-hand side of the design sketch indicates the top mock-up, which represents the editors' private financial support system. The center mock-up represents the public financial support system of the head of production and the secretary.

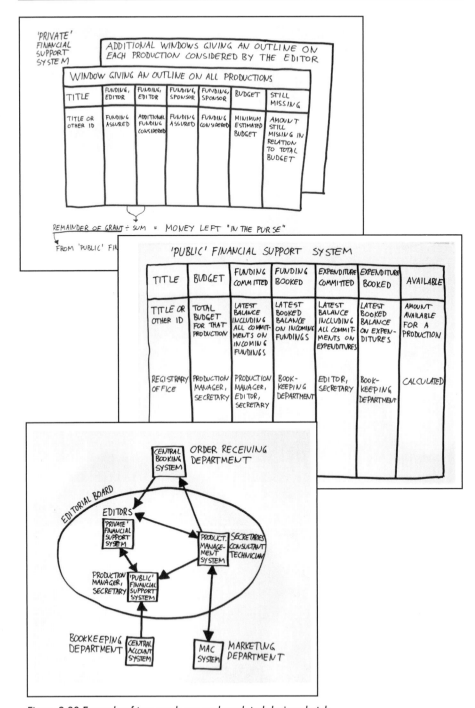

Figure 9.30 Example of two mock-ups and a related design sketch

Horizontal prototypes, mock-ups, and the like can only be tested in a simulated context. This requires creating an artificial context for the prototype and its projected incorporation into a workflow. Thus, knowledge gained from a test of a horizontal prototype is limited to knowledge area B (see figure 8.2). Accordingly, an IT designer should be very careful not to draw any definite conclusions from experiments with mockups and horizontal prototypes—in other words, the designer should always be aware of the limitations of the experiment. Nevertheless, as experience shows, making the design concrete and tangible early on in the process provides initial experiences that prove invaluable in the continuing design efforts.

Other early experiments can be made with demo versions of standard products. The in-line analysis phase of a design project may have identified an objective calling for the use of standard products. These products will often be available in demo versions, which are useful for experiments in a design project. Though their functionality and interface design are fixed, experimenting with demo versions will yield experiences with different ways of organizing the use of the system, as well as with how the system relates to other parts of the design or to existing IT systems in the relevant work domain. Figure 9.31 shows an example of the use of horizontal prototypes in a design project.

A design project was undertaken at the editorial unit of a radio station to clarify computer support for planning, broadcasting, and reporting on a daily program. After a period of exploration, a project group, comprised of three journalists, a secretary, and an IT designer, produced an idea for an overall design (see the example in figure 9.20).

The IT designer made a very simple horizontal prototype, in the form of screen shots developed in a word-processing program, illustrating how data generated in one context could be used at other points in the workflow. The prototype likewise illustrated how an IT solution would support cooperation between the producer and the presenter, as well as between them and the other journalists. This simple prototype, which was presented at a design workshop for the project group, became the basis for clarifying several aspects of a future work organization and potential ways of using the system.

On that basis, many aspects of the design were concretized and specified.

Figure 9.31 Example of experiments with horizontal prototypes

9.15.2 Vertical Prototypes

Later on in the innovation phase of the design project, when the overall form of IT usage is in place or when the project team wants to experiment with the specific shaping of a design aspect, experiments may involve more stable and finished versions—*vertical prototypes*. Such a prototype is a simple, but workable IT system that illustrates and simulates selected aspects of a total IT system. Vertical prototypes are developed using special tools that make developing and changing the prototype fairly economical in terms of resources. As this kind of prototype usually requires a stable data model, the process may involve data modeling within the relevant work domain.

A vertical prototype makes it possible to work with real data and use the prototype in actual work situations. Selected employees may work with the prototype for a designated period, after which the experiment is evaluated. Significantly, the experiment may also involve testing new patterns and forms of cooperation, to the extent they are supported by the prototype. This type of experiment may develop knowledge within knowledge area E (see figure 8.2). Figure 9.32 describes a process of experimentation with vertical prototypes in a design project.

In the design project in an editorial unit of a radio station mentioned in figure 9.31, the IT designer and a journalist collaborated to develop a vertical prototype for a specific aspect of the coherent vision. This involved an electronic file to support the work of individual journalists. The vision called for making it possible to search past features, books, or articles for information about people or topics. The vertical prototype was tested by three journalists who each used the prototype in their daily work over the course of a week.

The experiences revealed that information should always be linked to a specific person, not a topic, as the starting point for searches turned out always to be a specific person. The test also revealed a number of other conditions, including the significant limitations of the equipment available to the journalists at the time—for instance, the number of IT systems that could be left open at any one time.

Figure 9.32 Example of experiments with vertical prototypes

9.16 Developing Scenarios

Technique	Phases	Principles	Knowledge areas	Representation tools
Developing scenarios	4	1,4	B	Scenario

Source: Carroll (1995); Clausen (1993).

Developing scenarios is a technique that supports building coherent visions and thus helps anchoring these visions. A scenario is a textual representation describing a future work practice. The objective of scenario writing is to put a focus on the relationships between the IT systems and work organization proposed in a design vision and the resulting requirements for user qualifications. A scenario typically describes a specific business process.

For example, a premise for a design project may be a decision by the company to always use standard systems whenever possible. The project group may then start the innovation phase of the project by studying and selecting a couple of IT systems meant to support the relevant business process. The task then involves designing a work organization and mapping the qualifications required for the users to carry out their assignments with these systems. Scenarios can here be used to describe the projected usage of these systems in the company.

In other cases, the project group may have been given a freer hand to conduct the design project, or a market study may have revealed that the desired IT systems are not available. If this is the case, the project group should start by developing scenarios for various ways of organizing the work to meet the goals and needs documented in the previous phases. This task calls for describing functions and interfaces for one or more IT systems that could support the desired work organization. These systems can subsequently be tested by experiments with prototypes. Once the design project has been completed, received offers for different IT systems can be evaluated in relation to the scenarios. The scenarios or the IT systems may subsequently need to be adapted.

Finally, a scenario may also be used solely to illustrate the project group's visions in the design project report. However, in this case as well, the project group may find that the scenario reveals previously overlooked or insufficiently understood relationships. The project group then needs to backtrack and adapt the design of the work organization or the IT systems—or alter the mapping of user qualifications.

In any case, the purpose of a scenario is to illustrate relationships between IT systems, work organization, and qualification requirements in a way that enables management and staff to assess whether their goals and needs have been met. Likewise, in a tender or in the subsequent implementation of the design visions, suppliers may benefit from scenarios since they provide a good image of the situations where their products will become a part.

To illustrate the technique of developing a scenario, let us picture a project group in the middle of the innovation phase of a design project. Furthermore, let us assume that the project group has located two promising standard systems. In its efforts to evaluate these systems, the project group has produced a few collages showing the systems' functionality and selected central screen shots. A project group meeting is organized to discuss a certain business process that the systems are designed to support. The collages for one of the systems have been hung on the walls. The participants have prepared by rereading the previous reports and work documents, and two future users have been invited to the meeting to ensure that no significant details are overlooked.

The meeting reviews the different tasks involved in the business process. Each participant tries on one or more of the roles required for solving the future assignments. If the system prescribes a set structure for solving a task, such as a temporal division, the participant should follow this method. Otherwise, the participants should start with how the work is currently performed and proceed according to a typical daily rhythm. They will want to experiment with different alternatives for organizing the work using the facilities of the IT system, focusing on information included in the work, coordination among users, and any problems that might arise. When a problem occurs, the participants examine whether it can be solved immediately, either by a more expedient work organization or by requiring the system to react differently. If not, the problem is noted for later treatment. Any new qualification requirements and examples of deviations from the norm are likewise noted. One of the participants documents the decisions that are made. After the meeting, a participant takes on the task of writing the first draft of a scenario, which is treated and adjusted at the next project group meeting.

The scenario should illustrate the use of the IT system as seen from the perspective of many different users. The scenario should not lose itself in details, yet it should be specific enough to enable a reader to assess what consequences the introduction of the IT system and the new work organization will have for him or her personally. The style of a scenario may vary, but prose text in everyday terms is generally the most effective style. It is important, as much as possible, to operate with the terms that the users themselves rely on in their work. When that is not possible—for instance, because the system operates with new terms—any new terms should be specified. Moreover, it is often a good idea to include a design sketch of the proposed IT system.

Figure 9.33 is an example of a scenario from a design project at a radio station. The radio station is divided into a series of editorial units under joint management. An editorial unit consists of a producer, an on-air host, a number of reporters, a technician, and an assistant. IT systems that were included in the project group's design proposals are presented in italics and capitalized. These are also indicated in the design sketches in figures 9.22 and 9.23. The scenario describes the editorial unit's projected usage of the systems from overall planning through daily programming, broadcasting, and follow-up. The scenario has a timetable of one week.

Weekly programming starts on Friday when the producer meets with a reporter to establish an overview of the next week's four programs. They spend two to three hours searching for ideas by going over the *Event Calendar* and *List of Ideas,* browsing the *News Agency System* and the Internet, or by reading newspapers and magazines. They also have electronic access to past shows. Occasionally, they might use their computers to reserve books on-line from a library. Before they part, they write down any potential features for next week's programs in the *List of Ideas.*

A reporter comes to work at 8 A.M., Monday through Thursday. He starts by looking through the *Event Calendar* and the *News Agency System.* He reads the morning papers and adds topics to the *List of Ideas.* When the producer comes to work at 9 A.M. and turns on his computer, the *List of Ideas* automatically pops up on his screen. He sees that the list, apart from his own and the reporter's ideas, also contains a "suggestion" for an interview that his boss has logged in over the weekend. In the *List of Ideas*, he marks the stories that he is considering for today's broadcast then calls a meeting of the editorial unit.

After returning to his office, the producer moves the features selected at the meeting into the *Pool,* which subsequently comes to contain a number of *Program Elements.* He then calls up the day's *Manuscript* and plans the sequence of the features by making a link from the relevant *Program Element* to the point in the *Manuscript* where he wants it to go. A reporter, who is working on a feature, keys text into his *Program Element,* to which sound files (music and spoken words) may also be linked. Reporters can edit sound files (such as telephone interviews) on their computers. They only require assistance from a technician when special equipment is needed or when making an advanced montage. A reporter in the field may use a portable computer with similar functionality, and download and upload his *Program Element* directly to and from the *Pool* by modem.

The *Program Element* also indicates what music will be used during the broadcast. Pieces of music may be selected automatically from the *Music Manager,* or the host may select a title that better matches the show. The host links a piece of music to the *Program Element,* automatically transferring the name of the artist, the title, duration of the song, and so forth. If a piece of music is not available in the *Music Manager,* the host has to personally write this information down and bring the music into the studio. The host decides when the music will start or stop, where and how to fade, and also enters his or her spoken commentary into the *Program Element.*

The *Manuscript* evolves during the day, and everyone in the editorial unit can keep tabs on the program's status. Moreover, the producer may monitor the status of any *Program Element* that a reporter is working on. For instance, he or she can open the sound file of an interview and make cuts if he thinks it is too long. The producer decides when to make the *Manuscript* (or parts of it, in the form of selected *Program Elements*) available to management and other editorial units for coordination.

The *Manuscript* may be changed, even during a broadcast—if, for instance, an interview in the studio runs longer than originally planned. *Program Elements* are broadcast *one by one,* some automatically (digitally recorded and stored features and music), while others are started and stopped manually (such as news updates or interviews in the studio). When a feature is finished, the start and stop times of subsequent features are automatically adjusted. While the program is running, the producer, host, technician, and assistant each have a computer that highlights the information from the *Manuscript* that each one of them needs. When the program is over, the *Manuscript* contains all the information (text and sound) necessary for automatic generation of the reports that the editorial unit needs to submit to the radio station's administration.

Figure 9.33 Example of a scenario

Epilogue: How to Make Use of the Book

This epilogue focuses on two ways of applying the overall ideas and the concrete recommendations included in this book. First we provide an example and some of our general experiences in working with IT practitioners on disseminating the MUST method in ways that allow them to incorporate parts of the method into their repertoire for actions. Then we give an example of how we use it as a textbook for a university course.

Including the MUST Method in Practitioners' Repertoire for Action

Studies have shown that the introduction of new methods often fails. The example in this section builds on our positive experience from a dissemination endeavor that we carried out to introduce the MUST method in an internal IT department. We end this section by offering three lessons learned from this example and other dissemination projects in which we have been involved.

This example demonstrates that a combination of seminars, reflections on current and emerging practices, apprenticeship relations, and supervision of technical as well as personal skills was an instrumental approach. It helped a group of IT professionals to adapt and integrate relevant parts of the MUST method into their repertoire for action, to take on new roles, and to become more creative in fulfilling these roles.

We were invited to teach the MUST method to a group of IT professionals of an internal IT department. A project was formed in order for the IT professionals to adapt and integrate our method into their repertoire for action. The project was conceived to be important as the department strove to implement the organization's strategic plans. They included a call for major changes related to the IT department's responsibilities and its relations to the user departments. Among the strategic plans were four suggestions:

- The technological platforms for office work as well as for the production of the company's services and products should be merged.
- Business Process Reengineering (BPR), introduction of standard systems, and selective outsourcing of areas formerly taken care of by the IT department should be considered, some suggestions include development of applications not available at the market, networks, installation of PCs, support, and the running of installations.
- Future IT professionals should be trained in business analysis, technical issues, and personal management issues.
- The lack of knowledge and skills in the IT department calls for new employees, further education, or partnerships with external suppliers.

We approached method dissemination mainly from a learning perspective. Introducing the MUST method, we applied a combination of strategies. In doing so, we were inspired by Schön's (1983) studies of reflective practitioners. He provides a conceptual framework for the analysis and establishment of contexts for learning. He advocates that students and coaches conduct a reflective conversation with the materials of design situations in order to facilitate the acquisition of new skills. The work of Lave and Wenger (1991) was also an inspiration. They reconsider apprenticeship and situated learning and suggest legitimate peripheral participation as a conceptual framework for understanding how learning takes place in various trades. Nonaka's (1991) concept of learning organizations made us reflect on how to be instrumental in helping to institutionalize practices where learning becomes an ongoing concern.

First, we introduced the MUST method through seminars based on this book. Then two IT professionals started applying the method in a large IT design project. It was the first time they were part of a project of this scale and with such a close cooperation among IT professionals, managers, and users. We followed the project closely—participated in meetings, observed interviews, and reviewed plans and various intermediary results. This allowed us to observe the IT professionals while working, which made it possible for us to develop an appreciation of their strengths and weaknesses. Thus, when teaching and acting as coaches, we were able to relate to specific instances where the IT professionals' previous practices worked and where they fell short.

The next step was to introduce the MUST method to all of the IT department's employees. This included three types of activities:

1. Using the initial IT design project described in the previous paragraphs as an example, the method was introduced through four half-day seminars and supplemented by written materials.

2. For each of the IT professionals' ongoing projects, we worked as coaches. Together with the participating IT professionals, we started out evaluating the state of their current projects and related them to earlier experiences, focusing on problems perceived by the IT professionals. Then we selected parts of the MUST method that were appropriate in addressing the problems.

Next, we introduced an ongoing review process, where the IT professionals on a biweekly basis presented and discussed their project and received feedback. Sometimes further teaching on elements of the method was required. This went on until the IT professionals had adopted parts of the method. In addition, we conducted a future workshop. The themes of the workshop were the roles of the IT department in relation to user departments and external consultants, and the problems and possibilities internal to the department. The results of the future workshop were documented in a report, which was used to prioritize the areas where the IT department should strive to improve.

3. The MUST method includes a rather different style of working with users and managers than the IT professionals had practiced before. Therefore, new technical as well as personal skills needed to be developed. The technical skills were taken care of in activities described in points 1 and 2 of this list.

The personal skills involved handling unstructured, open-ended situations and much more oral and written communication with users and managers than the IT professionals were used to. This made these IT professionals somewhat uneasy applying the method. Therefore, in addition to the technically oriented review process described in point 2 of this list, we offered—on a biweekly basis—individual supervision addressing personal issues. We discussed the problems each perceived in fulfilling the role of an IT designer, and set up small-scale experiments for them to practice on in their ongoing projects. The results of the experiments were discussed in the following supervision session and new initiatives were taken.

These activities continued for a period of six months, until the IT professionals felt more secure in applying the method. Major elements of the MUST method became part of the organization's practices for conducting projects.

Lessons Learned

Our approach to method dissemination is based on two basic premises:

1. Introduction of a new method should be coupled with actual challenges in real design projects.
2. Traditional teaching cannot stand alone in method dissemination.

These premises have emerged from earlier projects. Drawing on our previous teaching experiences, we applied a combination of lectures, reflections on current and emerging practices, apprenticeship relations, and supervision of technical as well as personal skills. The central point is to get beyond a mode of detached reflection in the interaction between the IT professionals and the person responsible for the dissemination endeavor (from now on referred to as "the consultant").

Practitioners who are simply given a general presentation of a new technique are left on their own when trying to integrate the technique into their work practices. And a consultant who is simply told about events and changes in a recent project is left with the question about what really happened. So, to get beyond the say/do problem, we advocate that the consultant get involved in the work of the IT professionals through observations or ultimately through working together on a project. This makes it possible for the consultant to relate to problems in the practitioners' current practices when presenting a new technique or proposing changes in their design practice.

Finally, we turn to a closer inspection of lessons learned about method dissemination activities. We do this under three headings (commitment to change, observation led to a breakthrough in the dialogue, and accepting the stranger) that capture important issues in relation to the research question that guided our work: What are appropriate ways of introducing the method supporting IT designers in an industrial context? In the previous paragraphs, we drew on our experiences from an internal IT department. In the next sections, we also include our experiences at an IT consulting company and a university hospital—two additional partners who worked with us on research projects, addressing this central research question.

Commitment to Change

A commitment to change is an important factor in any change process, including method dissemination. The commitment should be established at the management level as well as among those whose practices are the subject of change—the IT professionals. It is general wisdom that management commitment to change is pivotal. In the IT consulting company that worked with us, for example, it was the department manager who originally took the initiative to try out the MUST method in a project. The manager was highly engaged in the project and served as its project manager. In the internal IT department that worked with us, the IT manager also took the initiative. When he left, however, two levels of management in the business unit with whom we also worked sustained his commitment.

Both companies knew beforehand that they could do things better and had decided to spend resources in trying to improve their design processes. Experimentation with the new method in the IT consulting company took place in a commercial project with an important customer. The project in the internal IT department had the attention of the highest level of management since it was part of a major investment. This encouraged the companies to take a serious and critical approach in learning, using, and evaluating the different activities and techniques proposed by the method.

In the university hospital, a large number of projects had been carried out following the outsourcing strategy. There was a very positive attitude to the need for changing work practices in design—the IT professionals openly discussed their problems in the projects at lunch and at weekly meetings. However, they did not have the time and resources to investigate these problems thoroughly and identify similarities across projects. For these reasons, we chose to approach the dissemination project at the hospital in two steps. Step one focused on identifying problems, investigating similarities, and proposing improvements. In the second step, the IT department would choose which of the proposals they wanted to implement.

The very organization of the project into these two steps reflects our understanding of another aspect of the importance of commitment to change: Changes should address areas where improvement is appreciated by the people involved. In order to locate such areas, we had to spend time identifying common problems and their nature across the projects. The projects chosen for detailed investigation were carefully selected to reflect the diversity of IT projects at the hospital. Great care was taken to present preliminary findings to the whole group of IT professionals before reporting to the management. Such presentations were done on a regular basis throughout the project; it was arranged as a meeting or a part of the IT professionals' weekly meeting, where our findings documented in a report had been distributed to the participants in advance. The discussion often resulted in changes and additions to our report.

Observation Led to a Breakthrough in the Dialogue

In order for a consultant to communicate effectively with practitioners, he or she benefits from observing the practitioners experimenting with the new work practices.

In our project with the IT consulting company, we made general presentations of the method before parts of it were used in a project with an important customer. In retrospect, we realized that these presentations were basically an account of abstract knowledge that the practitioners had to relate to their individual experiences. We could only relate to, and give examples from, our individual experiences from projects and situations in which the practitioner had not taken part. We often struggled to understand each other since both parties were interpreting the abstract method descriptions from the perspective of different practical and situated experiences.

This changed dramatically once a common ground was established. During the project at the customer site, we participated as an observer and a shared base of experience was developed. This led to a breakthrough in the mutual dialogue: Different aspects of the method (and its general guidelines) could now be related to common and situated project conditions. This shared base of experience established possibilities for discussing how the method could be applied in specific situations. Discussing the method based on shared experience also allowed the practitioners to develop faith in our ability to understand their work situation. In other words, this contributed to a confidence in us, which is another element that facilitates practitioners' commitment to change.

The same was the case in our work with the internal IT department. When presenting the MUST method at seminars to this group, we were able to relate to an earlier project carried out by some of the practitioners in which the method was used. From our observations in that earlier project, we had even learned about the products and services produced by the company. This established some kind of a common ground for the communication.

Accepting the Stranger

Accepting the stranger denotes that the company's IT designers have to accept that a stranger—the consultant—comes very close to their work practice. It is primarily a message for the participating industrial company—but also a lesson that presents food for thought for the consultant. Observing the activities of IT professionals is vital for the consultant in order to be able to communicate his knowledge and method to the practitioners (as discussed in the previous section). At the outset, project members from all three companies agreed to this condition. But this issue later became a reason for concern for some of the participants.

In the IT consulting company, the practitioners were all senior consultants with highly established and well experienced work practices. They felt concerned when the consultant, through his observations came close to their work practice and organization. One practitioner explained during the project that they in fact had already "written" 80 percent of the final report for the customer even before they had the first visit at the customer site. The consultant immediately recorded this, and later it turned out that the practitioner in question had felt very annoyed by this. He was concerned how the consultant would interpret this "work practice" and how it would be presented to other colleagues and managers. The "80 percent rule" could be explained in a very positive way: The practitioner was a highly experienced and knowledgeable domain expert and in general 80 percent of his findings had been experienced before with other customers. However, it could also be explained in a less positive manner: This practitioner had a tendency to jump to conclusions and recommend IT solutions to a customer based on his knowledge of the company's IT portfolio rather than on the needs and problems observed at the customer site.

The diagnostic analysis performed at the IT consulting company was based on a series of interviews and led to a report pointing out four problematic issues suitable for experiments involving the MUST method. One of these issues exposed an internal conflict within the company. The conflict was rooted in a dilemma of prioritizing the IT platform. On the one hand, they might prioritize the IT solution as a generic system where new releases could be offered to all customers. On the other hand, individual customer's specific needs might be prioritized in a way that could lead to different tailored systems, which might be hard to maintain through new versions of the generic system modules. The manager did not appreciate that this conflict was identified in the report and suggested that his employees had not read the report—a suggestion that did not align with the dissemination approach.

The university hospital's concern about accepting the stranger was also important. Our approach stipulated that changes in their current work practice had to be based on a common understanding of the areas for improvements. That clearly involved some kind of evaluation of past and present performance, which implied evaluations of specific individuals since the projects were often staffed with very few people. Strangers (i.e., the consultants) took part in this evaluation. Since our dissemination endeavor depended on a constructive dialogue with all parties involved, we needed to handle the evaluation with delicacy. Therefore, for a considerable part of the project period we spent full days in the IT department—which meant that we took part in lunch and various meetings, and thus became less of a stranger. Second, we always sent out interview summaries to the interviewed persons in order to allow them to correct mistakes in what would become the project's record. Third, we stressed again and again that the purpose was to identify general problems and not to identify success stories or failures. And finally, we took great care not to name individuals in reports or oral presentations.

The lesson seemed to be that establishing and maintaining a positive attitude toward dissemination projects requires considerable attention to confidentiality and personal integrity issues.

Using the Textbook for a University Course

In a course for graduate students in participatory IT design, the Danish version of this book (as well as earlier versions of it) has been used as the primary textbook in courses for graduate and undergraduate students in information systems and computer science programs. The example that follows is taken from a course offered to students as part of their master's program. Students earlier in their career may need more direct instructions and exercises than indicated here.

Motivation

Most companies and organizations rely on standard software rather than developing their own systems from scratch. Therefore, some IT designers focus on design of generic systems for the market. Others design for a specific customer's needs and opportunities, delivering what we refer to as "coherent visions for change." Thus, the latter group works on standard software as well as custom-made software in their overall design that also comprises changes in users' qualifications and in the organization of work. This course aims at developing students' competence within the latter type of jobs.

For many years, information systems and computer science programs have offered courses in software engineering and systems development focusing on technical and project management issues. However, we have found a lack of courses that develop students' competencies in designing coherent visions for change for a specific customer. This type of training also requires attending to organizational issues.

Objectives

Students in this course learn to plan and conduct the initial part of an IT project. After the course, successful students have the theoretical and practical qualifications to do several things:

- Explore and document needs and opportunities for a specific company
- Design one or more coherent visions for change
- Evaluate potential consequences of a realization of the visions
- Plan an IT design project as well as a subsequent IT realization project

Thus, students learn to design two things: a coherent vision for change, as well as the processes through which project participants get from initial ideas to actual IT applications in use. However, instructions on how to conduct an IT realization project is outside the scope of this course.

Size

The course is planned to take up one-third of the students' time during a term of twelve weeks, which in the European Credit Transfer System equals 7.5 ECTS. Generally speaking, this equals one-eighth of a student's work in a year, which we see as a necessary minimum. If students are able to spend more time on this subject, the list of literature later in this epilogue has proven to be a valuable resource in the past.

Prerequisites

Students are expected to have taken courses in programming and systems development or software engineering. A general understanding of organizations and of their IT usage is considered an advantage.

Contents

This course deals with theories of and methods for IT design, as well as IT design practices. Various accounts of IT design and how it may be approached are studied. The students plan and conduct a small IT design project according to the guidelines of the primary textbook.

The focus of this course is on design as a process: what are the main elements of design and their dynamics; adequate tools and techniques; results of a design process and their relations to other activities in systems and organizational development; and improving one's skills as an IT designer.

Format

The format of the course includes lectures by the professor and presentations by the students (see figure E.1). In addition, students work in groups of three to five people on an IT design project (see figure E.2). Each group finds a small company or a department within a larger company for which they produce a design report. The professor or a teaching assistant offers supervision to each group and advice on how to plan and conduct the project including which tools and techniques to apply.

Week One: An Introduction to the Course

Readings: Chapter 1 of this book and an example from the professors' own repertoire of IT design projects. If the professors do not have such examples, Kensing, Simonsen, and Bødker (1998) (see figure E.3) may prove helpful. Students should start forming groups and investigate potential companies for the IT design project.

Week Two: Concepts and Principles

Reading: Chapter 2 (except section 2.3) and chapter 3 of this book.

The groups for the IT design project should now be formed and the project companies chosen.

Week Three: Project Establishment and Strategic Alignment Analysis

Reading: Chapters 4 and 5 of this book, plus the tools and techniques described in sections 9.1–9.7.

The groups should work on their project charters and focus on the work domains that will be the subjects for further study.

Week Four: Ethnographically Inspired Analysis
Reading: Chapter 6 and section 2.3 of this book plus the tools and techniques described in sections 9.8–9.13.

The groups' first deliverable: a combined project charter and strategic alignment report.

Week Five: Vision Development

Reading: Chapter 7 of this book plus the tools and techniques described in sections 9.10.7 and 9.14–9.16.

The groups work on the in-depth analysis phase.

Weeks Six through Eleven: Student Presentations

Reading: See the list of recommended books and papers in figure E.3.

The students can present individually or in groups. They are encouraged to present the main points of the chosen readings and to relate these points to the textbook and their experiences so far.

We have experienced classes where students, in groups of two to three people, were comfortable preparing a talk based on one of the recommended books, while for other classes one to two papers per student or group were a challenge. In case the paper model is chosen, all papers are included in the curriculum. When students have presented whole books, we selected papers of the same author(s) or parts of the books for the curriculum.

Week Seven: The Groups' Second Deliverable: The Analysis Report

Weeks Eight through Eleven: The Groups Work on Developing Coherent Visions for Change.

Week Twelve: Course Evaluation and Deadline for Delivering the Final IT Design Reports

Figure E.1 Outline of a course for master's students

Groups of three to five students are to work on an IT design project for a specific company and apply the relevant elements of the MUST method to their projects. To reduce the level of complexity, the groups are advised to look for a small company or a department within a larger company for which they produce a design report of about twenty-five pages plus appendixes.

In our experience, a weekly or biweekly supervision session of thirty minutes to one hour is sufficient. Some groups need help on how to apply specific tools and techniques, while others are more uncertain about how to structure the process or how to cooperate with people in the company.

Students may also need help on how to delimit their project. On the one hand, a project should be complex enough for the method to be relevant to apply. On the other hand, it should be simple enough for the group to finish within the given timeframe. For this reason, it is important that each group finds a company within the first couple of weeks of the course.

As a rule of thumb, a student project may be divided into three phases combining the MUST method's phase one (project establishment) and phase two (strategic alignment analysis). After the first couple of weeks of the course, the groups should be prepared to work on the project. Over a period of one to two weeks, they work on the first deliverable (the project charter and strategic alignment report) for the company to ensure that the parties agree on the scope and other relevant prerequisites for the project (see figures 4.6 and 5.4). Among the important issues that require agreement are students' access to the company, how much time specific people within the company will be able to spend on the project, confidentiality, and so forth.

Having thus focused in on the relevant parts of the company, the group is ready for the ethnographically inspired analysis. For the next three weeks, students will spend time on interviews and observations at the company, on reading acquired material, and on group sessions developing a shared understanding of the company's needs and opportunities in relation to IT. These are summed up in a report (see figure 6.5) that is presented to the company and possibly adjusted after a discussion.

Finally, the group works for approximately four weeks on the design of one or more coherent visions for change. Students should be urged to involve managers and employees at the client company in their design activities as much as possible. The resulting visions are presented to the company and are likely revised after discussion. The students may use the final week for finishing the report (see figure 7.3), including perhaps improving the earlier deliverables as appendixes.

Sometimes representatives from the companies agree to come to either a joint or a separate session of the class where each group presents its final report and receives feedback on the report as well as on the ways in which the group managed its cooperation with the company.

Figure E.2 Project assignment

Finally, to help students further develop their own stance and identity as IT designers, it has proven instrumental to invite three or four professional IT designers to talk about their experiences from recently finished projects. The invitation may ask them to structure their talk around the issues related to the contents and focus of the course. These presentations may be offered to just those attending the course or to all students if appropriate.

Pedagogical Considerations

To help students develop skills as competent IT designers, we have found that a combination of the following four elements is instrumental:

1. Reading and discussing the literature on theories of and methods for IT design is essential (this should take the form of lectures and student presentations).

2. Small-scale exercises are helpful when practicing the application of specific tools and techniques (as part of the supervision for the projects or separate course exercises).

3. In order to learn how to deal with the complexities involved in real-life IT design projects, students need to experience these projects firsthand.

4. Finally, a diverse set of exemplary cases is a valuable resource when planning and conducting projects (the textbook, the students' own projects, and those offered by the invited professional IT designers can provide such cases).

If students are able to spend more than the implied one-eighth of a year on this course, we recommend that the reading list for the course be expanded (see figure E.3).

Examination

At the oral examination, scheduled for one-half hour, each student is requested to give an in-depth reflection on how his or her own experiences from the IT design project related to the literature studied in the class. This is followed by a discussion with the examiner. Alternatively, students may hand in such reflections as a written test.

Textbook:

Bødker, K., F. Kensing, and J. Simonsen. 2004. *Participatory IT Design. Designing for Business and Workplace Realities*. Cambridge: MIT Press.

A list of recommended books and special issues of journals to choose from:

Avison, D. E., and A. T. Wood-Harper. 1990. *Multiview. An Exploration in Information Systems Development*. New York: McGraw-Hill.

Beyer, H., and K. Holtzblatt. 1998. *Contextual Design: Defining Customer-Centered Systems*. San Francisco: Morgan Kaufmann Publishers.

Blomberg, J., and F. Kensing, eds. 1998. *Computer Supported Cooperative Work—A Journal of Collaborative Computing 7*, nos. 3–4. Kluwer Academic Publishers. (Special issue on Participatory Design.)

Greenbaum, J., and M. Kyng. 1991. *Design at Work: Cooperative Design of Computer Systems*. Hillsdale, NJ: Lawrence Erlbaum Associates.

Hammer, M., and J. Champy. 1993. *Reengineering the Corporation. A Manifesto for Business Revolution*. New York: Harper.

Muller, M. J., and S. Kuhn, eds. 1993. *Communications of the ACM, Special Issue: Participatory Design 36*, no. 4 (June).

Norman, D. 1990. *The Design of Everyday Things*. New York: HarperCollins.

Schön, D. A. 1983. *The Reflective Practitioner: How Professionals Think in Action*. New York: Basic Books.

Schuler, D., and A. Namioka. 1993. *Participatory Design: Principles and Practices*. Hillsdale, NJ: Lawrence Erlbaum Associates.

Simon, H. A. 1969. *The Sciences of the Artificial*. Cambridge, MA: MIT Press.

Suchman, L. 1987. *Plans and Situated Action: The Problem of Human-Machine Communication*. Cambridge: Cambridge University Press.

Trigg, R. H., and S. I. Anderson, eds. 1996. *Human-Computer Interaction 11*, no. 3. (Special issue on current perspectives on participatory design.)

Winograd, T. 1996. *Bringing Design to Software*. New York: ACM Press.

A list of recommended papers and book chapters to choose from:

Bansler, J., and K. Bødker. 1993. A reappraisal of structured analysis: Design in an organizational context. ACM *Transactions on Information Systems* 11, no. 2:165–193.

Blomberg, J., J. Giacomi, A. Mosher, and P. Swenton-Hall. 1993. Ethnographic field methods and their relation to design. In *Participatory Design: Principles and Practices,* eds. D. Schuler and A. Namioka, 123–155. London: Lawrence Erlbaum Associates.

Brown, J. S., and P. Duguid. 1994. Borderline issues: Social and material aspects of design. *Human-Computer Interaction* 9, no. 1:3–36.

Dreyfus, H. L. 1988. The Socratic and Platonic basis of cognitivism. *AI and Society* 2:99–112.

Floyd, C. 1984. A systematic look at prototyping. In *Approaches to Prototyping,* ed. R. Budde, K. Kuhlenkamp,
L. Mathiassen, and H. Zullighoven, 1–18. Berlin: Springer-Verlag.

Grudin, J. 1991. Interactive systems: Bridging the gaps between developers and users. *IEEE Computer* 24, no. 4:59–69.

Grudin, J. 1994. Groupware and social dynamics: Eight challenges for developers. *Communications of the ACM* 37, no. 1:92–105.

Grønbæk, K., M. Kyng, and P. Mogensen. 1997. Toward a cooperative experimental systems development approach. In *Computers and Design in Context,* ed. M. Kyng and L. Mathiassen, 201–238. Cambridge, MA: MIT Press.

Hammer, M. 1990. Reengineering work: Don't automate, obliterate. *Harvard Business Review* 68, no. 4:104–112.

Hughes, J. A., Randall, D., and Shapiro, D. 1993. From ethnographic record to system design: Some experiences from the field. *Computer Supported Cooperative Work* 1, no. 3:123–147.

Kensing, F., and J. Blomberg. 1998. Participatory design: Issues and concerns. *Computer Supported Cooperative Work* 7, nos. 3–4:167–185.

Kensing, F. J. Simonsen, and K. Bødker. 1998. Participatory design at a radio station. *Computer Supported Cooperative Work* 7, nos. 3–4:243–271.

Kyng, M. 1994. Scandinavian design: Users in product development. In *Proceedings of CHI'94,* 3–9. Boston: ACM Press.

Schön, D. A. 1992. Designing as reflective conversation with the materials of a design situation. *Knowledge-Based Systems* 5:3–14.

Simonsen, J. 1999. How do we take care of strategic alignment? Constructing a design approach. *Scandinavian Journal of Information Systems* 11:51–72.

Simonsen, J., and F. Kensing. 1997. Using ethnography in contextual design. *Communications of the ACM* 40, no. 7:82–88.

Stolterman, E. 1992. How systems designers think about design and methods: Some reflections based on an interview study. *Scandinavian Journal of Information Systems* 4:137–150.

Suchman, L. 1983. Office procedure as practical action: Models of work and system design. *ACM Transactions on Office Information Systems* 1:320–328.

Suchman, L. 1994. Do categories have politics? The language/action perspective reconsidered. *Computer Supported Cooperative Work (CSCW): An International Journal* 2–3:177–190.

Suchman, L. 1995. Making work visible. *Communications of the ACM* 38, no. 9:56–64.

Winograd, T. 1994. Categories, disciplines, and social coordination. *Computer Supported Cooperative Work (CSCW): An International Journal* 2–3:191–197.

Figure E.3. Course material

References

This section lists the literature that has been referenced throughout the book.

Andersen, N. E., F. Kensing, M. Lassen, J. Lundin, L. Mathiassen, A. Munk-Madsen, and P. Sørgaard. 1990. *Professional Systems Development. Experiences, Ideas, and Actions.* New York: Prentice-Hall.

Avison, D. E., and A. T. Wood-Harper. 1990. *Multiview. An Exploration in Information Systems Development.* New York: McGraw-Hill.

Bansler, J., and K. Bødker. 1993. A reappraisal of structured analysis: Design in an organizational context. *ACM Transactions on Information Systems* 11, no. 2:165–193.

Beck, K. 2000. *Extreme Programming Explained. Embrace Change.* Reading, MA: Addison-Wesley.

Beyer, H., and K. Holtzblatt. 1998. *Contextual Design. Defining Customer-Centered Systems.* San Francisco: Morgan Kaufmann Publishers.

Blomberg, J., J. Giacomi, A. Mosher, and P. Swenton-Wall. 1993. Ethnographic field methods and their relation to design. In *Participatory Design: Principles and Practices,* ed. D. Schuler and A. Namioka, 123–156. Hillsdale, NJ: Erlbaum.

Blomberg, J., and F. Kensing, eds. 1998. *Computer Supported Cooperative Work—A Journal of Collaborative Computing* 7, nos. 3–4. (Special issue on participatory design.)

Blomberg, J., L. Suchman, and R. Trigg. 1996. Reflections on a work-oriented design project. *Human-Computer Interaction* 11, no. 3:237–265.

Boehm, B. W. 1991. Software risk management: Principles and practices. *IEEE Software* (January):32–41.

Bowman, B. 1997. *RAD++. How to Achieve Excellence in Application Development.* Hartley Whitney: Antares Alliance Group.

Brown, J. S., and P. Duguid. 1994. Borderline issues: Social and material aspects of design. *Human-Computer Interaction* 9, no. 1:3–36.

Budde, R., K. Kautz, K. Kuhlenkamp, and H. Züllighoven. 1992. *Prototyping. An Approach to Evolutionary System Development.* Berlin: Springer-Verlag.

Bødker, K., and F. Kensing. 1994. Design in an organizational context—An experiment. *Scandinavian Journal of Information Systems* 6:47–68.

Bødker, K., and J. S. Pedersen. 1991. Workplace cultures: Looking at artifacts, symbols, and practices. In *Design at Work: Cooperative Design of Computer Systems,* ed. J. Greenbaum and M. Kyng, 121–136. Chichester: Lawrence Erlbaum Associates.

Carroll, John M., ed. 1995. *Scenario-Based Design. Envisioning Work and Technology in System Development.* New York: John Wiley & Sons Inc.

Ciborra, C. U. 1997. De profundis? Deconstructing the concept of strategic alignment. *Scandinavian Journal of Information Systems* 9, no. 1:67–82.

Clausen, H. 1993. Narratives as tools for the systems designers. *Design Studies* 14:283–298.

Dreyfus, H. L. 1988. The Socratic and Platonic basis of cognitivism. *AI & Society* 2:99–112.

Earl, M. J. 1993. Experiences in strategic information systems planning. *MIS Quarterly* 17, no. 1:1–24.

Ehn, P., and M. Kyng. 1991. Cardboard computers: Mocking-it up or hands-on the future. In *Design at Work: Cooperative Design of Computer Systems*, ed. J. Greenbaum and M. Kyng, 169–195. Hillsdale, NJ: Lawrence Erlbaum Associates.

Fairley, R. 1994. Risk management for software projects. *IEEE Software* (May):57–67.

Floyd, C. 1984. A systematic look at prototyping. In *Approaches to Prototyping,* ed. R. Budde, K. Kuhlenkamp, L. Mathiassen, and H. Zullighoven, 1–18. Berlin: Springer-Verlag.

Freedman, D. P., and G. M. Weinberg. 1982. *Handbook of Walkthroughs, Inspections and Technical Reviews.* Boston: Little, Brown and Company.

Goguen, J. A., and C. Linde. 1993. Techniques for requirements elicitation. *Proceedings of the IEEE International Symposium on Requirements Engineering,* 152–164. Los Alamitos, CA: IEEE Press.

Greenbaum, J., and M. Kyng. 1991. *Design at Work: Cooperative Design of Computer Systems.* Hillsdale, NJ: Lawrence Erlbaum Associates.

Grønbæk, K., M. Kyng, and P. Mogensen. 1997. Toward a cooperative experimental systems development approach. In *Computers and Design in Context,* ed. M. Kyng and L. Mathiassen, 201–238. Cambridge: MIT Press.

Grudin, J. 1991. Interactive systems: Bridging the gaps between developers and users. *IEEE Computer* 24, no. 4:59–69.

Grudin, J. 1994. Groupware and social dynamics: Eight challenges for developers. *Communications of the ACM* 37, no. 1:92–105.

Hammer, M. 1990. Reengineering work: Don't automate, obliterate. *Harvard Business Review* 68, no. 4 (July–August):104–112.

Hammer, M., and J. Champy. 1993. *Reengineering the Corporation. A Manifesto for Business Revolution.* New York: HarperBusiness/HarperCollins Publishers.

Henderson, J. C., and N. Venkatraman. 1992. Strategic alignment: A model for organizational transformation through information technology. In *Transforming Organizations,* ed. T. A. Kochan and M. Useem, 97–117. New York: Oxford University Press.

Hughes, J. A., D. Randall, and D. Shapiro. 1993. From ethnographic record to system design: Some experiences from the field. *Computer Supported Cooperative Work* 1, no. 3:123–147.

Jacobson, I., G. Booch, and J. Rumbaugh. 1999. *The Unified Software Development Process.* Reading, MA: Addison-Wesley.

Jungk, R., and N. R. Müllert. 1987. *Future Workshops: How to Create Desirable Futures.* London: London Institute for Social Inventions.

Kensing, F. 1986. Generation of visions in systems development—A supplement to the toolbox. *Proceedings of System Design for Human Development and Productivity: Participation and Beyond, ed.* P. Docherty et al., 285–301. Amsterdam: North-Holland.

Kensing, F. 1998. Prompted reflections: A technique for understanding complex work. *ACM Interactions* 5:7–15.

Kensing, F., and J. Blomberg. 1998. Participatory design: Issues and concerns. *Computer Supported Cooperative Work—A Journal of Collaborative Computing* 7, nos. 3–4:167–185.

Kensing, F., and K. H. Madsen. 1991. Generating visions: Future workshops and metaphorical design. In *Design at*

Work—Cooperative Design of Computer Systems, ed. J. Greenbaum and M. Kyng, 155–168. Hillsdale, NJ: Lawrence Erlbaum Associates.

Kensing, F., and T. Winograd. 1991. Operationalizing the language/action approach to design of computer-support for cooperative work. In *Collaborative Work, Social Communications and Information Systems,* ed. R. K. Stamper et al., 311–331. Amsterdam: North-Holland.

Kensing, F., J. Simonsen, and K. Bødker. 1998. Participatory design at a radio station. *Computer Supported Cooperative Work: The Journal of Collaborative Computing* 7:243–271.

Kvale, S. 1983. The qualitative research interview. *Journal of Phenomenological Psycology* 14, no. 2:171–196.

Kvale, S. 1996. *Inter Views—An Introduction to Qualitative Research Interviewing.* Thousand Oaks, CA: Sage.

Kyng, M. 1994. Scandinavian design: Users in product development. In *Proceedings of CHI'94,* 3–9. Boston: ACM.

Lanzara, G. F., and L. Mathiassen. 1985. Mapping situations within a systems development project. *Information and Management* 8, no. 1: 3–20.

Lave, J., and E. Wenger. 1991. *Situated Learning: Legitimate Peripheral Participation.* New York: Cambridge University Press.

Lederer, A. L., and H. Salmela. 1996. Toward a theory of strategic information systems planning. *Journal of Strategic Information Systems* 5, no. 3:237–253.

Madsen, K. H. 1994. A guide to metaphorical design. *Communications of the ACM* 37, no. 12:57–62.

Martin, J. 1991. *Rapid Application Development.* New York: Macmillan Publishing Company.

Muller, M. J., and S. Kuhn, eds. 1993. *Communications of the ACM* 36, no. 4.

Nonaka, I. 1991. The knowledge-creating company. *Harvard Business Review* (Nov.–Dec.): 96–104.

Norman, D. 1990. *The Design of Everyday Things*. New York: HarperCollins.

Porter, M. 1985. *Competetive Advantage*. New York: The Free Press.

Schmidt, K. 1986. A dialectical approach to functional analysis of office work. In *Proceedings of the 1986 IEEE International Conference on Systems, Man, and Cybernetics, 1586–1591.* Atlanta.

Schmidt, K. 1988. Function analysis instrument. In *Functional Analysis of Office Requirements: A Multiperspective Approach*, ed. G. Schäfer, 261–289. Chichester: Wiley.

Schön, D. A. 1983. *The Reflective Practitioner: How Professionals Think in Action*. New York: Basic Books.

Schön, D. A. 1987. *Educating the Reflective Practitioner*. San Francisco: Jossey Bass.

Schön, D. A. 1992. Designing as reflective conversation with the materials of a design situation. *Knowledge-Based Systems* 5:3–14.

Schuler, D., and A. Namioka. 1993. *Participatory Design: Principles and Practices*. Hillsdale, NJ: Lawrence Erlbaum.

Simonsen, J. 1994. *Designing Systems in an Organizational Context: An Explorative Study of Theoretical, Methodological, and Organizational Issues from Action Research in Three Design Projects*. Ph.D. thesis, Writings in Computer Science, no. 52. Roskilde: Roskilde University.

Simonsen, J. 1999. How do we take care of strategic alignment? Constructing a design approach. *Scandinavian Journal of Information Systems* 11:51–72.

Simonsen, J., and F. Kensing. 1997. Using ethnography in contextual design. *Communications of the ACM* 40, no. 7 (July):82–88.

Simonsen, J., and F. Kensing. 1998. Make room for ethnography in design. *ACM-SIGDOC Journal of Computer Documentation* 22, no. 1 (February):20–30.

Stolterman, E. 1992. How systems designers think about design and methods: Some reflections based on an interview study. *Scandinavian Journal of Information Systems* 4:137–150.

Suchman, L. 1983. Office procedure as practical action: Models of work and system design. *ACM Transactions on Office Information Systems* 1:320–328.

Suchman, L. 1987. *Plans and Situated Action: The Problem of Human-Machine Communication.* Cambridge: Cambridge University Press.

Suchman, L. 1994. Do categories have politics? The language/ action perspective reconsidered. *Computer Supported Cooperative Work (CSCW): An International Journal* 2–3: 177–190.

Suchman, L. 1995. Making work visible. *Communications of the ACM* 38, no. 9:56–64.

Trigg, R. H., and S. I. Anderson, eds. 1996. *Human-Computer interaction* 11, no. 3. (Special issue on current perspectives on participatory design.)

Venkatraman, N., J. C. Henderson, and S. Oldach. 1993. Continuous strategic alignment: Exploiting information technology capabilities for competitive success. *European Management Journal* 11:139–149.

Winograd, T. 1994. Categories, disciplines, and social coordination. *Computer Supported Cooperative Work (CSCW): An International Journal* 2–3:191–197.

Winograd, T. 1996. *Bringing Design to Software.* New York: ACM Press, Addison-Wesley.

MUST Publications

This section lists the literature that have been published within the MUST research program.

Bødker, K. 1989. *Analyse og design i et kulturperspektiv—udfordring til systemperspektivet* [Analysis and Design in a Cultural Perspective—Challenging the System Perspective]. Ph.D. thesis, Writings in Computer Science, no. 26. Roskilde: Roskilde University.

Bødker, K. 1990. A cultural perspective on organizations applied to analysis and design of information systems. In *Organizational Competence in Systems Development. A Scandinavian Contribution*, ed. G. Bjerkes et al., 211–232. Lund, Sweden: Studentlitteratur.

Bødker, K., and J. S. Pedersen. 1991. Workplace cultures: Looking at artifacts, symbols, and practices. In *Design at Work: Cooperative Design of Computer Systems*, ed. J. Greenbaum and M. Kyng, 121–136. Chichester: Lawrence Erlbaum Associates.

Bødker, K., and F. Kensing. 1994. Design in an organizational context—An experiment. *Scandinavian Journal of Information Systems* 6:47–68.

Bødker, K., F. Kensing, and J. Simonsen. 2002. Changing work practices in design. In *Social Thinking—Social Practice*, ed. Y. Ditrich, C. Floyd, and R. Klischewski, 267–285. Cambridge, MA: MIT Press.

Kensing, F. 1987. Generation of visions in systems development—A supplement to the toolbox. In *Systems Design for Human Development and Productivity: Participation and Beyond*, ed. P. Docherty et al., 285–301. Berlin: Springer-Verlag.

Kensing, F. 1998. Prompted reflections: A technique for understanding complex work. *ACM Interactions* 5, no. 1:7–15.

Kensing, F. 1999. Method design and dissemination. In *Proceedings of The Seventh European Conference on Information Systems, Copenhagen, Denmark,* ed. J. Pries-Heje et al., 386–402. Copenhagen, Denmark: Department of Informatics, Copenhagen Business School

Kensing, F. 2000. Participatory design in a commercial context—A conceptual framework. In *Proceedings of the Participatory Design Conference, New York,* ed. T. Charkasky, 116–126. Palo Alto, CA: Computer Professionals for Social Responsibility.

Kensing, F. 2003. *Methods and Practices in Participatory Design.* Copenhagen: ITU Press.

Kensing, F., and J. Blomberg. 1998. PD meets CSCW—Issues and concerns. *Computer Supported Cooperative Work—The Journal of Collaborative Computing* 7, nos. 3–4: 167–185.

Kensing, F., K. Bødker, and J. Simonsen. 1994. *An Emerging Approach to Systems Design—Experience from the MUST Program.* Writings in Computer Science, no. 94. Roskilde: Roskilde University.

Kensing, F., and K. H. Madsen. 1991. Generating visions—Future workshops and metaphorical design. In *Design at Work: Cooperative Design of Computer Systems,* ed. J. Greenbaum and M. Kyng, 155–168. Chichester, UK: Lawrence Erlbaum Associates.

Kensing, F., and A. Munk-Madsen. 1993. Participatory design: Structure in the toolbox. *Communications of the ACM* 36:78–85.

Kensing, F., and T. Winograd. 1991. Operationalizing the language/action approach to design of computer-support for cooperative work. In *Collaborative Work,*

Social Communications and Information Systems, ed. R. K. Stamper, 311–331. Amsterdam: North-Holland.

Kensing, F., J. Simonsen, and K. Bødker. 1998. MUST—A method for participatory design. *Human-Computer Interaction* 13, no. 2:167–198.

Kensing, F., J. Simonsen, and K. Bødker. 1998. Participatory design at a radio station. *Computer Supported Cooperative Work: The Journal of Collaborative Computing* 7:167–185.

Simonsen, J. 1992. Is it possible to combine a phenomenological and a functionalistic approach? In *Proceedings of the 15th IRIS*, ed. G. Bjerknes, T. Brattetelg, and M. Kautz, 75–82. Larkollen, Norway: Department of Informatics, University of Oslo.

Simonsen, J. 1994. *Designing Systems in an Organizational Context: An Explorative Study of Theoretical, Methodological, and Organizational Issues from Action Research in Three Design Projects*. Ph.D. thesis, Writings in Computer Science, no. 52. Roskilde: Roskilde University.

Simonsen, J. 1996. Involving customer relations in contextual design—A case study. In *Proceedings of the 4th European Conference on Information Systems*, ed. J. D. Coelho, T. Jelassi, W. König, H. Kromar, R. O'Callaghan, and M. Sääksjärvi, 1153–1161.

Simonsen, J. 1997. Linking design to business strategy through functional analysis. In *Proceedings of the 5th European Conference on Information Systems*, ed. R. Galliers et al., 1314–1327. Cork, Ireland: Cork Publishing Limited.

Simonsen, J. 1998. The anchoring concept. In *IRIS'21, Information Systems Research Seminar in Scandinavia 2*, ed. N. J. Buch, J. Damsgaard, L. B. Eriksen, J. H. Iversen, and P. A. Nielsen, 779–791. Aalborg, Denmark: Department of Computer Science, Aalborg University.

Simonsen, J. 1999. Anchoring visions in organizations. In *Evolution and Challenges in System Development*, ed. J. Zupancic, G. Wojtkowski, W. Wojtkowski, and S. Wrycza, 73–84. New York: Kluwer Academic Publishers.

Simonsen, J. 1999. How do we take care of strategic alignment? Constructing a design approach. *Scandinavian Journal of Information Systems* 11:51–72.

Simonsen, J., and F. Kensing. 1994. Take users seriously, but take a deeper look: organizational and technical effects from designing with an ethnographically inspired approach. In *Proceedings of the Third Biennial Conference on Participatory Design*, ed. R. H. Trigg et al., 47–58. Palo Alto, CA: Computer Professionals for Social Responsibility.

Simonsen, J., and F. Kensing. 1997. Using ethnography in contextual design. *Communications of the ACM* 40, no. 7 (July):82–88.

Simonsen, J., and F. Kensing. 1998. Make room for ethnography in design. *ACM-SIGDOC Journal of Computer Documentation* 22, no. 1 (February):20–30.

Simonsen, J., F. Kensing, and K. Bødker. 1997. MUST—En metode til forundersøgelse med brugerdeltagelse [MUST—A participatory design method]. In *Design af Multimedier* [Design of Multimedias], ed. B. Fibiger, 19–60. Aalborg, Denmark: Aalborg University Press.

Index